CW01661018

# THE SPIRIT OF HINDU LAW

Law is too often perceived solely as state-based rules and institutions that provide a rational alternative to religious rites and ancestral customs. *The Spirit of Hindu Law* uses the Hindu legal tradition as a heuristic tool to question this view and reveal the close linkage between law and religion. Emphasizing the household, the family, and everyday relationships as additional social locations of law, it contends that law itself can be understood as a theology of ordinary life.

An introduction to traditional Hindu law and jurisprudence, this book is structured around key legal concepts such as the sources of law and authority, the laws of persons and things, procedure, punishment and legal practice. It combines investigation of key themes from Sanskrit legal texts with discussion of Hindu theology and ethics, as well as thorough examination of broader comparative issues in law and religion.

DONALD R. DAVIS, JR. is Associate Professor in the Department of Languages and Cultures of Asia, University of Wisconsin-Madison.

# THE SPIRIT OF HINDU LAW

DONALD R. DAVIS, JR.
*University of Wisconsin-Madison*

CAMBRIDGE
UNIVERSITY PRESS

CAMBRIDGE UNIVERSITY PRESS
Cambridge, New York, Melbourne, Madrid, Cape Town, Singapore,
São Paulo, Delhi, Dubai, Tokyo

Cambridge University Press

The Edinburgh Building, Cambridge CB2 8RU, UK

Published in the United States of America by Cambridge University Press, New York

www.cambridge.org
Information on this title: www.cambridge.org/9780521877046

© Donald R. Davis, Jr. 2010

This publication is in copyright. Subject to statutory exception
and to the provisions of relevant collective licensing agreements,
no reproduction of any part may take place without the written
permission of Cambridge University Press.

First published 2010

Printed in the United Kingdom at the University Press, Cambridge

*A catalogue record for this publication is available from the British Library*

*Library of Congress Cataloguing in Publication data*
Davis, Donald R., 1970–
The spirit of Hindu law/Donald R. Davis, Jr.
p. cm.
ISBN 978-0-521-87704-6 (hardback)
1. Hindu law. 2. Hindu law–Philosophy. I. Title.
KNS127.3.D38 2010
340.5′34–dc22

ISBN 978-0-521-87704-6 Hardback

Cambridge University Press has no responsibility for the persistence or
accuracy of URLs for external or third-party internet websites referred to
in this publication, and does not guarantee that any content on such
websites is, or will remain, accurate or appropriate.

# *Contents*

# *Tables*

# *Preface*

A book with this title was supposed to have been written by my teacher, Richard Lariviere, in the University of Georgia's "Spirit of the Laws" series. His higher calling into academic administration left a gap in the series that I always lamented. When I approached Richard and, through him and with his permission, Alan Watson, who edited the series, it became clear that there was no hope of placing one more volume in the old series. To my great delight, Cambridge agreed to publish the book, which is certainly very different from what Richard would have done, though still inspired by his ideas and still very much in line with the series' intention to provide basic surveys of law and religion in the major traditions of the world.

There are three audiences for the book: Indologists and scholars of Religious Studies and Legal Studies. Indologists will find a certain amount of technical investigation of key discussions from the Sanskrit texts, though not as much as some may like and much of it in the notes rather than in the main text. Where possible, I use standard translations of the Hindu legal texts and do not provide the Sanskrit original there. In most cases, I give my own translations, especially of the medieval commentaries, in which case I also provide the original text in a note. Some of the Indological discussions attempt an original contribution to the field, while others simply restate the results of older work.

Scholars of religion should expect discussions of Hindu theology and ethics, though in (often legal) terms that they may not be quite used to. In many ways, this book is a further elaboration of my earlier thesis about the pivotal, indeed definitional, role of *dharma* in the Sanskrit legal texts within Hinduism. I am increasingly convinced that Hindu studies have become overly focused on mythological, philosophical, and ritual issues at the expense of other fundamental religious elements, including law.

Finally, scholars of law will find first an ambitious argument about law itself and its intimate connection to religion, especially theology, and to ordinary life. Within this argument, however, I try also to demonstrate important insights into persistent problems in legal and religious studies generally through an examination of the Hindu law materials. Here I primarily suggest lines of thought that might enable Hindu law to find a more secure and productive place within comparative legal studies and legal history.

My great hope for the book is that scholars in each group will find both something familiar and sound from their disciplinary perspective and something fresh and attractive about my use of disciplinary approaches and ideas that are new to them. I have brought these fields together in the hope of creating something innovative and useful for each of them, while acknowledging the risk of displeasing those who may not find such interdisciplinarity as persuasive and helpful as I do. Throughout the book, I have tried to restate complicated arguments in plain language and make use of everyday analogies in order bridge the disciplinary divides that have for too long prevented a more productive confluence of approaches to law and religion.

# *Acknowledgments*

The writing of this book was supported by fellowships from the Institute for Research in the Humanities (IRH) at the University of Wisconsin-Madison (UW) and from the National Endowment for the Humanities. I received additional funding from the UW Graduate School and the College of Letters and Science. I am extremely thankful for both the release time from and financial support of these institutions.

Portions of the book were presented at the IRH Colloquium and the Center for South Asia at UW, and at the Annual Meetings of the American Academy of Religion and of the American Oriental Society. I am grateful for the feedback and questions raised at those venues. Students in my Hindu Law course were subjected to a draft of this study in the fall term of 2008. I thank them for the refinements I was able to make as a result of their feedback and reactions.

I owe a continuing debt of gratitude to my teachers and mentors, Richard Lariviere, Patrick Olivelle, and Ludo Rocher, each of whom provided both specific opinions about and general ideas for portions of the book. Charlie Hallisey provided both moral support and uniquely served as a sounding board for many of my ideas. Timothy Lubin and I had several conversations about ideas in the book and his affirmations and criticisms helped me quite a bit. Rajeev Dhavan patiently spent a long afternoon with me while I presented the basic ideas of the book to him. His wise comments improved several chapters. I wish also to acknowledge my friend, Werner Menski, whose gracious and good-natured encouragement of my work, in spite of our intellectual disagreements, continues to be an inspiration for me personally and professionally. Ethan Kroll read through the entire manuscript at a crucial moment and provided very helpful reactions to the central ideas of the book. Of course, all errors and missteps remain my own. Finally, Fred Smith and Federico Squarcini provided much needed affirmation and criticism at the earliest and last stages of writing.

Members of the University of Wisconsin's South Asia Legal Studies Working Group, particularly Marc Galanter, Mitra Sharafi, Jim Jaffe, and Sumudu Atapattu, provided a most congenial context in which to present ideas and benefit from cognate work being done in the field. I must also thank Kate Brett of Cambridge University Press who sought this book out in the old-fashioned editor's way and patiently guided me through the publication process.

Finally, I owe my largest debt of gratitude and love to my best friend and always supportive wife, Mary Rader. Her natural suspicions of academic truths combine with her gentle and nurturing spirit both to keep me grounded and to keep me moving forward at the same time. The patience that she and our two sons, Jasper and Zimm, showed during the stressful periods of writing mean more to me than they'll ever know.

# *Abbreviations*

| | |
|---|---|
| BDh | *Baudhāyana-Dharmasūtra* |
| DhK | *Dharma-Kośa* |
| GDh | *Gautama-Dharmasūtra* |
| KA | *Kauṭilīya-Arthaśāstra* |
| MDh | *Mānava-Dharmaśāstra* |
| Medh | Manubhāṣya *of Medhātithi* |
| MNP | *Mīmāṃsānyāyaprakāśa* |
| NS | *Nārada-Smṛti* |
| PMādh | *Parāśara-Mādhavīya* |
| PMS | *Pūrva-Mīmāṃsā-Sūtras* |
| SC | *Smṛticandrikā* |
| VaDh | *Vasiṣṭha-Dharmasūtra* |
| YS | *Yājñavalkya-Smṛti* |

# *Introduction* (dharmaśāstra)

Law is the theology of ordinary life. It is both the instrument and the rhetoric by which the most familiar, repeated, and quotidian of human acts are first placed in a system or structure larger than individual experience. Law thus provides the initial movement toward a transcendence of personal consciousness and meaning that makes possible the higher order coordination of human activity, the vision of meaning in life abstracted, and the achievement of ethical, social, political, economic, and religious goods. Law, or rules if you prefer for now, are a key part of every child's socialization into a family, a school, or a team. The communal rules to which we subject our children and ourselves impart meaning and purpose to the collective of which we become a part. As the scope and scale of such rules increase to approach the level more commonly understood as law, the sense of achievement, good, and transcendence provided by the law becomes more abstract and distant. Nevertheless, at every level, the plurality of laws by which we lead our lives encode assumptions and ideas about what we aspire to as human beings and what we presume about ourselves and others. Those assumptions, ideas, and presuppositions I call theology, and they pertain to ordinary life, things near to us like family, birth, death, sex, money, marriage, and work – all common themes in the law.

In staking this claim, I am obviously asking the reader to set aside or extend commonplace notions of law that exist today. One cannot deny the increasing global acceptance of a once parochial notion of law as rules backed by sanctions enforced by the state. This very modern, very European notion of law is not natural, not a given; it was produced at a specific moment in history and promulgated systematically and often forcibly through the institutions of what we now call the nation-state, especially those nations that were also colonial powers.[1] Many now argue that

[1] See Harold Berman, *Law and Revolution: The Formation of the Western Legal Tradition* (Cambridge: Harvard University Press, 1983), p. vii; Gerald Postema, *Bentham and the Common Law Tradition* (Oxford: Clarendon Press, 1986), p. 15.

"particularly in the developed West, contemporary law posits a fundamental conceptual divide between sacred and secular ... [but] the assertion of that divide has its own history, one that defines Western modernity itself."[2] The restriction of law to state-based rules and institutions led in the twentieth century to a kind of backlash against understanding law exclusively as legal positivism. Two important results were the legal realism and, later, legal pluralism movements (among others). Legal realism emphasized the elements of law in practice that had little or nothing to do with the interpretation of legislative statutes and the application of rules in court. Legal pluralism in turn emphasized other normative domains that often served functionally similar roles to state-based laws but without or beyond the control or oversight of the state itself.

First and foremost, therefore, this is a book about the nature of law, and more specifically its dependence and influence on religion.[3] When thinking about law, many of us think exclusively in terms of what the law and its institutions do *to* us, rather than focusing on what the law does *for* us. In other words, we tend to highlight what law restricts and constrains rather than what law enables and achieves. This emphasis derives from the thoroughgoing efforts to "secularize" the law by removing all elements of religion from the law and placing exclusive control over the law in the hands of the state. "Secularization," a term that could mean simply the process of the emphasizing of this world and worldly affairs – a process that does not necessarily exclude religion – has also come to mean the process of eliminating religion from public and civic life. Two centuries of "secularization," however, have hardly removed all religious elements from the law, even in the most secular, liberal, democratic nations. The language of secular theology includes words such as justice, order, security, family, tolerance, equality. In other words, a very similar range of ideas as any transcendental theology.

The formulation of law as the theology of ordinary life may at first seem unusual, even strident, but it is an extension of existing scholarship on the relation of law and everyday life. The key in this scholarship has been to find a way to connect law and everyday life without collapsing them

[2] Martha Merrill Umphrey, Austin Sarat, and Lawrence Douglas, "The Sacred in Law: An Introduction." In *Law and the Sacred* (Stanford: Stanford University Press, 2006), p. 1.

[3] It is important, however, to state up front that I do not intend to reduce law to religion in the form of theology in any historical or chronological sense that might be taken as a crass Durkheimian originalism. Rather, the relationship of law and religion I examine here is conceptual and mutual, though it has important institutional consequences as well.

indistinguishably. What I propose in this book is that the practice of theology helps us see how actions and events of ordinary life first instigate law-making through theological reflection and are then in turn influenced by those very laws. Theology is the attempt to understand or to give meaning to the transcendent significance of acts. Normally, we think of theology as directed, as its etymology clearly tells us, toward God or gods, i.e., to otherworldly affairs. However, most, if not all, theological traditions in this sense also direct attention toward the affairs of the mundane world.[4] When they do so, I suggest that theological reflection takes shape as the law. The act of reflection converts a mere act, a movement of the body, into an obligation. This kind of reflection, focused as it is on the ordinary world and ordinary actions, is theological because it is a reflective attempt to impart meaning and purpose to quotidian acts.

There are many ordinary acts that are rarely, if ever, subject to theological reflection in the sense I intend – blinking, for instance – but many other acts of this kind do become the subject of theological concern – take urination, defecation, and even breathing (think here of the rules/laws for meditation). It is the intrusion of such theological consideration into an otherwise taken-for-granted action that brings it into the realm of law. When the act in question is more deliberate or by nature requires more attention, it is all the more likely to be considered theologically.

Take an example: walking one's children to school. It is obvious that this act by itself, no matter how often done, does not create law. However, as soon as one begins to think about or reflect upon why and how one gets children to school, a host of important questions arise. Suppose, for instance, that one decides that two factors, being a good parent and ensuring the child's safety, take precedence over all other factors in motivating this act. Immediately, two values, two ethical goods, have been identified through self-reflection and reflection on the mundane world. Now, unless such reflection is meant to remain idiosyncratic, motivating only one person, we are faced with a situation in which many people may agree that these are suitable motivations for walking one's children to school. Parents should be good and children should be safe. These crude, reductive conclusions when set in the context of reflection on the specific act of walking children to school beg in fact for the creation of legal restrictions and guarantees that people can achieve their goals to be good parents

[4] Compare, for example, Ball's notion of "nonreligious theology" as a "performance" necessary for any understanding of law. See Milner S. Ball, *The Word and the Law* (Chicago: University of Chicago Press, 1995), p. 2.

and have safe children. Thus arise severe speed limits for vehicles near schools and the provision of crossing-guards or crossing-flags at major intersections.

In the city where I live, the city government recently included appropriations to pay crossing guards. The mayor announced this decision with some fanfare at a local school saying, "This is one of those things that is, and should be, a priority; we should be protecting the health and safety of kids."[5] He also associated the move with public health and promoted it as part of the city's fitness initiative. A document prepared by three national organizations with guidelines for crossing guards further suggests, "The presence of adult crossing guards can lead to more parents feeling comfortable about their children walking or bicycling to school."[6] Most interesting to me was the fact that almost every picture of children crossing a street included in the brochure also pictured a parent. One might think that the presence of crossing guards would lead to fewer parents accompanying their children to school, but the opposite seems true. Clearly, more than safety is involved in the demands made for crossing guards, crossing flags, and vehicle speed limits. The demands and the laws that emerge from them result from assumptions and aspirations about what it takes today to be a good parent and to have safe children. Those assumptions and aspirations in turn are part of an effort at worldly transcendence, a way of making parts of the ordinary world meaningful and ethically good. In this way, the law encodes theological ideas about ordinary actions.

Surely, the two goals are shared by parents even in communities that do not demand legal limitations and enablings that support this specific act. But, it is a theological reflection on this specific ordinary action in a specific community at a specific time that leads to the creation of laws that are prompted by an attempt to give meaning to what might otherwise be an unreflective habit.

Take another example, this time from South Asia: bathing. It would certainly be a stretch for many people in Europe or the United States to see how bathing as an act of ordinary life could possibly be the subject of theological reflection and, thus, in my formulation, of law. However, almost every system of religious law contains rules for bathing, both the appropriate times or occasions for cleaning the body and the methods

[5] *Badger Herald*, October 4, 2005, "City Allows for Crossing Guards," available at http://badgerherald.com/news/2005/10/04/city_allows_for_cros.php.

[6] "Adult School Crossing Guard Guidelines," prepared by the National Center for Safe Routes to School, available at www.saferoutesinfo.org/guide/crossing_guard/pdf/crossing_guard_guidelines_web.pdf.

used while bathing.[7] Among most Hindus in India, for example, it would be unconscionable to worship at a temple without first having bathed. Traditionally, that bath itself would also have taken place in the temple tank. Bathing and rites of ablution are prominent in the Hindu law texts.

For instance, consider just some of the explicit instructions for bathing given in the *Laws of Manu* (5.134, 136–7):

> To purify oneself after voiding urine or excrement and to clean any of the twelve impurities, one should use a sufficient amount of earth and water ... A man intent on purifying himself should apply one lump of earth on the penis, three on the anus, ten on one hand, and seven on both. This is the purification for householders. It is twice that much for students, three times for forest hermits, and four times for ascetics.

Here again, there is no need to explain to people how to clean themselves. That is completely beside the point. The context at hand in the text is the purification of people and things in order for both to be effective participants in, or tools for, religious rituals, and also for social interactions. The ordinary action of bathing becomes through a theological connection to religious purification more than mere hygiene. It is now both a rite and a law that enhances and enables other acts, as also a set of restrictions that must be observed in order to participate in those acts.

Moreover, even hygiene, defined as both biological and social cleanliness, is at the root of rules, even laws, regarding bathing even in the West. One need only refer to showers being required before swimming, before returning to work, before incarceration, and so forth. Biological cleanliness is by no means the only criterion at work in such circumstances. It is the issue of social cleanliness and courtesy, being mandated through rules (admittedly rarely enforced), that take the simple act of bathing into the realm of theology. Yes, it is a worldly theology, but one that is as old as mankind, as Mary Douglas's work on dirt and defilement has shown.[8]

I have thus settled on this mode of thinking being *theological* reflection instead of ethical, ideological, or philosophical reflection for several reasons. First, theology signals the strongly religious element involved when turning ordinary acts into rituals and thereby giving them a transcendent, if still worldly, significance or meaning. Second, theology frequently connotes an abstract, even abstruse, intellectual activity. For

[7] Compare Abraham Cohen, *Everyman's Talmud: The Major Teachings of the Rabbinic Sages* (New York: Schocken, 1995 [1949]), pp. 241–59; Nu Ha Mim Keller (trans.), *Al-Maqasid: Nawawi's Manual of Islam*, rev. edn (Beltsville, MD: Amana, 2002), pp. 12–31.

[8] Mary Douglas, *Purity and Danger* (London: Routledge, 1966), pp. 34–40.

Gladstone, "Theology is ordered knowledge; representing in the region of the intellect what religion represents in the heart and life of man."[9] At its root, theology is the process of making sense of religious institutions and experience to oneself and to others. This definition would seem to beg the question of how to place a boundary around religion itself, but in my view theology is the very process of making that boundary. Everyone does this, but not everyone's ideas count for the same or have equal influence beyond themselves. Plural theologies emerge just as plural legal orders emerge, and in relation to one another. The abstract or abstruse quality of theology is associated with its more professionalized forms, the theologies of priests, rabbis, pandits, and mullahs, and these tend to be hegemonic for many people, though never fully so. Finally, theology also connotes an agenda informed by shared teleological ends toward which the system works. Those ends may be ethical, political, soteriological, or ideological, but the act of reflection that coordinates these ends I will call theology.

There are several advantages to conceiving of law as the theology of ordinary life. First, the gap between rule and behavior is acknowledged and recognized. Law and society studies have insisted on this point for some time. Law and the actions of ordinary life connect but do not collapse into one another. Second, the sometimes stark division between law and everyday life is bridged through the mediating concept of theology. That bridge insists neither on total interpenetration nor on real separation, but rather clarifies the manner in which the two tend to overlap or come together. Theology, even in classic formulations such as St Anselm's "faith seeking understanding" (*fides quaerens intellectum*), captures the liminal position of humanity in living between unconscious sentiment and rationalized discourse. Third, this conceptualization indicates that law is a special kind of theology focused on ordinary human activities, institutions, and events. Other theologies surely exist, but when the theological perspective is brought to bear on ordinary life, the result is law. Fourth and finally, the associations of theology with religion bring out the sense of higher purpose involved whenever law is invoked, and do so in a way that challenges all-too-easy understandings of religion itself as mere belief. If law is the theology of ordinary life, then religion is not a phenomenon directed solely at otherworldly ends, at God or gods, or at escaping or circumventing the practices of ordinary life. In this way, transcendence does not have to imply denial of or disengagement from the world. Law is both

[9] W.E. Gladstone, "Proem to Genesis," *The Nineteenth Century* 19 (1886): 1–21, quote from p. 19.

a means and an end for giving ordinary life meaning and value through a worldly transcendence. This is why law is often connected with other human goods such as order and justice.

Turning to the other element of the opening definition, whether we speak of everyday, ordinary, day-to-day, or workaday life, *Alltagsleben*, or *la vie quotidienne*, we are obviously grasping for something elusive – a way to capture the flux of human experience in its most immediate and most dominant sense. One might dispute whether we can do this at all given that this kind of experience changes faster than it can be fixed or named by language. Still, investigations into that flux are as old as the Buddha and we constantly strive to categorize and fix our lived experience in words. The now fairly large secondary literature on everyday life has argued for various ways to conceive of both the theoretical and the actual place of everyday life in relation to other more palpably defined human institutions. Some, like de Certeau, want to see everyday life as the social location for the contestation of power by ordinary people, the point at which coercive and oppressive social and political pressures are negotiated and resisted in the lives of people.[10] Others, like Das, want to find in everyday life a safe haven of routine and the social location for coping with the intrusions of social and political power.[11] So, when we turn to law, what are we looking for with respect to ordinary life?

In their seminal thematic essay on the topic, Sarat and Kearns argue that an examination of law in everyday life allows us to avoid what they call the "law-first" perspective on the role of law in society. Two basic views of law in everyday life have dominated legal scholarship. The first, the instrumental view, "posits a relatively sharp distinction between legal standards, on the one hand, and nonlegal human activities, on the other."[12] Instrumentalists are "centrally interested in law's effectiveness,"[13] or the degree to which laws achieve their intended effects on society. Moreover, in this view, "'Law' or 'the legal system' ... is a distinctly secondary body of phenomena. It is a specialized realm of state and professional activity that is called into being by the primary social world in order to serve that world's

[10] Michel de Certeau, *The Practice of Everyday Life*, trans. S. Rendall (Berkeley: University of California Press, 1984).

[11] Veena Das, *Life and Words: Violence and the Descent into the Ordinary* (Berkeley: University of California Press, 2006).

[12] Austin Sarat and Thomas Kearns, "Beyond the Great Divide: Forms of Legal Scholarship and Everyday Life." In A. Sarat and T. Kearns (eds.), *Law in Everyday Life* (Ann Arbor: University of Michigan Press, 1993), p. 21.

[13] *Ibid.*, p. 24.

needs."[14] The second, the constitutive view, "suggests that law shapes society from the inside out, by providing the principal categories that make social life seem natural, normal, cohesive, and coherent."[15] Constitutivists tend to see the effect of law in terms of "meaning and self-understandings rather than in the results of sanctions."[16] Following Geertz, the constitutive view argues that "law, rather than being a mere technical add-on to a morally (or immorally) finished society, is, along of course with a whole range of other cultural realities ... an active part of it."[17] Finally, advocates of the constitutive view usually take this view because they are in fact critical of the hegemony of law in Gramsci's sense, i.e., the way in which law pre-structures and predetermines nefarious social realities concerning race, gender, class, religion, sex, and so forth. The strong advocates of one view or the other aside, Sarat and Kearns make a compelling case that everyday life shapes the real effects of law, even as it is simultaneously constituted by law, if only partially. In other words, both the instrumental and the constitutive views are partially correct.

In the end, the instrumental and constitutive views of law and everyday life differ quite dramatically over the question of whether law and everyday life are separate and distinct or together and intermingled. Sarat and Kearns try to offer a way out of the either/or quality of the two views by asking us to step outside what the two views share, namely an emphasis on law as the first site of intellectual reflection. Viewed instead from the perspective of everyday life, it is easy to see how law is both an instrument that hammers away at human actions, sometimes very ineffectively, and a pervasive influence over the way we live our lives. So, asking questions from the perspective of everyday life toward the realms of law seems to avoid some of the problems in beginning with law. Still, I can't help thinking that the difference boils down to: if you want to see law everywhere, you can; if you don't, you won't. Instrumentalists emphasize the gap or separation between law and everyday life. Constitutivists emphasize rather their interpenetration. Is there another alternative?

When Sarat and Kearns claim that both views put law first, I think they really mean state law, primarily in the form of legislation and judicial precedent. What seems missing so far from their discussion of law and everyday life is a thorough consideration of legal pluralism. The fact

[14] Robert Gordon, "Critical Legal Histories," *Stanford Law Review* 36 (1984): 60.

[15] Sarat and Kearns, "Beyond the Great Divide," p. 22. [16] *Ibid.*, p. 27.

[17] Clifford Geertz, "Local Knowledge: Fact and Law in Comparative Perspective." In *Local Knowledge: Further Essays in Interpretive Anthropology* (New York: Basic Books, 1983), p. 218.

of plural legal regimes undermines clear boundaries between law and everyday life in the same manner described by the constitutivists, but it also reveals the definite limits of legal regimes of the state to make change and control action. Engel recognizes this in his use of the term "domain" to speak of coordinations of law and social context that vary widely in scope and power: "the continuum of normative orders ranging from the 'law' of the supermarket check-out line to the constitutional interpretations of federal courts."[18] Still, even Engel struggles to avoid collapsing law and everyday life without any distinction, and he recommends finally that we "reconsider one of the most obvious facts about 'official' law in relation to everyday life: its externality … the norms, procedures, and sanctions of law are generally extrinsic to particular social domains."[19] Engel is surely right to point to law's potential to be external to the social domain it purports to govern. At the same time, Engel has to revert to the notion of "official" law in order to make this point, a term that tends to be understood as "real" law, i.e., what we really mean by law, academic contortions aside.

The advantage of legal pluralism as a model for understanding law and everyday life is that it opens up the possibility for nuanced, multi-level descriptions that show a close relationship between law and ordinary practice at some levels and considerable divergence at others. The disadvantage of legal pluralism, however, is that we lose clarity about the boundaries of both law and everyday life, when we call several different normative orders "legal" and incorporate even wider swaths of human action under the label "everyday." Nevertheless, I want to accept that studies of law and everyday life must be more informed by the fact of legal pluralism because I think the trade-off is worth it and because I think categories like law and everyday life are always contestable and fluid. In fact, it is their very elasticity that helps make expansions and contractions of their scope productive intellectual endeavors for understanding the world around us. Moreover, and more importantly, thinking of law as the theology of ordinary life allows us to think of the same process operating at different scales and in different social contexts, while still maintaining a shared quality. The distinctiveness of law, therefore, is not to be found by arguing for some social

[18] David Engel, "Law in the Domains of Everyday Life: The Construction of Community and Difference." In Sarat and Kearns, *Law in Everyday Life*, pp. 125–6. Engel acknowledges his debt to Moore's well-known articulation of law as a "semi-autonomous social field."

[19] *Ibid.*, p. 168.

or institutional level as the best cut-off point, but rather by articulating the common process and subject matter of law – theology and ordinary life, respectively.

## RELIGIOUS LAW, HINDU LAW, AND DHARMAŚĀSTRA

Focusing on a religious legal system has the advantage of a contrary emphasis to that of thinking of law in terms of legislatures, courts, police, and the state.[20] Religious law emphasizes the role of law in the service of religious goals, or how the law helps accomplish religious ends.[21] One could just as easily look at other traditions of religious law such as Jewish law, Islamic law, or Canon law for similar cues about the close relationship of religion and law. In fact, several existing studies do just that.[22] Too often religious law is classified together with natural law, when in fact all religious legal systems recognize a diversity of the sources of law, including sources that are natural (reason, deity), positive (ruler's edict, legislation), and traditional (custom, precedent). Because of the way they persist in contemporary political and legal contexts as the province of clerics, priests, and rabbis, religious laws are regularly portrayed as dogmatic, primitive, irrational, and anti-modern. Modern nation-states can permit no competition in the domain of law and, for structural reasons, must seek to destroy the real pluralism that exists in every national jurisdiction. That structural commitment is based on a misrepresentation of religious legal systems as inherently against this world and only interested in the not-of-this-world transcendence associated, wrongly in my view, with Christianity.

[20] Robert M. Cover, "Foreword: *Nomos* and Narrative," *Harvard Law Review* 97 (1983–4): 4–68, suggests that these elements are "but a small part of the normative universe that ought to claim our attention" (4). In terms of law's fecund capacity for "jurisgenesis," Cover writes, "Law is a resource in signification that enables us to submit, rejoice, struggle, pervert, mock, disgrace, humiliate, or dignify" (8).

[21] To my mind, the change of emphasis from what law restricts to what law enables defines religious law. Part of the argument here is to suggest that every legal system must contain at least some religious elements and presuppose some goods and some ethics that may be understood in religious terms. Other scholars are less comfortable with the label "religious law." See Andrew Huxley (ed.), *Religion, Law and Tradition: Comparative Studies in Religious Law* (London: Routledge, 2002).

[22] For example, Berman, *Law and Revolution*; Bernard G. Weiss, *The Spirit of Islamic Law* (Athens: University of Georgia Press, 1998); Calum Carmichael, *The Spirit of Biblical Law* (Athens: University of Georgia Press, 1996); R.H. Helmholz, *The Spirit of Classical Canon Law* (Athens: University of Georgia Press, 1996); and Geoffrey MacCormack, *The Spirit of Traditional Chinese Law* (Athens: University of Georgia Press, 1996).

A study of religious law, therefore, has the potential to show first of all that a different kind of transcendence is possible that is worldly and yet still fully religious.[23] A comparative study of religious law, however, can also uncover and disentangle the complex interdependence of law and religion, even under systems that purport to be "secular" and, therefore, nonreligious. An easy way to conceptualize the distinction I make here is to recognize a difference between the separation of church and state and the separation of religion and law.[24] The former is a laudable and achievable goal for a political community, but the latter is both impossible and conducive to deceptive and false rhetoric about the law that can be politically misused and manipulated.[25] Extreme views about the need for law to be "secular" were regularly invoked in twentieth-century totalitarian regimes as part of the pogroms against particular religious communities, while covering up the highly religious underpinnings of laws promoted by such regimes.[26]

As a study of religious law, this book is not an attempt to demonstrate directly how religion still impacts law today and vice versa. Instead, I propose to examine the necessary and essential linkages between law and religion by studying a system of religious law largely unknown to nonspecialists, the tradition conventionally known as Hindu law. The benefit of looking at Hindu law lies precisely in the newness of it both for people interested in law and those interested in religion. Looking at the universal human phenomena of law and religion through the categories of a less familiar tradition forces us to pay closer attention to the details of the particular tradition itself and encourages a greater reflexivity because one cannot presume too much in advance. So, I am trying to take advantage of Hindu law's unfortunate exotic status to reveal underexamined presuppositions in current understandings of the nature of law and to

[23] The best study of this special sense of transcendence in the Hindu context is Francis X. Clooney, "Jaimini's Contribution to the Theory of Sacrifice as the Experience of Transcendence," *History of Religions* 25:3 (1986): 199–212. Clooney summarizes: "In short, it is anthropocentrism that is transcended in Jaimini's interpretation of sacrifice. Human meaningfulness is recognized and organized in balance with other equally important perspectives. Man realizes that he is part of something larger than himself – not the work of the gods or the order of the cosmos or what happened in the beginning, but the here and now, the perceived and repeatable performance of the Vedic sacrifice. By this realization he experiences the transcendent and recognizes that this experience itself is only a part of the ultimate meaning of the world" (p. 211).

[24] See Austin Sarat, Lawrence Douglas, and Martha Umphrey, *Law and the Sacred* (Stanford: Stanford University Press, 2006), p. 14.

[25] *Ibid.*, p. 15.

[26] See Hannah Arendt, *The Portable Hannah Arendt*, ed. Peter Baehr (New York: Penguin, 2000), pp. xvii, 119–40, and 471.

suggest certain beneficial lessons that may be learned from the Hindu legal tradition.

Let me be clear. It is not that *Hindu* law is the theology of ordinary life for *Hindus*. It is that the specifically religious foundations of all legal systems can be revealed through an examination of the Hindu legal tradition. The more narrow claim, while true and important for an understanding of Hindu law itself, perpetuates academic emphases on difference and uniqueness, rather than on comparability and shared imaginings. One purpose of this work is to suggest that the time has come for a different emphasis, one in which the distinctive and contextualized descriptions of Hindu law take second place to a rigorously comparative description.

In pursuit of this comparative emphasis, I repeatedly challenge the conceptualizations of both elements of Hindu law – Hinduism and law – as well as the constitutive concepts of the Hindu legal tradition.[27] In each chapter, I attempt to frame new questions about distinct concepts as part of the overall argument to re-imagine Hinduism in the light of law and law in the light of Hinduism. Each chapter has a threefold movement that begins with an explanation and analysis of a key concept from the scholastic tradition of Hindu jurisprudence. The concept is first explained insofar as possible in its own terms, that is, situating it in the context of the assumptions and worldview of the authors of Hindu legal texts. Next, the concept is linked to other Hindu jurisprudential ideas and the broader traditions of Hinduism. Finally, I consider a larger comparative issue such as ethics, meaning, property, or conflict, that emerges in connection with the Sanskrit term. The three sections of each chapter correspond to these three concerns. The book thus tacks between consideration of religion and law as presented in the Hindu legal texts and interpretive analysis of the comparative valence and value of Hindu jurisprudence. Though not particularly recommended, the book could be read by reading just the first section of each chapter if one were interested in basic technical descriptions of key Hindu legal concepts, or just the second section of each if one wanted an overview of the Hindu law tradition, or just the third sections if one's primary interest lay in the comparative and theoretical significance of the Hindu law tradition.

The fulcrum of the argument about the mutual modulation of both law and Hinduism is a specific genre of texts in the Sanskrit language known

[27] I am, of course, aware of the problematic conceptual history of the terms "Hindu" and "Hinduism," but for the purposes of the present work I use it as suitable and defensible description of this tradition of religious jurisprudence and law. See Donald R. Davis, Jr., "Hinduism as a Legal Tradition," *Journal of the American Academy of Religion* 75:2 (2007), pp. 241–67, for a specific discussion of my approach to the issue.

as Dharmaśāstra. In common parlance, though not without distortion, these texts are also called the Hindu legal texts or lawbooks. These texts contain what I will call Hindu jurisprudence, a way of thinking about law from a distinctively Hindu perspective.

For those who coined the label, Hindu law referred to the laws applicable to Hindus in British India as determined through translations of Dharmaśāstra texts by British Orientalists and the precedents of Hindu law cases brought before British judges in India. As a result of a well-known misinterpretation of what Dharmaśāstra texts were, the British used them as though they were legislated codes and applied them uniformly throughout their territories in India, according to their own classification of religious identity. This poorly conceived presentation of a "native" Indian legal tradition was subsequently backread as a convenient, and less intimidating, label for the system of religious jurisprudence given in Dharmaśāstra and also appropriated in the development of the still operative system of personal laws in India and elsewhere today. Although always either an anachronism or a distortion, the value in preserving the label "Hindu law" comes from its insistence that there is a legal history in Hindu traditions and that Hinduism does indeed have something to add to legal studies.

Understood as a long historical tradition, Hindu law can legitimately refer to different but related institutions and practices. Hindu jurisprudence, by contrast, is restricted almost exclusively to the legal theory of Dharmaśāstra texts. There is no real sense that a point of substantive Hindu law or of Hindu legal reasoning could emanate from anywhere else, unlike for instance the highly variegated theories of soteriology, ritual practice, cosmology, etc. that collectively and conventionally are seen as equally part of Hinduism. It is for this reason that I have come to define classical Hindu law in the following terms:

> Classical Hindu law was a variegated grouping of local legal systems that had different rules and procedures of law but that were united by a common jurisprudence or legal theory represented by Dharmaśāstra. In premodern India, the practical legal systems of any two given Hindu communities may have operated quite differently, but they were both likely to respect the "spirit" of Dharmaśāstra and incorporate it into their legal rules, processes, and institutions. The degree of correspondence between Dharmaśāstra and practical law made a system more or less Hindu.[28]

[28] Donald R. Davis, Jr. "Law." In S. Mittal and G. Thursby (eds.), *Studying Hinduism* (New York: Routledge, 2008), p. 225. Obviously, the propriety of the label Hindu for any particular legal system is a matter for empirical and historical investigation and judgment.

This definition attempts to account for clear historical variations in the practice of Hindu law and the distinction, even separation, of such practice from Dharmaśāstra rules, while still incorporating the unifying effects of Dharmaśāstra on patterns of legal thought and, to some extent, substantive rules of law. Ironically, Hindu law was never a simple matter of applying the Dharmaśāstra until the British tried to do so. So, what is Dharmaśāstra?

Recent research on the composition of the early Dharmaśāstra texts suggests that their origins come from three sources:

1 historically existing customary norms;
2 reformulations of earlier texts on *dharma* and sometimes other genres; and
3 innovative rules and frameworks of individual authors.[29]

Parsing out which parts of a text originate from what sources is very difficult, however, and is only achievable through extensive knowledge of other Sanskrit texts and further historical evidence.

A typical Dharmaśāstra text reads like a list of rules. A topic is announced and situated in some larger frame; for example, "I have described above the entire Law relating to decisions regarding boundaries. Next, I will explain how cases of verbal assault are to be decided" (MDh 8.266). Then a shorter or longer list of rules pertinent to that topic is given; for example, "For assailing a Brahmin, a Kṣatriya ought to be fined 100, and a Vaiśya 150 or 200, but a Śūdra ought to suffer corporal punishment. A Brahmin should be fined 50 for abusing a Kṣatriya, 25 for abusing a Vaiśya, and 12 for abusing a Śūdra" (MDh 8.267–8). Grammatically, the rules are usually stated in the imperative or command form known as the optative, though even many declarative statements are interpreted as commands. Due to this form and style, Dharmaśāstra texts give the appearance of being codifications set forth by lawgivers. However, the "lawgivers" here are all mythological figures and there is no historical evidence for either an active propagation or implementation of Dharmaśāstra by a ruler or a state – as distinct from other forms of recognizing, respecting, and using the texts. Thinking of Dharmaśāstra as a legal code and of its authors as lawgivers is thus a serious misunderstanding of its history.[30]

[29] See Richard W. Lariviere, "Dharmaśāstra, Custom, 'Real Law,' and 'Apocryphal' Smṛtis," *Journal of Indian Philosophy* 32:5–6 (2004): 611–27, Albrecht Wezler, "Dharma in the Veda and the Dharmaśāstras," *Journal of Indian Philosophy* 32:5–6 (2004): 629–54, and Patrick Olivelle, *Manu's Code of Law: a Critical Edition and Translation of the* Mānava-Dharmaśāstra (New York: Oxford University Press, 2005), pp. 5–49.

[30] Werner Menski, *Hindu Law: Beyond Tradition and Modernity* (Delhi: Oxford University Press, 2003) has been the most insistent scholar on this point.

Closer would be to think of the Dharmaśāstras as the textbooks for the Hindu scholastic tradition of religious jurisprudence. The simile works because textbooks serve first to instruct someone in a particular academic way of thinking and, therefore, are always at some remove from practical life. Textbooks deal with the constructed world of an academic subject – in the case of Dharmaśāstra, the ideal world of *dharma* properly performed. The constructed world is, of course, connected to the practical world, the world of ordinary life, but always through reflection and abstraction. In this way, the logic of everyday life is connected, as Holmes would have it, to the logic of law, but through the mediating lens of theology.

These textbooks of Hindu jurisprudence were written historically in four different formats.[31] The early texts (*c.*300 BC to 100 BC), known as Dharmasūtras, were prose texts consisting of aphoristic rules linked according to themes that were elaborated in later texts. The Dharmasūtras were also explicitly ascribed to, and in some cases originated within, one of the Vedic lineages, the traditions of recitation and ritual practice associated with branches of the sacred Vedas. The *Laws of Manu* (*c.*AD 200) introduced, for the first time, both a new format, namely versified rules, and a host of new topics, especially those pertaining to rulers, into the Dharmaśāstra tradition. Though not traditional, modern scholars often describe verse texts as Dharmaśāstras and *smṛti*s, "remembered" traditions or texts.[32] Both these early formats, prose and verse, are considered root-texts or source-texts for later commentaries and digests within the tradition, the third and fourth formats, respectively. It should be noted, however, that such root-texts continued to be produced until at least the eighteenth century. The earliest known commentary on a Dharmaśāstra root-text is that of Bhāruci on the *Laws of Manu* or possibly Asahāya on the *Laws of Nārada* in the seventh or eighth century AD. Commentaries are organized as complete glosses and interpretations of a single root-text, but they always incorporate verses from other root-texts as well as part of their explanations. In this way, they differ only in emphasis from the digests, which are organized by topic or theme, not according to a single

[31] An excellent survey of the Dharmaśāstra literature is found in the first half of Robert Lingat's *The Classical Law of India* (Berkeley: University of California Press, 1973). A shorter survey with a more up-to-date chronology of the texts is Patrick Olivelle, "Dharmaśāstra: A Textual History." In T. Lubin, J. Krishnan, and D.R. Davis, Jr. (eds.), *Hinduism and Law: an Introduction* (Cambridge: Cambridge University Press, forthcoming).

[32] On *smṛti*, see recently David Brick, "Transforming Tradition into Texts: The Early Development of *Smṛti*," *Journal of Indian Philosophy* 34 (2006): 287–302. One notes that Dharmaśāstra thus refers generally to a whole textual tradition and specifically to the versified root-texts such as the *Laws of Manu*.

source. Digests, however, also often include lots of explanatory glosses and interpretations in the manner of commentaries.

The tendency has been to see the formats as somehow replacing one another, but the reality is different. The earliest Dharmasūtra format continued in certain ways, for example in the *Laws of Viṣṇu*, though it was not a preferred mode of composition, while versified root-texts continued to be composed long after the earliest written commentaries were composed. We suspect, too, that every root-text probably had commentaries that have not survived or were transmitted orally right from the composition of the source. Digests as a textual form do seem to be an innovation of the twelfth century AD, but no satisfactory explanation has yet been given for this innovation. Nevertheless, digests did not displace other formats for Dharmaśāstra. With this cursory review of the style and the genres of Dharmaśāstra in mind, we might turn now to the subject at the heart of these texts, *dharma*.

In one way, the Hindu law tradition and Dharmaśāstra texts in particular are concerned with one complex thing: what is *dharma* and how do we know it and do it? It is beyond the scope of this book, or perhaps any, to fully explore the wide range of meanings and significance given to this term in the long history of India.[33] What I can do here, however, is give a basic idea of how *dharma* is understood in Dharmaśāstra texts and distinguish that idea from other prominent uses of the term. The general definition given long ago by P.V. Kane still captures well this specific meaning.

According to Kane, *dharma* in Dharmaśāstra means "the privileges, duties and obligations of a man, his standard of conduct as a member of the Āryan community, as a member of one of the castes, as a person in a particular stage of life."[34] In this definition, we see at least three important elements of *dharma*. First, *dharma* establishes and is oriented toward privilege, duty, and obligation rather than rights and uniform principles. Second, Dharmaśāstra views these duties almost wholly in terms of and from the perspective of men. As with every ancient jurisprudence, the ideal subject of legal and religious reflection is always male. Women are considered within the system at various points, but we should keep in mind the essentially agnostic, though sometimes downright misogynistic, attitude of the authors of these texts toward the condition and role of women. Third, *dharma* is linked to and varies according to one's membership in

[33] For a collective attempt to describe some of *dharma*'s various meanings and significances in South Asian religious history, see Patrick Olivelle (ed.), *Dharma: Studies in Its Semantic, Cultural, and Religious History* (Delhi: Motilal Banarsidass, 2009).

[34] P.V. Kane, *History of Dharmaśāstra* (Poona: BORI, 1962–75), Vol. 1, p. 3.

particular communities. Again, uniformity gives way to specific statuses and identities. It is worth noting, too, that none of these elements refers to or relies upon a supernatural source or a particular sense of morality. *Dharma* in Dharmaśāstra thus connects primarily to socially determined statuses, duties, and institutions, and only secondarily to the fixed, transcendent source of the sacred Vedas of the Hindu tradition discussed in the next two chapters.

One important aspect of *dharma* in Dharmaśāstra not addressed here by Kane is the idea that *dharma* is both rule and substance. Hacker made this point some time ago:

> We must imagine *dharma* as primarily a substance or a transcendental, immaterial thing. This substance, this immaterial thing is first of all in concrete duties, as they are passed down as fixed norms and prescriptions – indeed, these norms *are dharma*, that is, *dharma before its performance*. Because these norms already *are dharma*, however, *dharma* before its performance actually does not correspond to our concepts "norm," "rule," "law," or "duty." All of these are far too abstract. *Dharma* is rather a concrete *model of behavior* with positive significance for salvation that somehow exists already before its performance and waits for realization, or rather it is a collection of such models.[35]

The tenth-century Dharmaśāstra commentator Medhātithi made exactly the same point in his commentary on the *Laws of Manu*: "The authors of the traditional texts use the word *dharma* sometimes in the sense of actions which form the subjects of injunctions and prohibitions and sometimes in the sense of the thing that arises from the performance of those actions and persists until it has given its reward."[36] It is this ambiguity that allows *dharma* to be seen as both law and merit.

It may at first be surprising that very few definitions of *dharma* are given in the textual tradition devoted to its explication. The reason few definitions are given, however, lies precisely in *dharma*'s contextuality. Uniform statements of *dharma* are impossible. Instead, *dharma*'s sources must be established and its basic structure enumerated according to the contextual factors that cause *dharma* to vary from person to person and situation to situation. An example from the *Laws of Yājñavalkya* shows the emphasis on duty, contextuality, and society. The opening verse reads "The sages worshipped Yājñavalkya, the lord of yogis and said, 'Tell us in full the *dharma*s of the castes, the orders of life, and the others'" (YS 1.1).

[35] Paul Hacker, "Dharma in Hinduism," *Journal of Indian Philosophy* 24 (2006): 490.

[36] *dharmaśabdo 'yaṃ smṛtikaraiḥ kadācid vidhiniṣedhaviṣayabhūtāyāṃ kriyāyāṃ prayujyate, kadācit tadanuṣṭhānajanya āphalapradānāvasthāyini kasmiṃścid arthe* (Medh on MDh 2.6).

The commentator Vijñāneśvara tells us first that "the others" here refers to people of mixed caste. Then, he enumerates what *dharma* means by dividing it into six groups. The first five categories of *dharma* are:

1 caste;
2 life-stage;
3 caste and life-stage;
4 special; and
5 occasional.

The last category is (6) common. I separate the first five because these are the ones usually found in other texts. The groups identify the principal factor determining various *dharma*s such that some *dharma*s are effectively established by caste or life-stage alone, some by both caste and life-stage, some by special status such as being a ruler, and some by special occasion such as a festival or a personal penance. The sixth category refers to common virtues expected of all people including non-violence, honesty, and purification. Interestingly, but characteristically, the final category is enumerated in a single verse (YS 1.122) in the text. [37] The extremely concise treatment of this group signals its marginal position in the Dharmaśāstra understanding and presentation of *dharma*.

More revealing is the sixth verse of the *Laws of Yājñavalkya* (YS 1.6) which reads, "Whatever thing one gives with sincere faith to a worthy recipient at the right place, the right time, and by the right means, that is the entire definition of *dharma*." The poetic impact of the root-text, its distillation of every human duty into a simple act of giving, is immediately undermined by Vijñāneśvara's explanation of the verse. First, he glosses the word "gives" by saying that it means "relinquishing by bringing about the complete ownership of something in another person such that it may never return to its original owner." A beautiful image of sincere and simple piety is thus reframed as the legal transfer of property claims over an object. Vijñāneśvara continues, "This brings about *dharma*. But, is that the full extent of it? No, because of the word 'entire.' Even other things that are stated in the *śāstra* such as caste, special duties, libations, sacrifices, and so forth, these are the 'entire' cause of *dharma*." Again, the poetic simplicity suggested by the root-verse, in which the entirety of human obligation may be reduced to a single sincere act, is thwarted through a common

[37] The full list at YS 1.122 reads "Non-violence, truth, non-stealing, purification, control of the senses, giving, restraint, compassion, and calmness – these are means to achieve *dharma* for everyone." Compare MDh 6.92.

interpretive extension of the meaning of a single word to include, in this case, a host of other actions under the originally exclusive term "entire." The problem for Vijñāneśvara was this: the root-text can surely not mean what it says literally, because the remainder of the text becomes meaningless if it does. As prosaic as it may be, Vijñāneśvara, like all commentators in the tradition, is charged with making the whole text make sense as a whole. To do that in this case, he had to read all the other *dharma*s to be explained later in the text into the single word "entire." The point of this verse then is merely to provide one example of the productive causes of *dharma*.

This seemingly complete definition of *dharma*, therefore, becomes in the commentator's hands merely an illustrative statement of a much more complex web of privileges, duties, and obligations. The explanation emphasizes the practical social implications of the verse, namely the rules of property transfer and the large array of other *dharma*s that are similarly regulated. Other definitions of *dharma* in Hindu traditions emphasize its connection to Vedic ritual, religious salvation, or a fundamental moral principle such as non-violence or compassion.[38] Nevertheless, within Dharmaśāstra itself, we find a reluctance to define *dharma* at all, except in very general terms.[39] Instead, the texts provide elaborate systems for determining *dharma* (the subject of the next chapter) and extensive, but not exhaustive, elaborations of specific *dharma*s.

Historically, three frameworks have been used to divide *dharma* topically into discussions of specific duties. The oldest belongs to Manu, who divides *dharma* according to caste and life-stage. Another early scheme appears in Yājñavalkya, who divides *dharma* into three subtopics: household rites and duties, legal procedure, and penance. Finally, when digests of *dharma* material first began to appear in the twelfth century AD, extensive compendia on subtopics within older *dharma* schemes (legal procedure, gift, ancestral rites, kingship, etc.) came into vogue, though no fixed list of such topics existed. These three divisions are primarily ways to organize the contents of a text, but they further reveal the detail-oriented enumeration of rules for religious and legal practice that characterizes

[38] See Kane's review (*History of Dharmaśāstra*, Vol. 1, pp. 4–5) of the Pūrva-Mīmāṃsā (*codanālakṣano 'rtho dharmaḥ*), Vaiśeṣika (*yato 'bhyudayaniḥśreyasasiddhiḥ sa dharmaḥ*), and other definitions of *dharma* (*ahiṃsā paramo dharmaḥ*, *ānṛśaṃsyaṃ paro dharmaḥ*, *ācāraḥ paramo dharmaḥ*).

[39] Consider, for instance, Medhātithi's definition of *dharma* at MDh 2.6 "*dharmaśabdaś ca … yat puruṣasya kartavyaṃ pratyakṣādyavagamyavilakṣaṇena svabhāvena śreyaḥsādhanam* [*Dharma* is that which a man should do and which produces his welfare, with a nature that is distinguished from what can be known through perception and other worldly means of knowledge].

both theological and legal writing. And yet, we find few philosophical, especially ontological, discussions of the nature of the self or spirit that typify Hindu writing on Vedānta or Yoga. Nor do we find speculations about esoteric rites or realities of the sort found in Tantric texts. And we certainly see little that might be connected with the devotional, emotive, and participatory religious experience associated with Bhakti poetry and institutions. It is true that texts such as the *Laws of Viṣṇu* and the *Laws of Śaṅkha and Likhita* have clear sectarian affiliations, but even these texts conform in the main to a special Dharmaśāstra idiom and form of religious and legal expression. Despite the relative absence of these other important Hindu ways of being religious, it would be hard not to characterize a great proportion of the contents of Dharmaśāstra as religious.

An important point about commentaries and digests is in order. The Dharmaśāstra tradition is a form of scholasticism, meaning that it is a relatively closed intellectual system that focuses primarily on the correct understanding and transmission of a canon of texts through time.[40] Some scholars have claimed that Hindu law commentaries came into being in order to bring older root-texts up to date by adjusting old norms to new times and circumstances.[41] Others claim the opposite, that commentaries are solely part of a completely self-contained intellectual tradition, the transmitters of which paid little to no attention to changes in social history.[42] The truth, most now suspect, lies somewhere in between. Perhaps the best way to describe what commentators were trying to do is to say that they, like most academics, were first concerned to preserve and work within the established conventions for thinking and writing in their discipline. In other words, a proper interpretation of the texts was foremost in their minds. At the same time, it is both expected and unavoidable that changing social, political, religious, economic, and other circumstances would have influenced the commentators' interpretations. It appears that the impact of social history was sometimes conscious and sometimes not.

[40] In this respect, the tradition of Hindu law mirrors the significant scholastic origins of legal thought in Europe. See Berman, *Law and Revolution*, pp. 131ff.

[41] Ashutosh Dayal Mathur, *Medieval Hindu Law: Historical Evolution and Enlightened Rebellion* (Delhi: Oxford University Press, 2007) is only the most recent work to defend the notion that Hindu law commentaries were written to "suit the exigencies of the time and the particular requirements of various regions and groups" (p. xxiii).

[42] Though famous denials of any concern for historical reality in Hindu legal texts were made by authors such as J.H. Nelson and Govinda Das, the staunchest defender of a view of Dharmaśāstra authors as scholiasts, not lawyers, and of Dharmaśāstra texts as academic treatises, not records of a common law tradition has been Ludo Rocher. Though his views have moderated somewhat recently, see Rocher's early article, "The Historical Foundations of Ancient Indian Law:" "The entire commentarial tradition is totally separated from reality; nor was it ever intended

For the most part, however, the authors of Dharmaśāstra are not forthright about innovations or changes that they make to the tradition, whether these be text-critical, organizational, or interpretive in nature. In this way, history in Dharmaśāstra is rhetorically suppressed.

For this reason, though historical questions will arise occasionally in the course of this study, my primary interest will concern rather the jurisprudence, philosophy, or theory of Hindu law as presented in Dharmaśāstra. I make no claim to present in these pages a *history* of Hindu law. Right up front, it is important to emphasize the synchronous, even timeless or ahistorical, self-presentation of the Hindu legal texts. Like the scholars of Canon law, Dharmaśāstra scholiasts "indulged in a sublime disregard of history."[43] Concerns about historical and social context are, it would seem, systematically and scrupulously avoided. This is not to say that differences between and developments in the texts cannot be attributed, sometimes with fair certainty, to known historical or social factors; but, this is not how the texts themselves present matters. Instead, we find a somewhat open-ended group of foundational or root texts, on the one hand, and a series of commentaries on and thematic digests of these root-texts, on the other. We know almost nothing biographical about the authors of the root-texts and only slightly more about the commentators. Dating both root-texts and commentaries is fraught and existing chronologies hardly ever come closer than a century or two in most cases.[44] The result is a scholastic tradition that appears to operate outside the bounds of time and space. Of course, modern scholars need not accept the terms of self-presentation in Dharmaśāstra, but for the purposes of this book, I want to set aside significant historical questions in favor of appropriating a synchronic traditional view of Hindu jurisprudence in order to focus on conceptual foundations, assumptions, and structures that inform the Hindu legal imagination abstractly conceived. In particular, I avoid the very important historical work of correlating developments in Dharmaśāstra with changes in social history and cultural context. In the end, I provide an historically flattened view of well-developed medieval

to intervene in the reality of practical law and jurisdiction." See also a later lecture "Changing Patterns of Diversification in Hindu Law" for a detailed account. Both articles can be found in Ludo Rocher, *Studies in Hindu Law and Dharmaśāstra*, ed. D.R. Davis, Jr. (Delhi: Motilal Banarsidass, forthcoming).

[43] Stephan Kuttner, "Harmony from Dissonance: An Interpretation of Medieval Canon Law." In *The History of Ideas and Doctrines of Canon Law in the Middle Ages* (London: Variorum Reprints, 1980), p. 11.

[44] Kane, *History of Dharmaśāstra*, Vol. 2, pt. 1, pp. xi–xii provides the standard chronology of Dharmaśāstra texts. Olivelle, "Dharmaśāstra: A Literary History" gives the latest chronology of the major texts with a persuasive account of the appropriate methodology for dating.

views of Dharmaśāstra over either a history of the texts or of the law in practice. This approach to the texts is not without intellectual pitfalls, but it does have the virtue of mirroring traditional approaches to the same texts. More importantly, this approach permits us to see the remarkably stable conceptual frameworks of the tradition.

One of the most amazing things about these texts, in fact, is the longevity of the conceptual and interpretive frameworks used by their authors. Of course, it would be too much to say that a first-century author understood the texts in exactly the same way as a tenth-century commentator or a nineteenth-century pandit, but the fact remains that the commonalities of presuppositions, hermeneutic approaches, and conceptual foundations between these far outweigh the differences. The tradition very effectively passed on specific ways of writing and thinking that changed but little in the course of time. The historical certainty of massive social, religious, political, and legal changes outside this textual tradition is simply not easily discerned in the texts themselves. Since the purpose of this book is to understand the tradition, its self-understanding, and its self-presentation, questions of history, profound and necessary as they are, find only a marginal place in this book.

A final key point to understand about Dharmaśāstra is the place of this particular scholastic tradition in the larger realm of scholarship and scholasticism in India. Knowledge was divided into many different branches, each called a *śāstra*.[45] There are *śāstra*s for architecture, dance, ritual, poetics, grammar, drama, religious liberation, rulership, and love, among others. The special branch devoted to religious and legal duty, however, was Dharmaśāstra. This does not mean that this tradition and its texts had a complete monopoly on ideas about religion and law, but it does mean, first, that specialists in Dharmaśāstra made it their business to know the specificities of this tradition and to promulgate its hegemony as the central discipline concerning *dharma*, and, second, that any other speculations about *dharma* in other genres and other traditions, Hindu or not, had to contend with the paragon status of Dharmaśāstra views on *dharma*.[46]

When I speak of law in this work, I mean *dharma*. More specifically, I intend that the Sanskrit word for law is *dharma* and, more importantly, that the English word for *dharma* is law. Translation always

[45] On *śāstra*, see Sheldon Pollock, "The Idea of Śāstra in Traditional India," and "Playing by the Rules: Śāstra and Śāstric Literature," both in A.L. Dallapiccola (ed.), *Shastric Traditions in Indian Arts* (Wiesbaden: Steiner, 1989), pp. 17–26 and 301–12.

[46] I explain this argument more fully in Donald R. Davis, Jr., "Hinduism as a Legal Tradition," p. 258.

creates trouble. In this case, however, it is the best kind of trouble, in which a conceptual mismatch, a partial overlap, forces us to reconsider and rethink what we already know. I could instead speak of a restricted sense of law – limiting it to familiar ideas about courts, legislatures, and police – and an expansive sense of law – opening it to several kinds of social control, moral norms, and regularized behavior. But, I choose not to make this distinction because it lets us off the hook too easily in terms of seeing what is really interesting about the Hindu tradition, namely an insistence that both notions of *dharma*/law operate simultaneously. On the side of "law," therefore, I want to suggest that we neglect the law's *dharma* side and, conversely, on the side of "*dharma*" that we neglect its law side. For those interested in law, I will argue that *dharma* helps to reveal understudied interventions of law in ordinary life. For those interested in Hinduism, I will try to show that a focus on law uncovers a pervasive and power role for law in this often mythologically and esoterically defined religion.

The main social location of this other religious tradition in Hinduism, the household, is by no means unknown in scholarship. Rather, it is taken for granted or linked somehow to other religious practices. I believe this religion of the household has been subsumed or underemphasized, in part, because scholars have not considered it to have its own theology. My argument throughout this book is that Dharmaśāstra is that theology. It is a theological system focused on discovering and transmitting the religious significance of ordinary human activities, especially those linked with the family, household, and other localized institutions. Such a household theology, or theology of ordinary life, takes the form of law. From the Hindu law tradition, therefore, we may learn that the greater part of law everywhere incorporates a similar theology of ordinary life, and that this accounts for the inextricable links between law and religion.

A few final introductory remarks. I make no apology for the simultaneously Hegelian and Pauline title of the book, because I believe it invokes the right kind of associations for my argument. The authors of Dharmaśāstra themselves viewed the Veda as a quasi-Hegelian Spirit that guided and restrained the forward movement of humanity through history. At the same time, the Hindu tradition promotes a notion that Dharmaśāstra contained the spirit, the higher value, of the law as against the flesh, the merely worldly manipulation of law as political instrument or mechanical and lifeless ritual. We will see that this higher effect was called "the unseen" or the "unprecedented," a substantive benefit created through the ritually conceived practice of *dharma* as law.

Lastly, I have been influenced by several theoretical approaches to law and religion and I should identify those at the beginning. From legal studies, readers will find a reliance on ideas of legal pluralism, legal realism, law and society, and law and literature – each of which brings something distinctive to the study of Hindu jurisprudence. The often quoted maxim in legal studies that "we are all realists now" may characterize the thoughtful core of legal academics and some professionals. However, I am skeptical that most professionals and most students have internalized a basic insight of "law and society" studies, namely that most law happens outside of courts and legislatures. In religious studies, readers should expect more emphasis on intellectualist views of religion over psychological, sociological, or phenomenological approaches. The nature of the evidence partially determines this choice, but I also want to argue that theology and hermeneutics are as central to religious life as ritual, experience, and identity. Indeed, I want to suggest that all these characteristics of religion interpenetrate one another. By combining the insights of methodologies in both legal and religious studies, I hope to bring the rich material of the Hindu law tradition to bear on questions that matter today, issues that continue to attract and confound academics and professionals in their efforts to improve the world around us through better understanding.

CHAPTER I

# *Sources and theologies* (pramāṇa)

One of the most common and best ways to get an initial sense of a system of law is to examine the sources of law taken as authoritative in that system. Sources of legal authority speak to both the religious and social foundations of the law. In most legal traditions, the sources of law can usually be categorized in terms of morality, politics, and history or universal, legislative, and traditional rules, respectively.[1] The priority given to one of these or their balance differentiates legal systems from each other and also distinguishes periods of their internal history. Hindu law is no exception to this scheme, though, of course, the particular emphases given and how each source of law is described and conceived relate to the history of law in India and the development of Hinduism. In the case of Hindu law, the de-emphasis on legislation and the commands of political rulers strikes the modern reader as its distinctive characteristic.[2] This relative lack of legislative rules, however, emerges in part from the fact that Hindu jurisprudence names the household, and not the state, as the primary institutional location of law. More broadly, we can say that the Hindu legal tradition maintains that the main authority over, and responsibility for, law occurs at the level of community, not state polity, and that the paradigmatic community is the household or the family, especially the household of an educated Brahmin male.

In this chapter, I examine first the sources of law and their relation to each other identified in Dharmaśāstra as the legitimate means of knowing *dharma*. Knowing how and why these sources are justified as authoritative provides insight into how the household became the exemplary institution of religious and legal reflection in Hindu jurisprudence. I will argue

[1] I follow Harold J. Berman, "Toward an Integrative Jurisprudence: Politics, Morality, and History," *California Law Review* 76 (1988): 779–801, in using these categories.

[2] Robert Lingat, *The Classical Law of India*, trans. J.D.M. Derrett (Berkeley: University of California Press, 1996), p. 256, has made the most thorough examination to date of the traditional Indian king as an "administrator, not a legislator."

that the focus on the household and other local institutions facilitated the identification of shared goals and goods that informed and structured the Hindu view of law. Small-scale communities such as the household are more effective both at imposing common values and goods and, at the same time, convincing their members of the advantages and benefits of accepting those core ideas. The discussion of common goods will lead finally to an examination of how a cardinal legal principle of modernity, the rule of law, might be understood against the legal theology of the Hindu tradition. The comparison of two different formulations of what constitutes basic legal authority helps us see the weaknesses and strengths in each.

## HOW TO KNOW THE LAW

The Dharmaśāstra texts do not tell us about the sources of law, of course, but rather the sources of *dharma*. In this context, there are two words for source in Sanskrit. The first, *mūla*, means "root" and is used in the classic statements of the sources of *dharma* in early Dharmaśāstra. The second, *pramāṇa*, is a term used widely in philosophical texts to mean the valid bases for knowledge and thus the authoritative source for knowing something. The latter is frequently used as a gloss or synonym for the former in commentaries on the early texts. Therefore, the tradition generally understands the sources of *dharma* to be sources of knowing what *dharma* is.

Three sources of *dharma* are described in all Dharmaśāstra texts. The first and theologically most important is the Veda or Vedas. Whether singular or plural, this source refers to the four collections of oral texts of hymns, praises, and ritual instructions pristinely preserved for more than three millennia by Brahmin reciter-scholars. Nevertheless, there is an intriguing ambiguity between the meaning of the Veda singular and Vedas plural. The plural can only mean the texts just mentioned, but the singular also has a more abstract meaning of knowledge taken generally. It is all knowledge and the totality of perfect knowledge existent in the cosmos itself. The tradition generally acknowledges that not all Veda has been communicated in the Vedas. Neither may be impugned in the slightest, but the extant Vedas can sometimes be incomplete. Theologically, it is this incompleteness that allows other sources of *dharma* to exist at all.

The second source is called *smṛti*, or tradition, though it refers more specifically to particular texts that contain the collected traditions of virtuous and lawful people including the Dharmaśāstra texts themselves. The famous Indian epics *Rāmāyaṇa* and *Mahābhārata* are also part of this

Table 1. *The three sources of dharma*

| Source (*mūla/ pramāṇa*) | English equivalent | Common form |
|---|---|---|
| *veda* | revelation | oral text |
| *smṛti* | tradition | written text |
| *ācāra* | customary law | community norm |

group, as are the voluminous narrative and didactic texts known as the Purāṇas. When scholars speak of Hindu law, they most often mean the Dharmaśāstra texts that fall into this category.

More important to the practice of law at any given historical moment, however, is the final source, *ācāra*, or customary law. The significance and distinctiveness of this source to the overall system of Hindu law led me to devote Chapter 7 of this study to *ācāra*. For now, it will suffice to note, first, that *ācāra* has a strongly normative character and is much more than habit or unconscious behavior and, second, that it is always restricted to a particular community or group.

The classic root-texts that establish these sources of *dharma* are found in the Dharmasūtras. Compare the following three statements:

> The source of Law is the Veda, as well as the tradition and practice of those who know the Veda. (GDh 1.1–2)
>
> The Law is taught in each Veda, in accordance with which we will explain it. What is given in the tradition is the second, and the conventions of cultured people are the third. (BDh 1.1.1–4)
>
> The Law is set forth in the Vedas and the Traditional Texts. When these do not address an issue, the practice of cultured people becomes authoritative. (VaDh 1.4–5)

The most thorough explication within Dharmaśāstra of these three sources identified in each of the early Dharmasūtras comes not from a commentary on one of these texts, but rather from the extensive commentary by Medhātithi on the *Laws of Manu*.[3]

"The Vedas," says Medhātithi, "get their name because they are the source from which people learn (*vidanti*) the good defined as *dharma*, which cannot be known from any other source of knowledge."[4] A text is

[3] A comparison of Medhātithi with the work of his predecessor Kumārila in the other branch of learning that laid claim to *dharma*, the Pūrva-Mīmāṃsā, shows that Medhātithi borrowed heavily from Kumārila's explication of the sources. Nevertheless, in order to stay within Dharmaśāstra, I will focus here on Medhātithi's presentation of the three classic sources.

[4] Medh on MDh 2.6 gives here a folk etymology: *vidanty ananyapramāṇavedyaṃ dharmalakṣaṇam artham asmād ity vedāḥ*.

not accepted as authoritative merely because the name "Veda" is attached to it, "but rather, in the context of its being without any human author, because it teaches what actions must be performed and because it contains no errors."[5] This definition of the Vedas – including naming the four Vedas as the Ṛg-, Yajur-, Sāma-, and Atharva-Vedas – is common to most or all Hindu texts, and it is most closely associated with the Pūrva-Mīmāṃsā philosophical tradition, discussed in Chapter 2.

We might expect Medhātithi to go into the philosophical arguments made elsewhere for the unauthored, eternal, and transcendent nature of the Veda. All of this is simply presumed by referring to the Mīmāṃsā tradition.[6] Instead, Medhātithi distinguishes what can be known directly and what can be taught. Medhātithi begins with the surprising statement that Dharmaśāstra expounds the Veda as the first source of *dharma* not as a matter of revelation, but as a matter of logic or reason. Only the elite few can learn directly from the Veda that the Veda is the first and truest source of *dharma*. Dharmaśāstras are written to teach that fact to others who are incapable of such direct knowledge. The point here is that Dharmaśāstra is a second-order discourse with the respect to the Veda. Truths known from and by means of the Veda itself are merely reiterated in Dharmaśāstra for the edification of the less capable. Medhātithi's distinction exemplifies a very typical distancing of the Vedic and Dharmaśāstra traditions that simultaneously exalts the superior and symbolically central place of the Veda.

The role of the Veda as a source of *dharma* in Dharmaśāstra, therefore, is to act as the semiotic residue of an eternal and transcendent truth that carries over into every other source of *dharma*. The details of the Veda matter little for Dharmaśāstra, but the value and authority of the other sources rely on a semiotic projection of Vedic-ness into the sources. That semiosis constitutes the theological link between the Vedas and the details of the *dharma*s found in the texts and customary laws. Put differently, the spirit of the Veda pervades the sources of *dharma* and contains their authority.

Traditional texts, the *smṛti*s, are justified or made authoritative in two ways. First, a connection to a lost Vedic source is sometimes attributed to rules found in the traditional texts, the idea being that every rule should

[5] Medh on MDh 2.6: *kiṃ tarhi apauruṣeyatve saty anuṣṭheyārthāvabodhakatvād viparyayābhāvāc ca.*

[6] Medh on Mdh 2.6: "Why is no reason given (for the Veda being a source of *dharma*)? This is a text of traditional teaching and it states things which are well-established. Those who seek such reasons should learn them from the Mīmāṃsā. I have already stated that what is said here is directed to those are learning (about *dharma*) solely from traditional teachings. [*hetur nokta iti ced āgamagrantho 'yaṃ siddham artham āha. hetvarthino mīmāṃsāto vinīyante. asmābhir uktaṃ ya āgamamātreṇa pratīyanti tān praty etad ucyate*]."

have and must have had a real source in a Veda, but that some portions of the Veda have been lost over time.[7] Second, and more importantly, "acceptance by people who know the Vedas acts as the main criterion" for declaring something to be *dharma*. The argument is essentially sociological in character: since the same people who perform Vedic rites also perform other rites described in the traditional texts, then we may logically assume that they would not accept duties and practices that contravened the Vedas.[8]

The key for Medhātithi with regard to the traditional texts is the sanctity of the tradition itself. That sanctity is guaranteed by the character of its transmitters and the unbroken chain that links present knowers of the Veda to those of the distant past. Less important is the text itself. While commentators regularly remark on variant or disputed textual readings, the underlying guarantee of a text's authority is the person transmitting it, not the words or the form of the text itself. Medhātithi gives a plausible account of the historical process at work in determining the authority of a *dharma* text:

> When the learned uniformily recall as tradition or declare some person as being endowed in all ways with the stated good qualities, then the text held to be composed by him – even though it emanates from a human source – is an authoritative source (*pramāṇa*) of *dharma*. This is the meaning of "the tradition and practice of those who know the Veda." Even today, if a person endowed with these qualities compiles a text on the basis of those qualities, then later (generations) would accept it as an authority just like Manu, etc. But, people of this generation would not learn (what is *dharma*) from his text because they would also have whatever sources of information he had. To the extent that someone of this generation does not show his sources, the learned do not accept his word as authoritative. If the sources are shown, however, and the text is accepted as authoritative at a later time, then it is right to infer a Vedic basis for these because there is no other explanation except for its acceptance by the learned.[9]

[7] For more on the theory of lost Vedas, see Wilhelm Halbfass, *Tradition and Reflection: Explorations in Indian Thought* (Albany: SUNY Press, 1991).

[8] Medh on MDh 2.6: "There is a mutuality between traditional and vedic texts because they always have a mutual connection. The two do not diverge at all with regard either to performer or to act. Whoever performs what is taught in the extant Vedas, if they themselves do something else in a certain way, then that too is based on the Veda. Acceptance by those who know the Veda is the most important criterion for authority (in regard to *dharma*). [*smārtavaidikayor nityaṃ vyatiṣaṅgāt parasparam | kartṛtaḥ karmato vāpi viyujyate na jātu tau || pratyakṣaśrutinirdiṣṭaṃ ye 'nutiṣṭhanti kecana ta eva yadi kurvanti tathā syād vedamūlatā || prāmāṇyakāraṇaṃ mukhyaṃ vedavidbhiḥ parigrahaḥ*]."

[9] Medh on MDh 2.6: *sarvathā yam avigānena śiṣṭāḥ smaranti vadanti vā evaṃvidhair guṇair yuktam tena caitat praṇītam iti tasya vākyaṃ saty api pauruṣeyatve dharme pramāṇaṃ syād iti | smṛtiśīle ca tadvidām ity asyārthaḥ | adyatve ya evaṃvidhair guṇair yukta īdṛśenaiva ca hetunā grantham*

In this description of how a traditional text is composed and authorized, we again see the emphasis on scholarly acceptance as the final criterion for authority in *dharma*. Such acceptance imparts a Vedic quality to the text, despite the fact that subsequent generations come to know about these *dharma*s through a humanly authored text. The Vedic connection is indirect, but fully transitive. More importantly, we are left with a socially constituted source of *dharma* in the form of the scholarly community of *dharma* scholiasts – something akin to the idea of *ijmā'*, or consensus, in Islamic law.[10] It is not a big leap of historical imagination to view this textualized source that originates from a social institution as opening the door to changes, extensions, and innovations of the existing tradition. Of course, this must be denied as a matter of theology, but Medhātithi's description of the process of textual transmission and authorization shows how theology and history were held together and were compossible.

Customary law finds its authority in effectively the same way as the traditional texts, i.e., by positing a social and generational link between the earliest transmitters and practitioners of the Vedic *dharma*s and those of the present day. In Medhātithi's words, "When there are no (relevant) statements in the Vedas or traditional texts, but the learned, considering it to be *dharma*, perform it, then that act too must be understood as Vedic, just as in the previous discussion (of traditional texts)."[11] The only real difference then is textualization and the potential for long-term transmission enabled by taking shape as a text. Otherwise, all normatively accepted practices of the learned are themselves *dharma*s and sources of *dharma* for others. For the moment, we are simply noting that customary law is justified in the Dharmaśāstra texts first by an appeal to the Vedic quality imparted to such norms through the pristine transmission of tradition. Both texts and practical legal systems, however, recognized the legitimacy and authority of customary law via the social consensus of plural communities in India. In this chapter, we are interested in the first justification, saving the second for Chapter 7.

*upanibadhnīyāt sa uttareṣāṃ manvādivat pramāṇībhavet | idānīntanānāṃ tu yad eva tatra tasya bodhakāraṇaṃ tad eva teṣām astīti na tadvākyād avagatiḥ | idānīntano hi yāvan mūlaṃ na darśayati tāvan na vidvāṃsas tadvākyaṃ pramāṇayanti | darśite tu mūle pramāṇīkṛte granthe kālāntare ... tadā teṣāṃ śiṣṭaparigrahānyathānupapattyā tanmūlānumānaṃ yuktam.*

[10] On *ijmā'*, see Mohammad Hashim Kamali, *Principles of Islamic Jurisprudence*, 3rd edn (Cambridge: Islamic Texts Society, 2003), pp. 228–60.

[11] Medh on MDh 2.6: *yatra śrutismṛtivākyāni na santi śiṣṭāś ca dharmabuddhyā 'nutiṣṭhanti tad api vaidikam eva pūrvavat pratipattavyam.*

A final important aspect of the sources of *dharma* pointed to in this last quotation from Medhātithi is the fact that there is a clear hierarchy of sources and a clear sense that if a superior source regulates some action, then inferior sources may not modify it nor even be operative at all.[12] The first image here is one of conflict between the sources and the ranking of authority between them. All texts without exception rank the sources of *dharma* as follows:

1 Veda
2 Traditional Texts
3 Customary Law

This ranking and image of conflict, however, can easily be overstated, because of the fact that superior sources are frequently silent on matters affecting people and these are dealt with in inferior sources. In practice, what this means is that the three classic sources of *dharma* tend to apply to distinct and different realms of human action. Rites detailed in the Vedic texts are not reiterated in detail in the traditional Dharmaśāstra texts. Similarly, rules for eating, worship, inheritance, marriage, or penance as found in the Dharmaśāstra are not likely to be repeated again in the localized discussions of customary law. Dharmaśāstra itself thus tends to assign a different "scope of application" (*viṣaya*) to each of the sources of *dharma* in such a way that conflict between the sources tends to be minimal.[13]

### *Excursus on "what pleases oneself"*

The three classic sources of *dharma* were supplemented in two later influential Dharmaśāstra texts, the *Laws of Manu* and the *Laws of Yājñavalkya*, with the addition of a fourth, and possibly a fifth, source. In order to complete the enumeration of the sources of *dharma*, we must mention these. At the same time, I will argue that this fourth (and fifth) source failed to be accepted as a truly significant source of law by the later tradition. In other words, I suggest that Manu introduced a fourth source, that Yājñavalkya, who largely summarized Manu, maintained it, but that later authors and

[12] The hierarchy of *dharma*'s sources is stated directly by Vijñāneśvara (on YS 1.7) among others: "In case of conflict between these (sources of *dharma*) each earlier one mentioned is superior [*eteṣāṃ virodhe pūrvapūravasya balīyastvam*]."

[13] On the question of inferior sources becoming operative when other sources are silent and the assignment of different *viṣaya*s to the sources, see Donald R. Davis, Jr., "On *Ātmatuṣṭi* as a Source of *Dharma*," *Journal of the American Oriental Society* 127:3 (2007): 291.

commentators for the most part ignored it or diminished its significance to almost nothing.[14] First, the root-texts:

> The root of the Law is the entire Veda; the tradition and practice of those who know the Veda; the conduct of good people; and what is pleasing to oneself. (MDh 2.6)
>
> The Veda, tradition, the standards of the good, what is pleasant to one's own self, [and] the desire born of proper intention – these are the roots of *dharma*. (YS 1.7)

At first, the verses seem straightforward and seem to extend the list of *dharma*'s sources to the open-ended realm of human pleasure. But, the commentators will have none of it. With unusual consensus, the commentators aver that "what pleases oneself" and/or "the desire born of proper intention" must be severely restricted to:

1 people of impeccable character and training in the Vedas;
2 to situations in which the other sources are silent; and
3 to situations of technical option between two equally valid *dharmas*.[15]

In other words, the same extension of the Vedic quality associated with traditional texts and customary law also applies to "what pleases oneself." When all three restrictions are applied, little scope remains for this source of *dharma*, except in fairly trivial matters in which personal preference is a sufficient determinant. In other words, so long as all other sources have been consulted without finding a relevant rule, then one may just do what one wants.

The presence of "what pleases oneself" in two of the most important Dharmaśāstra texts demanded the attention of the tradition and, thus, our attention as well. However, it is clear that the tradition effectively explained the source away, assigning its significance to a strongly restricted and generally trivial realm. My best guess as to why it was incorporated in the first place would be to suggest that this source totalizes the "dharma-fication" of human experience. By giving personal pleasure and preference the status of *dharma* in certain limited circumstances, it would seem that every level of human action, no matter how insignificant, is connected to *dharma*. This view of *dharma* makes sense in the context of Dharmaśāstra, though less so in the stricter view of *dharma* associated with Mīmāṃsā in which *dharma* must deal with matters unknown by other means and

[14] For the full argument, with extensive translations from the medieval commentaries, see Davis, "On *Ātmatuṣṭi*."

[15] *Ibid.*, p. 287.

with transcendental results. Although Dharmaśāstra repeats these theological restrictions of Mīmāṃsā regularly, the tradition also projects an insinuation of *dharma* into every act of human beings. It is the latter projection that characterizes the special contribution of Dharmaśāstra to the larger *dharma* tradition of South Asian religious and legal history. Even "what pleases oneself" was linked back to the Vedas, but my reading of the root-texts and commentaries suggests that the root-texts were expanding *dharma* to the utmost limits of human experience, only to have that expansion itself limited in a different way by the later tradition.

## LAW AND THE HOUSEHOLD

The institution to which Hindu law mainly applies is the household, not the state. A focus on the household and family in Hindu religious thought extends deep into the earliest Vedic texts that we have.[16] While the rudiments of a theology of ordinary life, a legal view of all human action, can be found in these texts, the early Dharmaśāstra tradition gave a new meaning to the term *dharma*, one that expanded its scope and significance in early Vedic texts and answered the even more influential use of the term in early Buddhist theologies.[17] The new scope centered on the household, the family, and the day-to-day religious and legal duties incumbent upon various castes and other categories of people. Thus, while there may have been considerable continuity in household-oriented religious and legal practice from the Vedic to classical periods in Hinduism, a full-blown theology of the household and the common life associated with it appeared first in the Dharmasūtra texts, beginning in roughly the second century BC.

This focus on the household alone necessitates that Hindu law and jurisprudence be understood differently than legal systems predicated on a state's exclusive jurisdiction over the law. The fact that the household is the ideal institutional context for both the theory and practice of Hindu law does not mean, however, that the political state is ignored, but rather subordinated jurisprudentially to a larger legal theology. That theology is the law of castes and life-stages (*varṇāśramadharma*) that serves as a

[16] See, generally, Kumkum Roy, "Defining the Household: Some Aspects of Prescription and Practice in Early India," *Social Scientist* 22:1–2 (1994): 3–18; also Thomas J. Hopkins, *The Hindu Religious Tradition* (Belmont: Wadsworth, 1971), p. 77.

[17] Patrick Olivelle, "The Power of Words: The Ascetic Appropriation and Semantic Evolution of *Dharma*." In *Language, Texts, and Society: Explorations in Ancient Indian Culture and Religion* (Firenze: Firenze University Press, 2005), pp. 121–36.

Table 2. *Dharmas of the castes, showing the subordinate place of political rulership*

I. Brahmin
   a. six occupations – teaching and studying the Veda, offering and officiating at sacrifices, giving and accepting gifts (MDh 10.74–5)
II. Kṣatriya
   a. three occupations – studying the Veda, offering sacrifices, and giving gifts (MDh 10.77, 79)
   b. special *dharmas* = *rājadharma*, the *dharma* of a ruler (MDh 10.79–80)
      1. protection of the people (MDh 7.144; YS 1.323, 335)
      2. promulgation of the law of castes and life-stages (MDh 7.24, 35; 8.41, 390–1, 410–18; YS 1.361; NS 12.117, 18.5)
      3. punishment of the wicked (MDh 7.14–31; YS 1.338, 354–9)
      4. adjudication of disputes (MDh 8.23–4; YS 2.1)
III. Vaiśya
   a. three occupations – studying the Veda, offering sacrifices, and giving gifts (MDh 10.78–9)
   b. special *dharmas* (MDh 9.326–33; 10.79–80)
      1. trade
      2. animal husbandry
      3. agriculture
IV. Śūdra
   a. special *dharma* – "obedient service to distinguished Brahmin householders who are learned in the Veda" (MDh 9.334)

structuring principle for all Dharmaśāstra. Graphically, the subordination of polity to household may be shown as follows, in Table 2.[18]

Each of the first three so-called "twice-born" castes[19] shares the duties to study the Veda, offer sacrifice, and give gifts, with the Brahmins specially obliged to enable all of these occupations by teaching, officiating, and receiving. Śūdras are not permitted to undertake any of these practices. Instead, they have the special duty to serve Brahmins and the other twice-born castes. Kṣatriyas and Vaiśyas have, respectively, the special duties to protect the people/punish the wicked and to engage in trade, pastoralism, and agriculture. The important point for the moment is the fact that essential aspects of human survival and sociality pertaining to political

[18] A more complete presentation of the basic structure of Dharmaśāstra according to caste and life-stage can be found in Patrick Olivelle (ed. and trans.), *Manu's Code of Law* (New York: Oxford University Press, 2005), pp. 77–86. His outline of the topics of the *Laws of Manu* demonstrates very clearly the prominent and extensive, but structurally subordinate, place of political rulership in the scheme of *dharma*.

[19] "Twice-born" refers to the ceremony of thread investiture permitted to the three highest *varṇas* that marks their second birth. More often, however, the term is simply a synonym for Brahmin.

governance, commerce, agriculture, and labor are all subordinated in this scheme to a set of privileged religious obligations that together constitute the highest duty of a married householder. In particular, one should note that most of what counts as law in modern legal theory is placed under the purview of the ruler, the Kṣatriya, in this scheme and most descriptions of the ruler's *dharma* feel very familiar as law connected with a political state. To limit law to this realm, however, is from the Hindu perspective (and, I would argue, most historical legal systems) artificial and incomplete. The more salient institution in Hindu law is the household and it is the household that structures both the exposition of and the conceptualization of *dharma*.

In Hindu law, as in Islamic law, "the law presupposes that membership in a family is a natural condition among humans and that individuals will rarely become totally bereft of family connections."[20] In fact, the privileging of the household and the status of a married householder is directly prescribed in the earliest texts of the Hindu law tradition. Gautama, for instance, states, "There is, however, only a single order of life, the Teachers maintain, because the householder's state alone is prescribed in express vedic texts." (GDh 3.36). Giving a different reason, Baudhāyana states, "There is, however, only a single order of life, the Teachers maintain, because no offspring is produced in the others" (BDh 2.11.27, cf. GDh 3.3).[21] Manu, too, echoes his predecessors, "Student, householder, forest hermit, and ascetic: these four distinct orders have their origin in the householder ... Among all of them, however, according to the dictates of vedic scripture, the householder is said to be the best, for he supports the other three" (MDh 6.87, 89). The Hindu law texts express the priority and superiority of the household as the main focus and location of *dharma* through discussions of the Hindu orders of life or life-stages (*āśrama*). In other words, the texts privilege the householder stage or form of life as the best, rather than the household. Nevertheless, the larger implication is clear and is further corroborated by examining the list of topics dealt with in *dharma* texts.

In fact, the easiest way to demonstrate the connection of Dharmaśāstra and ordinary life, especially through its connections to the household and ritual, is to examine the list of topics dealt with in the texts. *Dharma* texts

[20] Bernard G. Weiss, *The Spirit of Islamic Law* (Athens: University of Georgia Press, 1998), p. 154.

[21] For a discussion of the technical issues at work in these two statements and their relationship to the theology of the orders of life or life-stages (*āśrama*), see Patrick Olivelle, *The Āśrama System: the History and Hermeneutics of a Religious Institution* (New York: Oxford University Press, 1993), pp. 83–91.

provide rules for eating, bathing, being a student, marriage, sex, contracts, sales, partnerships, wages, boundaries, ownership, life-cycle rites, five daily sacrifices, gifts, funerary rites, penances, and on and on. Almost all the topics have a connection to the household, to a ritual, or to both.

We are now able to come back to the question of the sources of Hindu law. The absence of legislation or royal edict as authoritative sources of law makes more sense, when we recognize the social context presumed by Hindu jurisprudence.[22] If *dharma* pertains firstly and primarily to the household, it makes little sense jurisprudentially to develop state-level rules, when the state is jurisprudentially part of the household *dharma* of the ruler.

The point that we must recognize is the seemingly inverted structure of law as found in Dharmaśāstra, in which mundane, household-related activities dominate the structural explication of *dharma* and seemingly larger social, political, and economic institutions and practices are placed within a description of the duties of householders. It is this inversion that strikes the modern reader as quite different from modern legal thought which has increasingly tended to publicly disavow interference in the so-called private realm, the realm of the household. The inversion within Hindu law, however, is in fact the norm for most systems of ancient and medieval law.[23]

This historically normal "inversion" reveals a blind spot in most contemporary jurisprudence, namely the relevance of everyday life in places such as the household to the operation of law at every social level. More specifically, still too much contemporary legal theory – heavy as it is with constitutional and high-level appellate legal matters – reifies the law as an abstraction that exists independently of its social moorings. In this way, the life of the law in real persons and its connection to questions of power and strategy are lost. Despite the efforts of the Legal Realists and the Law and Society movement to expose and emphasize the impact of everyday life on legal processes, the fact remains that we are still uncomfortable with a form of legal discourse and debate that focuses on the personal side of law, i.e., the way in which people actually make use of the law, what

[22] Edicts (*rājaśāsana*) did, in fact, exist in ancient and medieval India and they often fixed or established various legal regulations. Edicts are mentioned at various places in Dharmaśāstra as legitimate sources of *dharma*, though quite circumscribed in their effect. See Donald R. Davis, Jr., "Intermediate Realms of Law: Corporate Groups and Rulers in Medieval India," *Journal of the Economic and Social History of the Orient* 48:1 (2005): 103–6, and J. Duncan M. Derrett, *Religion, Law and the State, in India* (London: Faber, 1968), pp. 168–9 for discussions.

[23] J. Duncan M. Derrett (ed.), *An Introduction to Legal Systems* (New York: Praeger, 1968).

they do with and by means of it, how they participate in it, regardless of the law's intentions or theoretical purposes.

The privileging of the restricted view of law creeps even into work on religious law. For instance, Weiss demonstrates that Islamic jurists' "horizons were far-reaching, encompassing a whole way of life inclusive of many details of day-to-day living that lay beyond the sphere of what usually counts as law."[24] I do not disagree with Weiss's characterization of the expansive scope of interest on the part of Islamic jurists, but I do want to question his privileging of the parochial sense of law from modern theory as the best standard against which to judge the nature of Islamic law.

The best reason to challenge the restricted view of law is that modern legal theory tends to focus on law in its breach, the violations of law that expose how rules work in practice and how contraventions of the law are punished. Hindu jurisprudence, by contrast, concentrates on law in its fulfillment. Law is *dharma*, the "act of upholding." Even in a positive sense, the difference is between what law permits and what law enables: what can I get away with? vs. what benefit does this bring me? For this reason, modern legal theory is conceptually indisposed to consider the crucial question of how and why people do in fact follow the law most of the time. By examining legal systems like Hindu law that structure their systems through a focus on the household and sources of law that work most effectively through the institution of the house and family, we open a theoretically neglected aspect of law's authority and efficacy. The centrality of the household corrects not only certain views of law in India and elsewhere; it also challenges us to reconsider similarly restrictive accounts of Hinduism as a religious tradition.

An emphasis on the householder corrects prevailing emphases within the field of Hindu studies that continue to suggest that Hinduism is lived as much or more outside of home and family as inside.[25] The mere existence of a theology of ordinary life centered on the household points to the historical existence of an important religious tradition in Hinduism similarly centered on the household. But, we cannot confuse the two in the

[24] Weiss, *Spirit of Islamic Law*, p. 7.

[25] Consider two examples: Klaus K. Klostermeier, *Survey of Hinduism*, 2nd edn (Albany: SUNY, 1994), p. 5: "Hindu religion has, in spite of its all-inclusive character, a metaphysical core." Klostermeier acknowledges that the householder tradition, despite theological polemics against it, persists as an important path in Hinduism (p. 192), but he tends to write about this side of Hinduism in the past tense, as what Hindus used to do. Thomas J. Hopkins, *Hindu Religious Tradition* (Belmont: Wadsworth, 1971), p. 142, presents the householder tradition as a more or less unbroken tradition within Hinduism, but depicts it as having almost no points of interaction with other traditions, an orthodoxy unto itself.

manner perpetrated by early Indological scholars of Hindu traditions. We must not confuse a theology with a practice and thereby reduce Hinduism to any theology, much less the once-dominant view of classical Hinduism as governed in practice by Dharmaśāstra and its categories. But, just as we should not mistake Dharmaśāstra's theology for Hinduism in practice, so also should we avoid thinking that lived Hinduism can be described by Vedānta theological traditions, or theologies centered on the *Bhagavad-Gītā*, Tantric texts, or devotional literature. At the same time, we ought not to dismiss theologies and their categories because they confirm the historical existence of so much more than just scholastic traditions. In the case of Dharmaśāstra, we are presented with a theology of householder Hinduism.

The theology of the householder, even if sometimes not considered the highest or best religious path, is always the norm in Hinduism. Renunciation, ecstatic devotion, and extreme Tantric ritual have all been proffered as superior religious paths within the Hindu tradition, but their common point of departure is the religion of the householder. At the textual level, this meant an engagement with the theology of the household and family presented in Dharmaśāstra. These other traditions are each very significant, but they also either restrict their pursuit to a limited number of specially qualified people, ascetic or Tantric initiates for example, or they appropriate and refashion the terms of household and family in ways that depend upon the ethos of Dharmaśāstra. Olivelle summarizes this ethos as follows:

> A twice-born man, following his vedic initiation, studies the Vedas at the house of his teacher; after returning home he marries a suitable wife and establishes his sacred fires; he begets offspring, especially sons, by his legitimate wife; and during his entire life offers sacrifices, recites the Vedas, offers food and water to his deceased ancestors, gives food to guests and mendicants, and offer food oblations to all creatures. [26]

Whether it is the procedures for initiation and study or the concepts and methods for worship, other theological traditions regularly draw upon the orthodox exposition of householder religion. Moreover, Dharmaśāstra itself took notice of novel practices and rites that were unknown to earlier Hindu traditions, thus incorporating and, in a sense, legalizing them. It is the interplay between Dharmaśāstra and other Hindu traditions that

[26] Olivelle, *Āśrama System*, p. 55.

signals its importance in the Hindu religious imagination, especially in theological circles, but also in practical contexts.[27]

The principal elements of this householder religious tradition within Hinduism may be summarized as follows:

1 Sacramentary Rites – birth, naming, thread investiture, marriage, death, etc.
2 Domestic Rites – *pūjā*s and other rites done in the home, especially those involving family deities (*kuladeva*).
3 Actions of the body, e.g., eating, bathing, sex, etc.
4 Social life that affects the household/family, e.g., caste status, family property transactions, debts, membership in corporate groups (guilds, trading groups, castes, military, etc.).
5 Expiation and purification for transgressions or contextual impurities.

Each of these categories of householder religious practice is subjected to extensive regulation in Dharmaśāstra and its commentaries. Taken together, it profits our view of Hinduism to understand these elements as constituting a theologically demarcated religious tradition in which law, in the form of *dharma*, plays the pivotal role by imbuing these actions of ordinary life with meaning and/or purpose.

Returning from religion to law, we might ask what advantage there is in thinking of the household as the foremost institutional location of law. What the household as a community can possess more easily than almost any other form of community is a set of common goods that shape the legally constituted world of its members. The teleological or goal-oriented view of law in such contexts, as old as Plato and Aristotle, is realistically achieved at this scale. In modern societies, the element of community and shared goods in the law is most often the responsibility of a system of popular representation, such as a parliamentary democracy.

For as yet underexplored reasons, it is easier to define common goods for all humanity – human rights, the rule of law, etc. – than it is to define common goods for any actual polity or other legal economy. The focus on the household in Hindu jurisprudence may afford us an opportunity to view a social level at which a teleological structuring of law is practicable and, in addition, to see what implications such teleologies have for both the macro and intermediate levels of legal economy.

[27] A contemporary example of the practical resonance of Dharmaśāstra's theology is described in Leela Prasad, *Poetics of Conduct: Oral Narrative and Moral Being in a South Indian Town* (New York: Columbia University Press, 2007).

## THE RULE OF LAW AND THE RULE OF THE LAWFUL

The idea of *pramāṇa* extends beyond the sources of law into the nature of authority itself. Indeed, the word and its derivatives are very often translated as authority. The household is the link between the question of *dharma*'s sources and the question of legal authority, to be examined here under the familiar heading of the rule of law. In this section, I will first compare the explication of the authority of *dharma*'s sources with general discussions of authority in contemporary jurisprudence.[28] I will then extend this discussion by suggesting that one way to characterize the Hindu law view of authority is to say that the rule of law must be supplemented by the rule of the lawful.[29] The emphasis on the rule of the lawful in Hindu jurisprudence only makes sense when read against the privileging of the household as the primary social location of law.

Standard accounts of authority dating back to Hobbes describe two criteria of legal authority: peremptoriness and content-independence.[30] Peremptory legal commands are those that preclude any debate or refusal about their obligatory character. Content-independent legal commands are commands given with the idea that they will be obeyed simply because they are commands, and not because the content of the command is justifiable, demonstrably beneficial, or rational. Many, even most, ordinary commands seem to fulfill both requirements: "Clean up your room!" "Go to bed!" How legal commands acquire the same quality has been a perennial question in legal theory.[31]

Hindu jurisprudence articulates exactly the same requirements or criteria for authority, but only with regard to two of the three classical sources of law. Peremption is declared in certain terms by the *Laws of Manu*:

[28] For another recent account of authority in Hindu law with comparisons to contemporary jurisprudence, see Timothy Lubin, "Authority." In T. Lubin, J. Krishnan, and D.R. Davis, Jr. (eds.), *Hinduism and Law: an Introduction* (Cambridge: Cambridge University Press, forthcoming).

[29] Compare the recent essay by Jonathan K. Ocko and David Gilmartin, "State, Sovereignty, and the People: A Comparison of the 'Rule of Law' in China and India," *Journal of Asian Studies* 68:1 (2009): 93: "the dichotomy between the rule of man and the rule of law opened up an inescapable paradox. In practice, the rule of law could never, of course, be separated from the rule of man, because without human administration the law means nothing." The conclusions of this essay support those made here, I believe, though I find the formulation "rule of man" less precise and burdened with a problematic conceptual history.

[30] H.L.A. Hart, *Essays on Bentham* (Oxford: Clarendon, 1982), pp. 253–5.

[31] Scott J. Shapiro, "Authority." In Jules Coleman and Scott Shapiro (eds.), *The Oxford Handbook of Jurisprudence and Philosophy of Law* (New York: Oxford University Press, 2002), provides a thorough, but concise survey.

"Scripture" should be recognized as "Veda," and "tradition" as "Law Treatise." These two *should never be called into question* in any matter, for it is from them that the Law has shined forth. If a twice-born disparages these two by relying on the science of logic, he ought to be ostracized by good people as an infidel and a denigrator of the Veda. (MDh 2.10–11, emphasis added)[32]

Medhātithi confirms that "what is being prohibited here is criticism that involves improper arguments based on bad logic," not hermeneutic inquiry itself, which instructs us as to how to receive the arguments and counter-arguments of tradition. In other words, one can challenge the scholastic interpretation of the commands found in these sources, but not the commands themselves. The unassailable character of Vedic and Dharmaśāstric commands derives in part from their content-independence.

Medhātithi gives two examples of how the authority of *dharma*-related commands cannot depend on what they actually command, i.e., their content. First, he points to worldly affairs such as agriculture and labor which prove their benefits to mankind through directly perceivable results such as crop-yields and wages.[33] The results of *dharma*s are not like this. The connection of dharmic action and results cannot be shown by logic or direct experience, but rather only through the authoritative attestations of the texts. Here, the experience of tradition, not of the individual, witnesses to the truth of the textual statements. Second, and more pointedly, Medhātithi responds to an important point of contention between Hindu and non-Hindu traditions regarding the killing of animals. As I will describe in more detail in Chapter 2, Medhātithi accepts a general rule that "all killing is sinful," but also insists that direct scriptural injunctions of the killing of animals in the context of ritual sacrifice are not only permissible but obligatory, and are a crucial exception to the general rule. More importantly, he does not frame his case by insisting upon a moral validity for the general rules against killing. Instead he declares that "the fact of killing itself is not what makes it a sinful act, but rather the prohibition (against it)."[34] The moral quality of the killing is, for Medhātithi,

[32] It is only fair to note that some Dharmaśāstra authors take a different reading of the key term *amīmāṃsye*, "not to be questioned," reading instead *mīmāṃsye*, "to be subjected to Mīmāṃsa interpretation." The manuscript tradition clearly supports the first reading, however (Olivelle, *Manu's Code of Law*, pp. 244–5). Moreover, the following verse separately confirms the peremptoriness of the first two sources of *dharma*.

[33] "In the case of agriculture and the like, we come to know about the production of rice and other products through direct perception and experience. But, the achievement of a ritual sacrifice and so forth ... cannot be learned through direct perception." Medh on MDh 2.6 (also *anvayavyatirekābhyām avagamyate* connected with agriculture, etc.; cf. with *vyavahāra* on YS 2.20–1).

[34] Medh on MDh 2.6: "*yato na hiṃsātvaṃ pāpahetutve kāraṇam api tu pratiṣedhena viṣayīkaraṇam*"

irrelevant to the authority of the general rule prohibiting it or the exceptional rules commanding it. In other words, the content does not matter at all, only the fact that it has been commanded in an authoritative source.

We notice that only the Veda and the Dharmaśāstra are directly declared to be unassailable authorities. We must infer that the living tradition in the form of customary law would also be immune from any challenge to its authority, because its legitimacy derives from its theological continuity with the textual sources. In Hindu law, as in Islamic law, "the authority of the empirical dimension is dependent on its relationship with the transcendental and metaphysical *ḥukm* [command]."[35] Nevertheless, as Medhātithi's comment above makes clear, there is a difference between the commands themselves being beyond challenge and the interpretation of those commands being open to debate and dispute. One cannot challenge the fact that one must perform what is commanded and avoid what is prohibited, but how one satisfies the requirements of the command or prohibition is open to interpretation.

Authority thus has two levels that are at the heart of legal obligation and the prevailing common sense about law. First, one can't buck the system; one can't simply refuse or challenge the law on its face. Second, however, one can work within the law's constraints to create unique, often merely technical, fulfillments of the law's commands and prohibitions. The guarantee that the second level will not contradict the first is the submission of law's interpreters to the commands of the first level. Here, I submit, is the persuasive and crucial sleight of hand at work in all legal systems: the subtle shift back and forth between the authority of commands and the authority of persons who have specialist or expert knowledge of those commands and who should ideally also live by them.[36]

Of course, the inclusion of or the acknowledgment that people themselves have authority that is separable from the law has great potential for the corruption of power. For this reason, a near universal approbation of the "rule of law" over the "rule of men" now holds sway in political and legal circles at all levels. The allegedly incorruptible standard of the written law has been deemed superior and unequivocally necessary for modern

[35] Ebrahim Moosa, "Allegory of the Rule (*Ḥukm*): Law as Simulacrum in Islam?" *History of Religions* 38:1 (1998): 7.

[36] The idea that a king is above the law was a mooted point in medieval Europe, as indicated, for example in Rutherford's *Lex, Rex* in the seventeenth century. Aside from occasional references prohibiting punishment of rulers, I find nothing in Hindu jurisprudence to suggest something similar and I doubt whether any religious legal system could seriously entertain this possibility, given the superiority of divine law.

legal and political systems. Nations and institutions almost never challenge the idea and entry into the presumptive goodwill of others entails a prior and public commitment to the rule of law.

At the same time, the rule of law is one of the most disputed and yet widely used concepts in contemporary legal and political discourse. Though many notions of the rule of law have been offered in Euro-American political philosophy,[37] its most frequent function in present discussions is to serve as a kind of universal litmus test to evaluate the fairness and legitimacy of nation-states, especially in the context of human rights debates. So, a nation under attack for aggressive military or police actions will reassure international observers by asserting that the rule of law remains intact and that what seem like human rights abuses are in fact legitimate uses of state force carried out under rules of law. Conversely, observers of atrocities and political critics regularly speak of the breakdown in the rule of law as a prime factor in permitting violations of human rights to happen.

In his recent synthesis, Tamanaha identifies three common themes in discussions of the rule of law: government limited by law; formal legality; and rule of law, not men. While the first seems to be a more or less unequivocal good when stated generally, the other two pose problems because "laws are not self-interpreting or applying … [and] cannot be sequestered from human participation."[38] Formulating a common substantive idea of the rule of law has so far proved elusive, even within individual nation-states.

In the Dharmaśāstra exposition of the sources of *dharma*, we find a formulation for the authority of law that confronts the latter problems directly. Texts and traditions are conceptually privileged but are, at the same time, set in the embodied form of "good persons," of the lawful in society. A conceptual superiority of laws is tempered by a practical privileging of *lawful* persons. The formulation, which I call the rule of the lawful, tries to avoid the problems with a total depersonalization of law, specifically a tendency to disengage from questions of power.

Rule of law discussions inevitably degenerate into debates about the nature and content of the rule of law itself.[39] Rule of the lawful discussions, by contrast, force the discussion to center on the actions of real people and debates about the legality of specific acts rather than about abstract questions of law's authority. It has been a great service of the intellectual

[37] Brian Z. Tamanaha, *On the Rule of Law: History, Politics, and Theory* (Cambridge: Cambridge University Press, 2004).

[38] *Ibid.*, p. 123. [39] *Ibid.*, p. 3.

movement known as Law and Society to insist that such abstractions frequently miss the point about how law operates in practice.[40] It is people's application of rules of law and participation in the roles of law, in combination with a host of other contextual and intervening factors, that matter in actual legal practice.

The rule of the lawful concept promotes political and legal control by members of a community who have already benefited from the creativity and accomplishment afforded by law. The lawful in this context should mean those who have the least to gain from corruption, violence, or other exploitations of the law's power. In most ancient legal systems, including Hindu law, that group was invariably identified with the ruling, elite class. Their education, wealth, and discipline were held to make them less likely to fall prey to the enticements and corruption of power and greed that undermine the law – a historically questionable view, to say the least. The revelation and revolution of modern democratic governance has been to identify the lawful with the populace as a whole through some mechanism of representation. In other words, those *not* charged with guiding and administering the legal system are least likely to be susceptible to corruption and power-mania.

Nevertheless, the emphasis in rule of law rhetoric is on the burden of the state or other lawmaking power to enforce paper rules in real situations of conflict, violence, and desperation. The setup is one of fear and controlling violation or transgression. The emphasis in rule of the lawful rhetoric, by contrast, is on the burden of individuals and pluralistic communities to accept sometimes difficult rules and roles in order to participate in the higher order coordination and achievement offered through this kind of collective sacrifice.

Both rule of law and rule of the lawful are necessary for a legal system to operate effectively. At the extremes, the need for one or other can be made with greater clarity and ease, but the balance in between is the messy middle wherein the hard work of law's administration becomes most crucial. In the household, the idealized location of law in Hindu jurisprudence, rule of the lawful surely dominates, but not without a considerable conceptual importance granted to the house rules. Similarly, international treaties and national-level uses of violence and so forth clearly require rules that transcend the fiat or rule-making capacity of one person or one corporate body. Still, it is often the lawful character of the actors in such situations that complements the stagnant rules, giving them life and contextual purpose.

[40] See, for instance, Richard L. Abel (ed.), *The Law & Society Reader* (New York: New York University Press, 1995).

If we examine the idea of authority in Hindu jurisprudence, we do not find a formulation of the rule of law at all close to that developed in Europe beginning in the Enlightenment. There are statements calling on a ruler to always conform to the dictates of the legal texts and tradition,[41] but others that seem to place the ruler and Brahmins above the law.[42] Nevertheless, both traditions lead us to a related, but little-discussed, conclusion that pertains to the question of legal authority and the rule of law.

The authority of law depends upon the progressive elimination of choice in the contexts of ordinary life. Much of legal theory works under the assumption that "people who submit themselves to authority are free not to follow them if they so wish. Nevertheless, these people *choose* to obey. Each act of compliance involves a choice to comply."[43] In fact, this sort of conscious choosing in the context of law and action is the exception rather than the rule.[44] Legal rules are "not tools for making decisions – they are a way of preventing decisions from being made ... When someone submits to an authority, they must sincerely attempt to constrain their future selves ... They make choices to commit themselves to authority – but those choices are choices not to make future choices."[45] The main choice is the one made to participate in the "legal cosmology" or to accept the "rhetoric of law" in which certain roles clearly defined by the law become both the protection and the constraint on a person. However, even that choice is obviously constrained by the difficulties involved in wholly opting out of the social world to which a legal system pertains. In this way, as Reinhart has put it, "people act as they do more because of roles than because of rules."[46] In other words, legal rules tend to create legal roles that in turn obviate or mitigate the need to know the rules.

[41] For example, *Laws of Manu* 7.31–2: "Punishment can only be administered by someone who is honest and true to his word, who acts in conformity with the Treatises (*yathāśāstrānusāriṇā*), who has good assistants, and who is wise. Within his realm, he should act in accordance with the rules (*nyāyavṛttiḥ*); upon his enemies, he should impose harsh punishments; towards his friends and loves, he should behave without guile; and to Brahmins, he should show compassion" [Sanskrit parentheses added]. See also *Laws of Nārada* 18.8.

[42] *Laws of Nārada* 15–16.21: "In this world there are only two persons who are exempt from accusation and punishment – the brāhmaṇa and the king – , for these two support the world."

[43] Shapiro, "Authority," p. 417.

[44] Peter Berger, "Sociology and Freedom," *The American Sociologist* 6 (1971): 1–5: "Society protects our sanity by pre-empting a large number of choices – not only choices of action but choices of thought ... were social life in its entirety to be charged with profound meaning, we would all go out of our minds" (p. 4).

[45] Shapiro, "Authority," pp. 418, 430.

[46] A. Kevin Reinhart, "Transcendence and Social Practice: *Muftīs* and *Qāḍīs* as Religious Interpreters," *Annales Islamologiques* 27 (1993): 5.

In a similar way, the sources of *dharma* and the traditional discussions of *pramāṇa* also serve to eliminate choice. Olivelle makes this point in the context of the historical movement away from a choice-based conceptualization of the orders of life (*āśrama*) to one in which selectable orders of life become sequential stages of life. He writes, "The clear implication of this hermeneutical principle is that choice or option in matters relating to *dharma* should be avoided almost at any cost."[47] Each successive source of law in Hindu jurisprudence expands the scope of what is covered by *dharma*. In this way, options and choices that may have been available had there only been the Vedas are then constrained by the Dharmaśāstra and matters about which Dharmaśāstra leaves choices are in turn constrained by local customary law. It is in this context that we should also understand Manu's introduction of "what pleases oneself" as a source of law. This source is ironically intended to act as a final constraint against completely free choice by appealing to the substantive Vedic quality of people, the transmutation of tradition into character, that actually constrains choice even in situations of technical option under the law.[48]

As with the life-stages in particular, the injunctions of *dharma* texts tend to define roles for people as much as they specify rules for them. Once those roles have been established and then accepted or imposed on people, then the question of choice under law's authority becomes less and less significant. The rule of law in the form of Vedic and Dharmaśāstra injunctions and the rule of the lawful in the form of contextually defined "good persons" combine to minimize the capacity for individuals to make truly free choices. The specific rules formulated under these authoritative sources, however, remain open to interpretation and it is here that the important system of hermeneutics developed in another distinct philosophical tradition centered on *dharma*, the Pūrva-Mīmāṃsā, becomes important. The ritual hermeneutics of Mīmāṃsā also work to eliminate choice, and thereby mistakes, in the context of Vedic rituals. It is to the incorporation or translation of Mīmāṃsā into the idiom and teleology of Dharmaśāstra that we turn in Chapter 2.

[47] Olivelle, *Āśrama System*, p. 135.
[48] See Davis, "On *Ātmatuṣṭi*," pp. 287, 291.

CHAPTER 2

# *Hermeneutics and ethics* (mīmāṃsā)

The word *mīmāṃsā* means the "desire to think," or more colloquially, "how to think through or interpret things." Most of the time, it refers specifically to a philosophical and hermeneutic tradition of classical India, in which case it indicates Mīmāṃsā texts and ideas. Mīmāṃsā is distinct from Dharmaśāstra, but it – along with grammar, the "queen" of traditional Indic scholarship – is also foundational for a full understanding of the latter because of the legal hermeneutics it supplies. Beyond technical rules for the proper interpretation of texts, however, Mīmāṃsā expresses a theology that displaces the individual from the center of religious concern.[1] Personal soteriology is an afterthought in both Mīmāṃsā and Hindu law; discussions of personal salvation are either subordinate or accretively attached to the central focus of Mīmāṃsā in a larger system of meaning, namely the sacrificial ritual of the Vedas. In the Hindu law tradition, however, the authors of Dharmaśāstra shifted the focus from sacrifice to the system of classes and life-stages called *varṇāśramadharma*. In other words, Hindu jurisprudence reformulated the Mīmāṃsā theology by staking a claim that what is good for the individual must be "de-centered" in favor of what is good for the social system of castes and life-stages.

Compelling recent arguments suggest that *dharma* was made a central and contested theological category in South Asian religious history only after the time of the Mauryan king Aśoka (third century BC). Olivelle has demonstrated that, contrary to most current understandings and traditional representations, *dharma* was not an important theological category in the Vedic literature.[2] What has been called the "*dharma* in the

[1] For this argument with respect to Mīmāṃsā, I rely on the excellent work of Francis X. Clooney, *Thinking Ritually: Rediscovering the Pūrva Mīmāṃsā of Jaimini* (Vienna: De Nobili, 1990). This work informs or inspires much of the present chapter.

[2] Patrick Olivelle, "The Power of Words: The Ascetic Appropriation and Semantic Evolution of *Dharma*." In *Language, Texts, and Society: Explorations in Ancient Indian Culture and Religion* (Firenze: Firenze University Press, 2005).

Veda,"[3] therefore, is a misnomer and is in fact the *dharma* analyzed within the Mīmāṃsā tradition. In Mīmāṃsā theology, *dharma* is "a good indicated by Vedic command" (PMS 1.1.2)[4] and deals almost exclusively with the correct and timely performance of rituals described in the Vedic texts. In Dharmaśāstra, by contrast, a different *dharma* was conceived, one that was more expansive in scope and more social in orientation.[5] Thus, at roughly the same time, two distinct Hindu theological views of *dharma* were created. The tradition quickly found ways to reconcile any apparent contradictions or problems between the different conceptions of *dharma*. That reconciliation and its hermeneutical and ethical implications for Hindu jurisprudence are the subject of this chapter.

## RITUAL HERMENEUTICS IN MĪMĀṂSĀ

Mīmāṃsā sets as its purpose the knowledge and practice of *dharma*.[6] Too often the full system of Mīmāṃsā has been ignored in favor of analyses of the epistemological and ontological commitments of Mīmāṃsā that inform the system's view of ritual and personhood.[7] Arguably the most important of these commitments is the acceptance of a special kind of revelation, the uncreated and eternal Word called Veda that provides the structure for all personal and universal actions and purposes. The denial of any author for the Vedas liberates its Mīmāṃsā interpreters from having to seek out the author's intentions. Like all texts subjected to hermeneutic practice, therefore, the Vedas possess a "semantic autonomy."[8] Moreover,

[3] Albrecht Wezler, "Dharma in the Veda and the Dharmaśāstras," *Journal of Indian Philosophy* 32 (2004): 629–54.

[4] The translation is taken from Lawrence McCrea, "Hindu Law and Scriptural Hermeneutics." In T. Lubin, J. Krishnan, and D.R. Davis, Jr. (eds.), *Hinduism and Law: An Introduction* (New York: Cambridge University Press, forthcoming).

[5] Some early texts, such as the great commentary of the grammarian Patañjali, classified Dharmaśāstra as a worldly (*laukika*) tradition and the related Arthaśāstra tradition also eschews any theological connection to the Veda. See Patrick Olivelle, "Explorations in the Early History of Dharmaśāstra." In P. Olivelle (ed.), *Between the Empires: Society in India 300 BCE to 400 CE* (New York: Oxford University Press, 2006), pp. 174–6. It was the incorporation and self-presentation of Dharmaśāstra in Mīmāṃsā terms that permanently redefined Dharmaśāstra as a theological project, though its connections to broader socially, not theologically, constructed religious and legal truths were never fully lost.

[6] PMS 1.1.1: "Now, the desire to know *dharma*. [*athāto dharmajijñāsā*]."

[7] I have relied on the recent critical edition and translation of the *Mīmāṃsānyāyasaṃgraha* by James Benson in preparing the ensuing summaries of the Mīmāṃsā traditions. I thank him for sharing a copy of the work with me in advance of its publication.

[8] Paul Ricoeur, *Interpretation Theory: Discourse and the Surplus of Meaning* (Fort Worth: TCU Press, 1976), pp. 30–1. Though there are certainly important philosophical differences, the similarity between Ricoeur's idea of the "semantic autonomy of the text" and the Mīmāṃsā idea of the

revelation communicates not the story of a deity or deities, but rather it teaches a process, the procedure of ritual sacrifice. *Dharma* in the Mīmāṃsā is the "upholding," the constant performance, of that sacrifice with all its attendant specifications, modifications, and accommodations. For the full Mīmāṃsā, to know *dharma* primarily prepares one to do *dharma* correctly. As we have seen in the preceding chapter, Dharmaśāstra accepts and repeats the means of knowing *dharma* described in Mīmāṃsā as theological givens, while at the same time shifting the central focus of *dharma* away from the procedures of ritual toward the dynamics of society.

In the Mīmāṃsā view of language, words are eternal and forever connected to particular meanings, because to think otherwise means to postulate the existence of specific individuals who have contrived the meanings of words. As such the givenness of the words of the Veda implies that humans should respond automatically and purposefully to what the Veda tells us. Primarily, this means that humans must follow the injunctions of the Veda. A metaphor is often employed here in which the familiar experience of being commanded by a parent, teacher, or boss in ordinary life is transposed into the cosmic frame of commands that are simply out there, woven into the fabric of the universe itself, and requiring our dutiful response. Just as we obey the inevitable commands of ordinary life in order to obtain the benefits of love, training, and remuneration, so also should we obey these revealed commands in order to obtain myriad benefits to ourselves, our families, and the world at large. To ignore those commands implies a denial of the uniquely human capacity to understand and respond to them – effectively, a rejection of the greatest human purpose of all.

The first key to understanding the Vedic commands is learning to recognize what is primary and what is secondary. Mīmāṃsā provides hermeneutic rules for determining the principal and subsidiary elements of a rite through a hierarchical list of language features that signal priority, including:

1 direct textual statement, grammatically understood;
2 similar or overlapping word-meaning;
3 syntax;
4 context;
5 position of a word in the text or an item in the ritual performance; and
6 presence of mere name.

*svataḥprāmāṇya*, the self-authorizing character of the Vedas sets forth a parallel framework for hermeneutics in both cases in which authorial intention and dialogic engagement is practically eliminated.

Rites can be very complex, multi-day affairs and one must know from the start what the main event is in order to ensure the proper execution of the rite that will result in the desired effect. The determination of the primary and secondary elements of a rite in turn depends upon an awareness of what is prompting the rite and how it must be organized to be effective. It matters, for instance, whether one is performing a rite because it is a mandatory and regular part of ritual practice, say the five daily fire-sacrifices, or because one desires a specific and personal outcome, say the birth of a child. The motivation of the ritual is thus intimately connected to its overall organization and the big picture of what one is trying to do. Heavily involved in that organization is the precise order and sequence of the little acts that comprise the whole rite. As with fixing what is primary, therefore, Mīmāṃsā provides hermeneutic rules for properly ordering the subsidiary actions of a rite, again through a careful analysis of the language of the text and practices in a model rite from which elements may be borrowed.

Significantly, it is only at this point that Mīmāṃsā introduces the ritual performer, whom we might otherwise have presupposed as central to all rites. The main question for the Mīmāṃsā is who is entitled to perform these various rites and thus reap their rewards. Entitlement also implies responsibility and duty, however. Thus, while reward induces and prompts dutiful response to Vedic commands, Mīmāṃsā interprets the inducement of rewards as merely one among numerous elements that come together in the ritual process. The reward of a rite is not its goal, or at least not its only goal. The determination of who is entitled to perform sacrifice resembles the determination and arrangement of other constituent pieces of the rite. The identity of the sacrificer impacts other aspects of the rite.

According to Mīmāṃsā, Vedic rites are all variations on two basic rites, the *soma* and the *iṣṭi*, and all others are elaborations, extensions, or modifications of these, even though many other rites are also considered archetypal bases for others. As a result, every rite is a reworking of another and borrowings are rampant. The bulk of Mīmāṃsā as a system, therefore, deals with rules for transferring procedures and items from one rite to another. Transfer is considered both abstractly and concretely with sophisticated logics developed to justify transfer and minute consideration given to the details of particular transfers. As one would expect, such transfer must have frequently meant modification as well, owing to the need to amalgamate pieces of different archetypal rites into a new form. Hence derive the rules for modifying transferred elements and for prohibiting transfers and modifications under certain circumstances. Finally,

Mīmāṃsā considers what we might call two cross-over situations. In the first cross-over, limited rules are provided that permit a single action or single group of actions to in effect count twice by being simultaneously part of two conceptually distinct rites. The first cross-over is a rule of economy that obviates the need for repeated action in instances where the injunction may be fulfilled through common actions. In the second, rules are given to allow subsidiary elements of one rite to serve as part of the performance of another. Here, the borrowing is not the more important derivation of ectypal rites from archetypes in the process called transfer, but rather the importation of subsidiaries from one ectype to another.

The summary of the full Mīmāṃsā system given so far follows the traditional ordering found in the earliest text of the tradition, the Pūrva-Mīmāṃsā-Sūtras of Jaimini. Alternative schemes for describing the complete system are available, however, both from within the tradition itself and from modern scholarly accounts.[9] Among the former, probably the most important for understanding the spirit of Hindu law is the Mīmāṃsā division of authoritative textual statements into five categories, namely injunctions, explanatory statements, prohibitions, formulas, and names.

Injunctions are divided most often into four further subcategories that include originative, applicatory, performative, and qualificatory. An originative rule tells us what a primary rite is, while applicatory rules specify what is subsidiary to those primary rites and how they are to be applied in different contexts. Performative rules clarify the ordering of rites both in terms of timing and sequence. Finally, qualificatory rules specify who it is that is entitled to the benefit of a rite and the necessary qualifications of one who performs a rite. Injunctions are the heart of the Mīmāṃsā system because of the theology of cosmic command that informs its epistemological and ontological presuppositions. When interpreting any text, therefore, one is primarily seeking to discover what it is that is being commanded. The essential force of words in the Mīmāṃsā view pertains to the communication of what to do. All other categories of textual expression subserve this theology of command.

The second category of text, the explanation and/or praise, functions as a support for injunctions, specifically by explaining some otherwise opaque element in the injunction or by exhorting the fulfillment of the injunction. The relation between injunction and explanation/praise is sometimes not

[9] Clooney, *Thinking Ritually*, pp. 96ff. provides perhaps the best modern scholarly re-description of the complete Mīmāṃsā system by thematically arranging key Mīmāṃsā concepts into nine discrete processes at work in the hermeneutics of Vedic ritual.

immediately clear, but the assignment of a particular piece of text to one category or other dramatically and fundamentally changes its significance in the theology of command. An explanation basically has no compulsory element about it at all. Classifying texts in this category thus neutralizes any binding force they might appear to have, without denying them a marginal supporting role.

Prohibitions act, as one would expect, as negative injunctions, rules against doing something. The interpretation of prohibitions thus mirrors much of what applies to injunctions, though obviously without any need for subcategorical rules that elaborate or qualify the prohibited acts. The existence of prohibitions raises two common hermeneutical issues that affect Hindu jurisprudence. The first issue pertains to circumstances in which the straightforward interpretation of a textual statement as a prohibition would necessitate other more problematic interpretations of surrounding statements. For instance, if a section purports to list a series of acts to be done, as opposed to being avoided (or not done), then interpreting any individual act as something prohibited contradicts the general purport of all the rules and would call into question the other rules in the list. Instead, Mīmāṃsā suggests that such rules should be understood as exclusions, i.e., injunctions to perform the indicated actions while excluding the prohibited element.[10] The second issue relates to the first in that it concerns the other principal case in which interpreting a textual statement as a prohibition causes more hermeneutic problems than it solves, namely the case in which a prohibition contradicts another injunction. For the Mīmāṃsakas, this is absolutely the worst possible hermeneutic situation to recognize for it fails to resolve contradictions in the texts that are almost always understood to be apparent rather than real. In rare cases, however, directly opposed injunctions and prohibitions generate a situation of option – one may simply choose which of two contradictory injunctions to follow. As dissatisfying as they are, resorting to options occasionally untangles very thorny interpretive issues raised by unassailable revealed texts.

The final two categories of textual statement in Mīmāṃsā are more straightforward in that both deal with interpretively neutral forms, formulas and names. Formulas, or mantras, comprise a significant proportion of some Vedic texts, although they supply next to nothing for the overall purpose of the rite, according to the Mīmāṃsā. Formulas merely serve

[10] Technically, the negative indicator should be applied to some element in the statement other than the verbal ending. See MNP 330.

to remind ritual performers of some element connected to the rite being performed. Their recitation is mandatory according to the relevant injunctions, but formulas themselves do not serve the transcendent effect of the sacrifice. Names, by contrast, do supply a level of meaning to the overall rite by acting as one means of specifying new rites, acts, deities, or implements that then take on a concrete denotation. As with all other aspects of Mīmāṃsā, interpreting certain words as names is subject to clear criteria that systematically excludes other possibilities and avoids undesirable hermeneutic consequences.

Taken together, the five forms of textual expression recognized in Mīmāṃsā theoretically describe any possible statement or utterance and provide an initial set of rules for understanding it. Both summaries of the complete Mīmāṃsā system given above operate in the presence of other important hermeneutic rules that are developed in the course of the larger descriptions of the whole system.

To get a better sense of how Mīmāṃsā works, we might compare it to a contemporary situation in which a seemingly impenetrable mass of complex rules (like the huge Vedic textual corpus) is made manageable by a set of interpretive rules in order to do something that everyone from a teenager who works part-time to a gigantic multinational corporation must do: pay their taxes. For the average person paying taxes, Mīmāṃsā would refer first to the explanatory booklet that accompanies the official tax forms and describes step-by-step, through a series of questions and subforms, how to determine and then to pay one's taxes. Mīmāṃsā, in the second place, would also signify the mental labor and procedures by which people actually manage to fill out their forms. As with a particular rite, for a particular individual's tax situation only a very small portion of the overall tax code will apply. Mīmāṃsā is the tool that assists a person in determining which rules do actually apply. More specifically, it consists of an ability both to recognize one's situation in the excerpted portions of the tax code found in the accompanying interpretive booklet and to deftly mold one's situation so as to maximize the benefits potentially offered by the rules. As with religious rites, omissions and violations nullify the beneficial effects.

The tax preparation booklet, like Mīmāṃsā, instructs its reader as to what is primary and what is secondary. For example, one has to determine various entitlement factors that will make certain rules apply or not (age, marriage, blindness, children, military status, etc.), before one can address the specific details of tax exemption, credits, and so forth. Subsidiary forms or worksheets are sometimes required in order to properly complete the main forms and the booklet helps the taxpayer determine exactly which secondary forms (for capital gains, dividends, medical deductions, child-care expenses, etc.) are required. Even within the main form, one must calculate income before determining various deductions. In other words, there is a definite order in which the rules must apply and a number of subsidiary forms required to support and complete the main form.

Moreover, certain tax situations are considered paradigmatic – models for other taxpayers and tax forms. In terms of Mīmāṃsā, the US tax form 1040 is the archetypal tax form for individual taxpayers and other forms, both more and less complex (1040A, 1040EZ, etc.), are the ectypes of this basic form. Many elements are transferred or carried over from one form to another, along with the relevant interpretive framework for filling them out. In some cases, a single form can serve two purposes or filling out one form can subserve the completion of another as, for instance, when a completed federal tax form is used to prepare a state tax form in the United States.

I have elaborated the metaphor between Mīmāṃsā and modern tax-paying at some length in order to make the intimidating technicality and detail of Mīmāṃsā seem less foreign to certain ways of thinking and acting that persist in our own time. Of course, the presuppositions and objectives of Mīmāṃsā have distinct, perhaps even unique, features that limit facile comparisons to other interpretive systems, but the ordinary quality of paying taxes, its familiarity, and its tremendously wide range of complexity make it an apt modern metaphor for the socio-religious position and function of Mīmāṃsā. It was and is perfectly possible to perform a rite, especially a familiar one, without recourse to Mīmāṃsā at all, but that fact does not diminish the value of its hermeneutics. Everyone should perform rites and everyone should pay taxes, but very few can or need to master the full regulatory system in order to do what they must do and what they want to do. Small pieces of the system must be consulted or mastered by ordinary people. Still, the full system is there for particular reasons and, in times of need, having experts who can handle the whole thing is essential and useful.

## MĪMĀṂSĀ IN HINDU JURISPRUDENCE

The reception of Mīmāṃsā into the scholastic tradition of Dharmaśāstra occurred from the very beginning and clear reliance on Mīmāṃsā principles is attested in all of the early Dharmasūtra texts, especially that of Āpastamba. Dharmaśāstra adopted the Vedic ethos of Mīmāṃsā, its epistemology, and its hermeneutics. However, Dharmaśāstra also translated these core elements of Mīmāṃsā into the mundane world of human society. Thus, while theological acknowledgements of the Veda's perfection and absolute authority are repeated regularly in *dharma* texts, the new center of theological reflection was the system of *varṇāśramadharma*, a theological partner for the Veda. There is some dispute as to whether Dharmaśāstra reimagined and reconfigured an older, more limited, sense of *dharma* in the Vedas[11] or whether it created for the first time an idea of *dharma* that was central theologically.[12] In either case, it is clear that Dharmaśāstra, in contrast to Mīmāṃsā, contains a strongly social element in its overall theology of *dharma*.

The unshakeable process at the heart of Mīmāṃsā is the event of a sacrifice. In Dharmaśāstra, it is the event of ordinary life. The unquestionable authority for Mīmāṃsā is the Veda, especially its commands. For Dharmaśāstra, it is tradition, defined in terms of an unbroken transmission of ideas and institutions, all said to be imbued with the substance of the Veda. The connection of Dharmaśāstra with the Veda is an important, but secondary, theological justification of its authority. Human tradition is the focus of reflection in Dharmaśāstra. In this way, the appropriation of Mīmāṃsā in Dharmaśāstra occurs by means of a metaphor: ordinary life in the household is a sacrifice and the traditions of "good people," both their writings and their habits, are the continuing form of the Vedic texts.[13] Having established this axiomatic theological metaphor, however, the subject matter of Dharmaśāstra diverges sharply from that of Mīmāṃsā, even as its hermeneutical principles are applied to a different domain, a different event or process.

The Mīmāṃsā denial of God as creator and its placement of the impersonal, eternal Veda at the center of its authority structure had major implications for the development of Hindu jurisprudence. Law could never be subordinated to any personal force. In place of the Veda, the abstracted community of tradition was accorded pride of place as the *impersonal* force of stability in law, its moral compass so to speak. In this way, the overall authority of Hindu law derives from a distinctive conceptualization

[11] Wezler, "Dharma in the Vedas and in the Dharmaśāstras."

[12] Patrick Olivelle, "The Semantic History of Dharma: The Middle and Late Vedic Periods," *Journal of Indian Philosophy* 32 (2004): 491–511.

[13] The terminological link between the two is the much-discussed idea of *karma* (more precisely, *karman*). Stated simply, *karma* in the Vedas and in Mīmāṃsā almost always means a ritual sacrifice of one kind or another, while in later texts including the Dharmaśāstra *karma* signifies the broader range of human action that we typically associate it with today.

of *impersonal persons*. The impersonal element guarantees the theological connection of the rules of Dharmaśāstra with the impersonal and infallible Veda. The personal element ensures a capacity for adaptation and contextualization in practical ritual and legal contexts. Hindu law's recognition of impersonal persons, that is people who more or less perfectly continue and represent the impersonal authority of non-human origin, offers something new here. Generally, legal theorists argue that "the authority of the law, as opposed to the expert, is impersonal."[14] By contrast, Hindu law envisions that persons who are sufficiently educated and disciplined can act as pristine conduits of the impersonal authority attached to the Veda and yet still be more than mechanical vessels of Vedic truth. Mīmāṃsā serves to emphasize the impersonal element as an axiomatic theological truth of Hindu jurisprudence.

The presence of Mīmāṃsā in Hindu jurisprudence is seen most clearly in the work of the scholastic commentators, though it surfaces regularly in the root-texts of the tradition as well. The commentators on Hindu law are primarily interested in the correct interpretation of its basic texts. Mīmāṃsā is thus a system of textual interpretation and of the application of rules to circumstances. It is not a scheme for judicial interpretation as a whole, which requires consideration of specific facts, but rather a kind of preliminary and/or postliminary ascertainment of what legal rules govern a particular factual case. I emphasize this fact because the legal role of Mīmāṃsā is essentially separate from any element of a trial itself, being rather closer to questions of jurisdiction and sentencing in the modern world.

A by-now classic example of the use of Mīmāṃsā in the sphere of Hindu law is the issue of the human modes of life, or life-stages. In his thorough study of the Hindu life-stages, Olivelle demonstrates how two different positions about the modes of life appropriate to men (especially Brahmins) both derive from an application of basic Mīmāṃsā principles.[15] In the older original position, interpreters understood the textual statements prescribing four distinct modes of life (student, householder, forest-dweller, and renouncer) as four life-long choices open to young men. They argued this position by applying the Mīmāṃsā principle of option, which states that when equally authoritative sacred texts prescribe

[14] Scott J. Shapiro, "Authority." In Jules Coleman and Scott Shapiro (eds.), *The Oxford Handbook of Jurisprudence and Philosophy of Law* (New York: Oxford University Press, 2002), p. 401.

[15] Patrick Olivelle, *The Āśrama System: the History and Hermeneutics of a Religious Institution* (New York: Oxford University Press, 1993), p. 34 *passim*.

two different and potentially contradictory acts, one may simply choose which to undertake. The later and classic position, however, applies a different Mīmāṃsā principle, aggregation, to the set of four. This principle states that enumerations of similarly declared acts must all be followed, in this case sequentially over the course of a person's life. This classic position, accepted generally as the better interpretation because it upholds all the textual statements and avoids the last resort of simple option, formed the theological foundation for the well-known four life *stages* of Hinduism referred to in every primer on the subject.

Another example, this time from a specific commentary, shows the application of Mīmāṃsā to rules about the killing of animals and the eating of meat. The tenth-century commentator Medhātithi addresses a series of seemingly contradictory rules about animal slaughter and meat eating at the beginning of the fifth chapter of the *Laws of Manu*. The key word for any commentator is *seemingly*. The main verses in question are as follows:

> He may eat meat when it is sacrificially consecrated, at the behest of Brahmins, when he is ritually commissioned according to rule, and when his life is at risk. (5.27)
>
> "The sacrifice is the reason for eating meat" – this, the tradition says, is the rule of the gods. Doing it for any other purpose is called the rule of fiends . . . The Self-existent One himself created domestic animals for sacrifice, and sacrifice is for the prosperity of this whole world. Within the sacrifice, therefore, killing is not killing. (5.31, 39)
>
> If he gets the urge, let him make an animal out of butter or flour; but he must never entertain the desire to kill an animal for a futile reason. (5.37)
>
> One can never obtain meat without causing injury to living beings, and killing living beings is an impediment to heaven; he should, therefore, abstain from meat. (5.48)
>
> There is no fault in eating meat, in drinking liquor, or in having sex; that is the natural activity of creatures. Abstaining from such activity, however, brings great rewards. (5.56)

In reconciling these apparent contradictions, Medhātithi turns to one of the most common Mīmāṃsā-based techniques for interpreting texts: the distinction between a rule and an explanation/exhortation.[16] He labels

[16] The similarity between the distinction of rules imposing obligations and those making exhortations in Hindu law and in Islamic law is striking. In Sanskrit, Mīmāṃsā authors were concerned with the grammatical effect of the imperative verb (called the *liṅ-tva*). The corresponding categories in Islamic law and grammar were *iqṭa'ū* and *if'al* (Bernard G. Weiss, *The Spirit of Islamic Law* (Athens: University of Georgia Press, 1998), p. 103). Furthermore, just as Hindu law distinguished mandatory rules (*vidhi*) from recommendatory praises, exhortations, and explanations

almost all the verses from 5.28–5.55, the vast majority of the verses in this discussion, as mere explanations, repetitions, praises, or condemnations of the real rules explained essentially in 5.27 and 5.56, effectively eliminating their injunctive force.[17] In some places, he enters into a more substantive discussion of what is primary and what is secondary (e.g., *guṇatva* and *śeṣatā* in 5.37 and 5.48), concluding finally that the question of eating meat is primary and the act of killing is secondary.[18] Throughout his commentary on these verses, Medhātithi makes use of Mīmāṃsā categories to lessen or eliminate the injunctive force of some verses and to insist on the injunctive force of others. In the end, he relies on arguments elaborated in Mīmāṃsā to interpret this collection of verses as pointing to the legal permissibility of eating certain kinds of meat coupled with the legal and moral enticement to abstain from it (5.56).[19] More specifically, he interprets the phrase "there is no fault in eating meat" as correcting the impression created by some passages that meat should never be eaten. Medhātithi takes a restricted view of when meat may be eaten, namely the contexts mentioned at MDh 5.27, but always affirms its legality in those contexts. Moreover, since eating meat is the primary act over the act of killing, the question of killing itself can never trump the permissibility of eating meat. Beyond that, Medhātithi makes much of the statement "abstaining from such activity, however, brings great rewards." For him, this statement brings the whole discussion together. Such "unspecified rewards must be understood, following the Mīmāṃsā, to be heaven," according to

(*arthavāda*), so also did Islamic law distinguish obligatory rules of the Shari'a (*farḍ*, *wājib*) from exhortations (*nadb*, *mandūb*) that provided only recommendations (*ibid.*, pp. 103–6). See also Mohammad Hashim Kamali, *Principles of Islamic Jurisprudence*, 3rd edn (Cambridge: Islamic Texts Society, 2003), pp. 416–21. J. Duncan M. Derrett, *Religion, Law and the State in India* (London: Faber, 1968), p. 87, compares this distinction to the difference between Halakhah and Haggadah in traditional Jewish law.

[17] Medh 5.56: "The verses from 'food for the lifebreath' to this verse are simply a group of *arthavāda*s (explanatory/commendatory statements). Only two or three verses intend to set forth an injunction [*prāṇasyānnam ity ata ārabhya yāvad ayaṃ śloko 'rthavādasaṃghāta eva | dvitrāḥ ślokā vidheyārthāḥ*]." A full translation of this discussion can be found in Ganganath Jha, *Manusmṛti: with 'Manubhāṣya' of Medhātithi*, 10 Vols., 2nd edn (Delhi: Motilal Banarsidass, 1999 [1920–39]).

[18] Medh 5.48: "This verse shows that the whole group of verses prohibiting killing is auxiliary to (the prohibition against) eating meat [*sarvasya hiṃsāpratiṣedhaślokasaṅghātasya māṃsabhakṣaṇaśeṣatām darśayati*]."

[19] For Medhātithi, killing and eating meat in specified contexts is legally permissible, but the law does not stop there. Instead, a fully hermeneutic understanding of law demonstrates that the law calls on us to abstain from these actions for the "great rewards" that abstention brings. Both are the law, *dharma*, but the *dharma* that produces higher reward is to be preferred over that of mere acceptability.

Medhātithi. In this way, the legal permissibility of eating meat is tempered by an equally legal encouragement to abstain from it insofar as possible.

Now, my characterization of an encouragement to abstain as legal will certainly and hopefully strike some readers as wrong.[20] But, this brings us to the central issue involved in understanding the value of Mīmāṃsā for the spirit of Hindu law. Law consists not only of enforceable rules and the recognition of permissible actions, i.e., norms of restriction, but also of rules that enable certain benefits and the recognition of the good accomplished through the practice of both enforceable and unenforceable rules, i.e., norms of production. We find a parallel juxtaposition of obligatory and recommended rules in Islamic law. Complying with a recommendation earns a Muslim "spiritual reward (*thawāb*), but no punishment is inflicted for failure to perform."[21] Like the many explanatory/exhortatory statements in Medhātithi's discussion, "in a general sense the *mandūb* [what is recommended] serves as an aid to the *wājib* [what is obligatory], either in the capacity of a prelude or as a reminiscent to *wājib*."[22]

It seems largely a matter of choice as to whether unenforceable, unsanctionable rules may count as law. There is little doubt that there are serious terminological and conceptual difficulties involved, as we see in Weiss's characterization of the matter in Islamic law:

> categorizations of human acts as recommended or disapproved are regarded in the classical texts as entailing no sanction ... [and] are thus decidedly not rules; they decidedly do not lend themselves to being subsumed under the heading of law. We thus have ... a major component of the Shari'a that cannot with good reason be called law, and yet this component is as integral to the Shari'a as is the strictly legal component. It is important always to bear in mind that the Shari'a is as much concerned with recommending and disapproving as it is with prescribing and forbidding.[23]

In the study of Hindu law, Derrett used the same criterion of sanction and enforceability to argue for a distinction of religious and legal commands,[24] also arguing that only enforceable rules may legitimately be called legal.

[20] Compare Robert M. Cover, "Foreword: *Nomos* and Narrative," *Harvard Law Review* 97 (1983–4): 40. "The reader may have tired by now of my insistence upon dignifying the internal norms, redemptive fantasies, briefs, positions, or arguments of various groups with the word 'law' ... It is the multiplicity of laws, the fecundity of the jurisgenerative principle, that creates the problem to which the court and the state are the solution."

[21] Kamali, *Principles of Islamic Jurisprudence*, p. 419.

[22] *Ibid.*, p. 420.

[23] Weiss, *Spirit of Islamic Law*, p. 19.

[24] Derrett, *Religion, Law and the State*, pp. 75–96.

The same problem afflicts both characterizations, namely that the English category *law* is privileged as fixed before it is applied, while the target term, whether *dharma* or *shari'a*, is made to seem ambiguous or conceptually fatty because it collapses the "natural" distinctions made in English. What happens if we play the game in reverse? Is it possible that what we call *law* actually contains lots of recommendations and disapprovals, many acknowledged as unenforceable in practice, without recognizing these as part of the law? Even if we may agree that the tendency has been for European and American legal systems to excise such recommendations and disapprovals over the last 200 years or so, is it not equally fair to characterize those systems then as lacking something important to most other legal systems, namely the supporting "moralities of law" that are seen in those systems as integral, inseparable, indistinguishable parts of the law itself?[25] Furthermore, did not the Western tradition itself see obligations and recommendations as completely intertwined, if heuristically distinct, as seen in the well-known maxim of Horace *quid leges sine moribus vanae proficiunt*, what good are laws without morals?

A final example concerns the nature of ownership according to the Dharmaśāstra. As part of his influential discussion on ownership by birth, Vijñāneśvara, author of the twelfth-century *Mitākṣarā* commentary on Yājñavalkya, argues that ownership arises through worldly (*laukika*) means and not through transcendental (*dhārmika*, *vaidika*) means. Although Vijñāneśvara advances several arguments in support of this view,[26] I want to focus on the third in which he relies on Mīmāṃsā interpretations of PMS 4.1.2, the so-called *lipsā-sūtra*, the beginning of the Mīmāṃsā distinction between *puruṣārtha* and *kratvartha* elements of the ritual.[27] Here, we need only note that Vijñāneśvara appears to rely on the eighth-century Mīmāṃsā commentator Prabhākara's discussion of the *sūtra* in his *Bṛhatī* which asserts that the acquisition of property (*dravyārjana*) must affect the person, not the ritual in order for any valid rites to occur at all. That is to

[25] On the ill-conceived efforts to distinguish religion and law in the realm of *dharma*, see Ludo Rocher, "Hindu Law and Religion: Where to Draw the Line?" In S.A.J. Zaidi (ed.), *Malik Ram Felicitation Volume* (New Delhi: Malik Ram Felicitation Committee, 1972), pp. 167–94, and Richard W. Lariviere, "Law and Religion in India." In Alan Watson (ed.), *Law, Morality, and Religion: Global Perspectives* (Berkeley: University of California, 1996), pp. 75–94.

[26] Ludo Rocher and Rosane Rocher, "Ownership by Birth: the *Mitākṣarā* Stand," *Journal of Indian Philosophy* 29 (2001): 241–55.

[27] *Puruṣārtha* elements subserve the sacrificer performing the rite, while *kratvartha* elements subserve the other elements of the rite itself.

say, without owning something, one cannot sacrifice it, and if ownership itself occurred only via transcendental means, there would be no way to enter the system, so to speak. Ownership, therefore, must be a mundane affair. Vijñāneśvara uses this argument in support of his larger argument in favor of sons acquiring ownership by birth, rather than by the death of their father.

So what do these examples tell us about the good of Hindu law, i.e., its purpose or useful end? Each example shows that the goal or telos of Dharmaśāstra commands is not the sacrificial ritual at the heart of Mīmāṃsā. Rather, it is something more encompassing, namely *varṇāśramadharma* itself.[28] The good that *dharma* texts presume and, to some extent, describe is the stability, social order, hierarchy, and generally worldly benefits conceptualized in *varṇāśramadharma*. Upholding of the Vedas and of the sacrifice is now only a part of a religio-legal project centered on worldly affairs. Maintenance of the sacrifice through Vedic learning is a part of this larger project, but this is now a purpose (*phala*/*artha*) at least one remove from the more immediate purpose of balance, order, and righteousness in human cultural life achieved through knowledge of the traditions of the learned (*śiṣṭācāra*). Dharmaśāstra speaks of questions about killing and eating meat and the determination of ownership. These are concerns affecting the general realm of human action, not merely the ritual. *Varṇāśramadharma* is the shorthand for that realm.

Stated in technical terms, schematically represented in Table 3, we might say that the *artha* has subtly shifted from Mīmāṃsā to Dharmaśāstra. The shift is hard to discern because both traditions focus on *dharma*. But *dharma* for the Mīmāṃsā is very clearly the *artha* indicated by Vedic command, namely the *yajña*. For Dharmaśāstra, by contrast, *dharma* is the *artha* indicated by *śiṣṭācāra*, namely the system of *varṇa* and *āśrama*. The parallels are striking, but the contents are distinct. We have in both a distinctive goal (*artha*) that is pursued by means (*karaṇa*) of a set of commands or rules (*vidhi*s) that emanate from an authoritative source (*mūla*). The goal and the source diverge, or perhaps one encompasses the other, but

[28] The Sanskrit term used widely in Dharmaśāstra for an ethical good in this sense is *śreyas*, which seems to have had this meaning at least since the Kaṭha Upaniṣad (2.1–2): "The good is one thing; the pleasurable another." It is my contention that *śreyas* in the *dharma* tradition signifies the human benefit represented by a flourishing adherence to and practice of *varṇāśramadharma*. See Priyanath Sen, *The General Principles of Hindu Jurisprudence* (Calcutta: University of Calcutta, 1918), p. 25.

Table 3. *Technical scheme of how law is parallel to ritual*

| | *artha* good/goal | *karaṇa* instrument | *mūla* source |
|---|---|---|---|
| Mīmāṃsā | *yajña* sacrifice | *vidhi/śāstra* injunction/text | *Veda* revealed truth |
| Dharmaśāstra | *varṇāśramadharma* law of caste/life-order | *vidhi/śāstra* injunction/text | *śiṣṭācāra* norms of the good |

it is the common nature of the means that allows Mīmāṃsā hermeneutics to be important to Dharmaśāstra as well.

The appropriation of Mīmāṃsā's theology by Dharmaśāstra gave the latter the ability to take advantage of the intricate philosophical justification for the classical Vedic ethos while at the same time broadening that ethos into what we might justifiably call classical Hindu theology. Mīmāṃsā imparted to Dharmaśāstra a way of identifying and theologically justifying a shared good toward which all elements of the religious system point. By substituting *varṇāśramadharma* for sacrifice, however, *dharma* texts set forth an all-encompassing system for human action. Instead of being purposed solely for the sacred, yet circumscribed, arena of the sacrifice, *varṇāśramadharma* was a good that possessed simultaneously otherworldly and this-worldly value and incorporated more or less the entire scope of human activity, at least for those eligible to pursue it. The centerpiece of the *dharma* system in this refashioned form, then, is a structure of synchronic (*varṇa*) and diachronic (*āśrama*) social arrangements (*dharma*) in which individuals find meaning in life through their efforts to appropriately place themselves in the larger scheme. It is this commonly agreed upon good of Hindu law, its axiomatic acceptance, that held together the legal and religious systematizations of Dharmaśāstra over time. *Dharma* texts made deft use of the theological and philosophical presuppositions of Mīmāṃsā, so much so that one might say that there's an implicit "see Mīmāṃsā" footnote on every page of Dharmaśāstra text.[29] At the same time, Dharmaśāstra constructed a theological and jurisprudential system that focused on what is essentially a set of worldly social and personal actions.

In terms of law, Mīmāṃsā helped define first of all what might be called the spirit of Hindu law, the idea that all the religio-legal elements of Dharmaśāstra ultimately served as further support for the eternal truth of the Veda, even though the contents of *dharma* texts were not directly

[29] For Medhātithi's explicit statement to this effect, see Chapter 1, fn. 6, this volume.

concerned with Vedic rites. Further, the appropriation of Mīmāṃsā by *dharma* authors put hermeneutics at the center of jurisprudence. Proclaiming, promulgating, and enforcing the law all took a back seat to interpreting the law, at least in the scholastic tradition. In classical Hindu legal texts, therefore, law is both constitutive of the good life and the instrument for establishing the good life for oneself and for others. The emphasis is on what law enables, rather than what law restrains. Taken together, rules of law both prescribe and constitute *varṇāśramadharma*, the figurative sacrificial ritual of human society itself and the ultimate good of Hindu law.

## ETHICS IN A PROCESS-CENTERED THEOLOGY

Mīmāṃsā thus imparts to the tradition of Hindu law three things:

1 a philosophical and theological justification of the authority of Dharmaśāstra in relation to the Veda;
2 a set of hermeneutic or interpretive principles that can be applied to legal matters; and
3 a view of law as analogous to ritual.

Having discussed the first in Chapter 1, we must now examine the further implications of the latter two. Both issues connect to ethics as conceptualized in Hindu law, or, stated more broadly, what do hermeneutics and ritual have to do with a legalistic view of the good life?

The cultivation of skill in interpretation, specifically the hermeneutic ability to bring textual sources to life in the present moment, is understood as an essential element in the ethics propounded within the spirit of Hindu law. It is the ethical ideal to be harmoniously in tune with the spirit of the Veda, the tradition of prior sages, and the present political and social contexts when making ethical decisions about how to act. How is an act of legal interpretation related to ethics? From the perspective of Hindu law and most religious laws, hermeneutic constraints in fact predetermine a good proportion of what goes into ethics. One's prejudgments or prejudices dominate ethics and those should therefore be formed and shaped in advance of having to make ethical decisions in such a way that one no longer makes ethical mistakes. Hermeneutics is thus the art of bringing tradition to bear on the contexts of ordinary life, of making a place for surprise on the landscape of prejudice.[30]

[30] On surprise as an element of hermeneutics, see Charles Hallisey, "The Surprise of Scripture's Advice." In Judith Frishman, Willemien Otten, and Gerard Rouwhorst (eds.), *Religious Identity and the Problem of Historical Foundation* (Leiden: E.J. Brill, 2004).

The centrality of hermeneutics to ethics in Hindu law is a feature shared with other religious laws. In Islamic law, for instance, "The adoption of prophetic hadith as a major source of law second only to the Qur'an resulted in the transformation of the exposition of law into a largely exegetical enterprise."[31] More importantly, "the Law as a topically-organized finished product consisting of precisely-worded rules is the *result* of juristic interpretation; it stands at the end, not the beginning, of the interpretive process."[32] It is hard to over-emphasize the importance of the idea that law is what results from interpretation rather than being the basis for interpretation. Rules in Hindu, Islamic, and Jewish traditions are not themselves law, but they help law come about. Each of these traditions defines law (*dharma*, *shari'a*, *halakhah*) as consisting of positive and negative commands or rules (*vidhi/niṣedha*, *amr/nahy*, *mitzvot aseh/mitzvot to la'aseh*) and some sort of explanatory, exhortatory, or recommendatory set of rules and stories that supplement the obligatory rules (*arthavāda*, *mandūb/sunna*, *aggadah*). Of course, the parallels are not perfect, but the commonalities are sufficient to show a widespread view of law in which law is a path or a way that is forged through acts of interpreting legal sources. Experiential knowledge of the traditional path itself is imparted to people by their acceptance of the rules, an acceptance that entails both the acquisition of the substance of the tradition and the burden to continue its constant upholding through the hermeneutic application of tradition to current contexts. Again, each tradition recognizes an ideal person who embodies both the process and the ethical good involved in consciously entering the hermeneutic life. Hindu law texts call that person a *śiṣṭa*. In Islam, it is the *mujtahid*; in Rabbinic Judaism, a *ḥākāṃ* or *tzadik*. The question from an ethics standpoint is how does one become such an ideal person?

The answers are once again similar: by submitting or subordinating oneself to the tradition itself, to the path of the law already set forth by previous good persons.[33] In the *Laws of Manu*, we find this account of ethical submission by a student: "As a man discovers water by digging with a spade, so a student, offering obedient service, discovers the knowledge contained in his teacher" (MDh 2.218). The word for "obedient service"

[31] Weiss, *Spirit of Islamic Law*, p. 14.

[32] Bernard Weiss, "Interpretation in Islamic Law: The Theory of *Ijtihād*," *American Journal of Comparative Law* 26 (1977–8): 200.

[33] Jonathan W. Schofer, *The Making of a Sage: a Study in Rabbinic Ethics* (Madison: University of Wisconsin Press, 2005) argues that "subordination" is the key process of ethical formation in rabbinic thought and provides a subtle account of the constituent elements of such subordination.

here is *śuśruṣu*, literally "being one who ardently desires to serve," is the same word used of the lowest caste, the Śūdras, in the predictably dismissive and curt summary of their *dharmas* in the same text (MDh 9.334–5). By serving a teacher unconditionally, the way a Śūdra serves the higher castes, a student attains unparalleled knowledge and those servile habits cause that student to acquire the *habitus* of ethical goodness that defines the ideal person.[34] The content of those habits is defined by the set of rules operating within the larger concept of the law.

The process of ethical subordination in religious legal systems entails a related process that distinguishes the creative power of law as presented in such systems from the way it is presented in modern legal theory. In the context of Mīmāṃsā, Clooney calls the process the "de-centering of the human." Clooney states, "The sacrifice is not subordinated to a teleology articulated from a human point of view; sacrifice is not undertaken simply for the sake of the acquisition of heaven and other results, even if human beings talk about sacrifice in that way. Rather, human participants in the sacrifice are considered and evaluated in terms of their place in the larger framework."[35] If we recall that the sacrifice in Mīmāṃsā becomes the "ritual of society" in Dharmaśāstra, we must imagine that the system of castes and life-stages, the summary scholarly description of ideal social life, also shifts focus away from the individual without denying him or her a necessary role in the larger scheme.[36]

Situational ethics or the by-now proverbial contextuality of Indian thought might better be classified as an event-oriented ethics, meaningful expenditures of personal substance in the light of discrete, but often repeated, circumstances in everyday life. Here one's person is not central, one's action is. The question of one's eternal, abstract person or self – the famous *ātman* of Indian philosophy – is held to be a separate issue for separate consideration.[37] Dharmaśāstra is rather concerned with a person

For Islam, beyond the well-known etymology of "Islam" and "Muslim" is a root meaning submission, the notion of *ibadah* and *'abd*, devoted service and slavery, looms large, for example, in Ghazālī's account of human autonomy within divinely governed heteronomy. See Ebrahim Moosa, *Ghazālī and the Poetics of Imagination* (Chapel Hill: University of North Carolina Press, 2005), pp. 232–3.

[34] On habits and *habitus* in relation to religious ethics, see Saba Mahmood, "Ethical Formation and Politics of Individual Autonomy in Contemporary Egypt," *Social Research* 70:3 (2003): 852.

[35] Clooney, *Thinking Ritually*, pp. 193–4.

[36] A good technical example of how the individual is displaced from the center of hermeneutical reflection is the reanalysis of the paradigmatic injunction of Mīmāṃsā *svargakāmo yajeta* "the person who desires heaven should sacrifice" as *yāgena svargaṃ bhāvayet* "by sacrifice heaven should be brought about." See MNP 123.

[37] Francis X. Clooney, "Jaimini's Contribution to the Theory of Sacrifice as the Experience of Transcendence," *History of Religions* 25:3 (1986): 204.

in action, the karmic actor, whose substantial configuration is perpetually changing and whose purpose in life revolves around its discrete actions. More important in fact than the actor is the action. One's primary concern should be the propriety of the act. If action is right, then good will follow to its performer. The contexts of proper action, i.e., *dharma*, are not unlimited, however. Contextuality is restricted by tradition, both in the form of normative texts and normative habits.

Ethics from the hermeneutic perspective of Mīmāṃsā and as applied in Dharmaśāstra, therefore, begins when a person understands this de-centered place of the individual in the processes of *dharma*.[38] Hermeneutics is the process of bringing the various pieces of the puzzle together to "perform society." That performance involves the coordinated effort of not one, but many people, a set of substantive commands about what to do, the materials to do it, and a separate set of rules to bring these all together.[39] Ethics very definitely exceed the boundaries of the individual person in Hindu jurisprudence. In fact, it is here that we meet the transcendence offered in Mīmāṃsā and transformatively appropriated in Dharmaśāstra. The focus on the event over the person demands a self that is reduced to a series of functional roles that subserve the event of the sacrifice or of society. Like the seemingly dehumanizing feeling of reducing oneself to the set of numbers submitted to the tax authorities in the metaphor above, so the ethic of *dharma* necessitates a displacement of humanity from the center of attention. Transcendence is the very act of ethical subordination to the standards of *dharma*, because that subordination transforms the fragmented person presented in the ritual of society into a complete human, a person who knows the place of humanity in the the transcendent frame of worldly social life and comes to embody the discipline required of that de-centered place in order to achieve the higher purpose of the "ritual" itself. People

[38] It is the diverting of attention away from the individual that distinguishes the Hindu law view of ethical formation from that of Aristotle, for instance. Aristotle's account of how habits create character and virtue (*Nicomachean Ethics* 2.1) is predicated on the individual's habitual repetition of just action as opposed to analyzing just action in terms of its constituent parts, only one of which would be a given individual.

[39] Adapted from Clooney, "Why the Veda Has No Author: Language as Ritual in Early Mimamsa and Post-Modern Theology," *Journal of the American Academy of Religion* 55:4 (1987): 663: "Mīmāṃsā's response to the whole range of [Buddhist and Jain] criticisms was to rethink its world without reliance on any single viewpoint, effectively undercutting the possibility of a single perspective. It sought a justification for sacrifice that needed no external validation, either from active gods or satisfied humans, and that required the positing neither of any supernatural realities nor a reliable world order beyond that of good Sanskrit texts, well-performed sacrifices, and a set of rules for integrating the two."

who undergo this transformation through subordination in turn become the mediators of this worldly transcendence to others.[40]

The metaphor of law as ritual transferred from Mīmāṃsā to Dharmaśāstra opens up a set of important points of comparison between Hindu law and other religious laws. First, the idea that law is a ritual forces us to see that law is comprised not only of the rule, but also of the precedent of tradition and of the performance of the appropriately determined rule. Hacker has called this *dharma* before, during, and after its performance or fulfillment (Vollzug).[41] Hindu law would insist, as with ritual, that no *dharma* is done, that there is no law, until and unless the legally determined act has been performed, because law is more than rules. It is a complex, and very often subtle, process of appropriating tradition for the purposes of carrying out ordinary actions. The process is best understood with the aid of substantive metaphors. *Dharma* as tradition is a thing, a pool of goodness or merit, a constructed pathway. *Dharma* as action is the physical contribution one makes through one's deeds to the merit pool or the straight path. When tradition informs action through the medium of hermeneutics, the result is law. Like the rituals at the core of Mīmāṃsā, however, hermeneutics is a process to be repeated and never to be finished.

Second, law according to this view should have a purpose and should bring about a good. We see this most clearly in the idea that *dharma* is, among other things, merit or righteousness. The controlling definition of *dharma* from Mīmāṃsā ("*dharma* is a good indicated by Vedic command" at PMS 1.1.2) unequivocally states that *dharma* is a purposeful activity, a good, or an end (*artha*) that is defined by a special kind of command. In the full Mīmāṃsā system, *dharma* appears to be the coordinated harmonization of three distinct purposes pertaining to people, actions, and results through the assistance of hermeneutics.[42] This internally diverse, but still unified, end within Hindu jurisprudence connects Hindu law to other traditions of legal thought that demand a shared teleological goal.

The purpose or telos of *dharma* according to Dharmaśāstra is the preservation and perpetuation of the system of castes and life-stages (*varṇāśramadharma*). The notion that legal systems should possess an

[40] Compare A. Kevin Reinhart, "Transcendence and Social Practice: *Muftīs* and *Qāḍīs* as Religious Interpreters," *Annales Islamologiques* 27 (1993): 24: "In the self-description of the '*ulamā*' we see that, in Sunni Islam, scholars mediated transcendence and made it immanent in the ordinary world."

[41] Paul Hacker, "Dharma in Hinduism," *Journal of Indian Philosophy* 34 (2006): 490.

[42] Clooney, "Jaimini's Contribution," pp. 208–10, on *dharma* as the combination of *puruṣārtha*, *kratvartha*, and *śabdārtha* – purposes of "human intention, the integrity of action, and the intelligibility of words" (p. 210), respectively.

internally coherent purpose or goal has been debated endlessly between formalists and instrumentalists in legal theory.[43] Various ways out have also been suggested.[44] For the purposes of this chapter, however, it is sufficient to note that having a relatively unitary goal in a legal system links law to ethics and morality without claiming that one is necessarily superior to the other. Under such conditions, law and ethics tend to converge because the telos of the system acts as the common standard against which to judge both legal and ethical rules and actions. The common standard also makes space for a debate grounded in hermeneutics, but a debate that never challenges the axiomatic goals of the system as a whole.[45]

It is important to remember that Hindu jurisprudence recognizes a telos that was essentially separate from and superior to politics. The ruler's role is to create the conditions for the system of castes and life-stages to flourish and, if necessary, to enforce it on those who deviate from it. The ruler, like all individuals, is not at the center of the system, and yet the ruler has a greater responsibility for its protection and flourishing.

A final key issue that links law, ritual, and hermeneutics is what might be called the theology of command at work in most, or all, religious legal systems. In the Mīmāṃsā view, the Veda exists as an authorless corpus of commands. The "cosmic" quality of these commands, their eternality, and their claim on human action all combine to present a vision of law that is theologically understood to be the human response to Vedic commands. A similar theology of command characterizes Islamic law in that *ḥukm*, rule or command (especially God's), "is simultaneously the carrier of both a transcendental and an empirical communication."[46] More specifically,

> The *ḥukm* is rightly understood not as something known, nor a ruling drawn and applied from a body of rules, but as something theoretically indeterminate until performed. *Fiqh* is the consequence of that performance, it is "understanding" (the literal meaning of "*fiqh*") produced by the religiously legitimate process of

[43] Brian Z. Tamanaha, *Law as a Means to an End: Threat to the Rule of Law* (New York: Cambridge University Press, 2006), pp. 215–26.

[44] Among many possible examples, see Clifford Geertz, "Local Knowledge: Fact and Law in Comparative Perspective." In *Local Knowledge: Further Essays in Interpretive Anthropology* (New York: Basic Books, 1983) and Pierre Bourdieu, "The Force of Law: Toward a Sociology of the Juridical Field," *Hastings Law Journal* 38 (1986–87): 814–53.

[45] The most persuasive defense of teleology in the realm of politics and ethics in the modern world is Alasdair MacIntyre, *After Virtue: A Study in Moral Theory*, 2nd edn (Notre Dame: University of Notre Dame Press, 1984).

[46] Ebrahim Moosa, "Allegory of the Rule (*Ḥukm*): Law as Simulacrum in Islam?" *History of Religions* 38:1 (1998): 23.

measuring the situation at hand against the corpus of Revelation, and applying or extending the information in Revelation in certain specified ways.[47]

This understanding, the product of legal hermeneutics, is intimately tied to the ethics of self-formation.[48] In both traditions, an indisputable set of commands, a Revelation, must be brought into the ordinary world. Hermeneutics is the process by which revelation is continuously remade in the contexts of ordinary life. Conformity to rulings of hermeneutics, meaning the performance of the actions determined to have been commanded, constitutes the core of ethics. Finally, the whole process from revelatory command to hermeneutic specification to conformable performance is collectively called the law, *dharma* or *sharī'a*. Each element is necessary for law to emerge in its fullest sense.[49]

The relation of Mīmāṃsā hermeneutics and Hindu ethics in the context of Dharmaśāstra leads to the related question of how the theology of command affects the human being. What is the effect of this sort of cosmic command and how does it manifest in people's lives? The response within Dharmaśāstra is debt or obligation, the Sanskrit concept of *ṛṇa* to which we now turn.

[47] Reinhart, "Transcendence and Social Practice," p. 8.

[48] Reinhart makes this connection beautifully in A. Kevin Reinhart, "Islamic Law as Islamic Ethics," *Journal of Religious Ethics* 11:2 (1983): 186–203.

[49] Compare Paul Ricoeur, *The Just*, trans. D. Pellauer (Chicago: University of Chicago Press, 2003), p. xxii: "[T]he meaning of justice, which conserves its rootedness in the wish for a good life and finds its most ascetic rational formulation in procedural formalism, does not attain concrete plenitude except at the stage of the application of the norm in the exercise of judgment in some situation."

CHAPTER 3

# *Debt and meaning* (ṛṇa)

The relationship between persons is one of two traditionally conceived forms of human interaction governed by law. The other is the relationship of persons and things, to be considered in Chapter 4. Together, we might use the Hindu jurisprudential views of these two legally recognized forms of human interaction with the world as a kind of summary of the substantive law in the Hindu tradition. In particular, it is in these interactions that we will find the most visible connections of law, theology, and ordinary life that undergird the legal imagination in Hinduism and, as I have argued, in all legal systems.

Various types of relationship exist between people and these can all be reified or instantiated by the law. Think only of the historical significance and tragedy of laws pertaining to masters and slaves. Other ordinary relationships, too – between parents and children (more often father and sons), husband and wife, between classmates or business partners, or even between individuals and corporations – occupy a huge and central place in every legal system. The law promotes or prohibits these relationships according to certain fundamental views of human nature and life itself that are literally written into the text of the law. Famously, the nineteenth-century legal historian Henry Sumner Maine argued that the historical progress of law may be described as "a movement from Status to Contract."[1] Essentially, Maine suggested that earlier legal systems recognized and reinforced traditional privilege, wealth, and custom, while later systems increasingly asserted greater equality before the law in the form of autonomous individuals whose status was legally unmarked and whose relationships to one another were governed by freely chosen contracts they made.[2] Scholars have struggled with the beautiful, but treacherous, simplicity of Maine's idea ever since.

[1] Henry Sumner Maine, *Ancient Law: its Connection with the Early History of Society and its Relations to Modern Ideas* (London: John Murray, 1861), p. 141.

[2] Maine's own notion of Status drew heavily from his studies of India, but suffers both from an inadequate knowledge of history and language and from the fraught position from which he wrote

Following Maine, we might ask whether any root metaphor dominates the discussions of human relationship in Hindu jurisprudence. Perhaps the closest we can come is the notion of debt, or *ṛṇa*. Debt or obligation becomes in Hindu legal texts a paradigmatic metaphor for describing all human relationships. Human life in the view of the texts is positioned between two kinds of debt or obligation: debts given by birth, the so-called triple-debt, and debts voluntarily taken on. Debt in this latter, more technical, sense is the first and main subject of the first title of law in Hindu legal procedure and is thus paradigmatic for others. Underlying both uses of *ṛṇa*, however, is a vision of life as a continual process of discharging inborn debts by means of accepting day-to-day obligations. This vision suggests an ethics of the controlled self-emptying of one's personal character and substance into the world as a way of pursuing religious salvation. In this chapter, we will examine the religious and legal implications of the notion of debt in Hindu legal texts and explore how debt underlies and structures legal procedure and constantly circles back into the connection of law and ordinary life.

## CONGENITAL DEBTS AND CONTRACTUAL DEBTS

The theology of debt in Hindu traditions has its first textual manifestations in the *Taittirīya Saṃhitā* and the *Śatapatha Brāhmaṇa*, both texts dating to the middle Vedic period (*c.*800–600 BC).[3] The *Taittirīya* formulation has been more influential on later traditions: "A Brahmin, at his very birth, is born with a triple debt – of studentship to the seers, of sacrifice to the gods, of offspring to the fathers. He is, indeed, free from debt, who has a son, is a sacrificer, and who has lived as a student" (6.3.10.5).[4] Malamoud calls this the "theology of debt in Brahmanism," the idea that "man's congenital debt ... has no origin ... debt is already there fully formed ... fundamental debt affects man and defines him from the moment he is born."[5]

The first thing to notice in this formulation of the triple debt is the ordinary quality of the debts owed congenitally. All three are part of the

as a kind of apologist for empire. See Karuna Mantena, *Alibis of Empire: Social Theory and the Ideologies of Late Imperialism* (Princeton: Princeton University Press, forthcoming).

3 The best studies of the theology of debts in early Hindu traditions are Charles Malamoud, "The Theology of Debt in Brahmanism." In *Cooking the World: Ritual and Thought in Ancient India*, trans. David White (Delhi: Oxford University Press, 1996), pp. 92–108, and Patrick Olivelle, *The Āśrama System: the History and Hermeneutics of a Religious Institution* (New York: Oxford University Press, 1993), pp. 46–55, 176–82. My presentation of the doctrine of congenital debts relies heavily on these two studies.

4 Translation from Olivelle, *Āśrama System*, p. 47. TS 6.3.10.5 begins: *tribhir ṛṇavā jāyate.*

5 Malamoud, "Theology of Debt," p. 95.

normal course of the ideal Brahmin's or twice-born person's life in the context of household and family. Vedic study is expected of all twice-born males.[6] Sacrifice in this context almost certainly refers to the five "great sacrifices" incumbent on every twice-born male.[7] These are rites performed in the household and, indeed, define what it means to be a householder for the Dharmaśāstra. Similarly, marriage is the rite of passage for becoming a householder and the means to obtain children.[8] This view of marriage as normal and obligatory is characteristic of religious legal systems. In Islamic law, for instance, "the classical jurists considered marriage to be the normal ultimate state of human beings, and they saw marriage as inevitably resulting under normal circumstances in offspring."[9] Religious laws thus imagine the typical subject of the law to be a married male householder, a kind of core identity or role presumed throughout the legal texts.

The three debts are a chain of transmission of *dharma* linking the households connected with a man at different times in his life. As a student, he learns from and in the household of his teacher all the values, rules, and roles of tradition through a rigorous self-submission to the teacher's guidance and command. After marriage, he establishes his own household, carrying the knowledge he now has into a new context, quite literally into a new microcosm of all that is most important in his life. With the birth of his sons and their eventual studentship and marriage, the father passes on the same congenital debts and, in fact, depends upon their fulfillment for his own flourishing before and after death. The chain of *dharma* thus moves from father to son, but, more importantly, from household to household.

The *Laws of Manu* sets forth the doctrine of triple-debt as follows:

> Only after he has paid his three debts, should a man set his mind on release; if he devotes himself to release without paying them, he will proceed downward. Only after he has studied the Vedas according to rule, fathered sons in keeping with the Law, and offered sacrifice according to his ability, should a man set his mind on release. (MDh 6.35–6)

[6] MDh 2.164–5.

[7] Olivelle, *Āśrama System*, pp. 53–5. The five *mahāyajñas* are, according the *Laws of Manu*: "The sacrifice to the Veda is teaching; the sacrifice to ancestors is the quenching libation; the sacrifice to the gods is the burnt offering; the sacrifice to beings is the Bali offering; and the sacrifice to humans is the honoring of guests" (MDh 3.70). The parallel between the triple-debt and the structure of these five sacrifices is sufficient to suggest some connection between them.

[8] MDh 3.2, 4 (on marriage); 9.137–8.

[9] Bernard G. Weiss, *The Spirit of Islamic Law* (Athens: University of Georgia Press, 1998), p. 155.

Manu here connects the triple-debt with the system of life-stages. Paying the three debts becomes the prerequisite for entering the fourth and final stage of a renouncer. Each of the three debts implies, even demands, a specific mode of life or set of roles that a man must take on in life. The debt owed to the ancient sages impels a man to take on the knowledge and the habitus of tradition as symbolized by the study of the Vedas. Through Vedic study, a man brings his *past self* into line with tradition. The ideal man thus takes on the role of student in order to reinsert himself into the lineage of "good people." The debt owed to the gods is "special in that the gods are but substitutes or intermediaries of another creditor, which is death, or else Yama ... All debt is the presence of death."[10] One essentially buys back one's life from death through the offering of sacrifices. The role of sacrificer defines a man centrally in terms of his *present self*. Similarly, "the debt owed to the manes is central to brahmin ideology. It is an essential element in the religious definition of man. But further, it is made to account for the fundamental drive that is the desire to reproduce."[11] Marriage and children, and the roles of husband and father, thus emerge from this debt, but payment of the debt to one's ancestors ironically secures the flourishing of one's *future self*. Together the triple-debt presents a man with the requirements necessary to become fully human and thus serves as one kind of epitome of the religious life in the Hindu view.[12]

The *Laws of Nārada* (1.5) calls the triple-debt the "higher" debt and others the "lower": "Fathers wish for sons for their own sakes, thinking, 'He will release me from both the higher and lower debt'."[13] The commentator Asahāya gives as examples the rice-balls and water offered to ancestors and gold and grain, respectively.[14] Nārada differentiates congenital

[10] Malamoud, "Theology of Debt," pp. 100–1. [11] *Ibid*., p. 104.

[12] Another epitome of the good life is the scheme of the three or four "aims of life" (*puruṣārtha*) found abundantly in early Sanskrit texts. Unlike the theology of debts, however, the aims of life seemed not to have become a part of Hindu theological agendas until later in Indian religious history. Specifically, the addition of liberation (*mokṣa*) to the list of aims, difficult to pinpoint chronologically, seems to mark a shift from an anthropological to a theological conception. See Donald R. Davis, Jr. "Being Hindu or Being Human: a Reappraisal of the *puruṣārthas*," *International Journal of Hindu Studies* 8:1–3 (2004): 1–27.

[13] The translation of the verse modifies Lariviere's slightly. Lariviere translates the two debts as "sacred" and "worldly." Also compare Vijñāneśvara's differentiation (at YS 2.36–7, following NS 1.1) of seven forms of debt, five that are "lower" (*adhamarṇa*) and two that are "higher" (*uttamarṇa*). The latter, he says, consist of the rules for giving and receiving mentioned at NS 1.1.

[14] Asahāya on NS 1.5: *yathā ... uttamarṇaṃ pitṛpiṇḍodakādikaṃ dadāti tathā hiraṇyadhānyādikam adhamarṇaṃ ... dadāti*. Asahāya first uses these terms in this sense at NS 1.1; see Lariviere's comments in his translation at p. 273.

and contractual debts as a summary of what a son provides to the family or household, but the link he provides between congenital and contractual debts is important for demonstrating the conceptual connection of the triple-debt theology and the pragmatic presentations of debt as a title of law in Dharmaśāstra. We turn, therefore, to a consideration of debt in Hindu jurisprudence with a focus first on the title of law called The Non-payment of Debts.

The most prominent definition of this title of law comes from the *Laws of Nārada*: "The subject of Non-payment of Debts covers: which debts are to be paid and which are not to be paid, and by whom, when, and how, along with the *dharma*s for giving and receiving" (NS 1.1).[15] Several specific topics are covered under this expansive definition.[16] First, we find descriptions of various forms of interest: periodic, stipulated, compound, and usufructuary, including limitations on the overall amount (usually twice the principal), maximum term, and repayment schedules. Next, the texts discuss the question of the liability of sons and other relatives to pay a man's debts, including a specific order for reassigning the debts and legal limitations on the responsibility. Third, there are long discussions of security and guarantees associated with contractual debts. The governing rule in this connection comes from the *Laws of Nārada*: "There are two means of [contractual] security, a surety and a collateral pledge. A document and witnesses are the legal proofs that make [contracts] clear" (NS 1.103). Legal sureties are human guarantors against default on a loan. Similarly, we have the descriptions of collateral sureties in the form of various mortgages, principally custodial and usufructuary, but incorporating also sub-mortgages, leases, and hypothecations. Finally, the text also discusses the proper procedures for the recovery of debts, both judicial and non-judicial; these rules also specify the order of who gets paid back first and in what form.

Despite the fact that the *Laws of Nārada* places gifts and their receipt under the topic of debt, the important topic of gift-giving is not dealt with extensively under this title of law. Instead, we find descriptions of gifts in the delineation of the caste *dharma*s of the Brahmin[17] and in

[15] I have again modified Lariviere's translation of this verse. In this case, there is a textual variant in the third foot of the verse, which reads either *dānagrahaṇa-dharmāc ca/dharmāś ca/dharmābhyāṃ*. Even in the first reading, which Lariviere accepts, he does not account for the particle *ca*, which adds to the list of other elements of debt already enumerated. Therefore, the verse should be read as listing seven elements of this title of law as mentioned above by Vijñāneśvara.

[16] See Heramba Chatterjee Śāstri, *The Law of Debt in Ancient India* (Calcutta: Sanskrit College, 1971) for extensive descriptions of each of these topics.

[17] See, for example, MDh 4.186–94, 4.226–37, 4.247–56 and YS 1.198–216.

the title of law called the Resumption of Gifts.[18] It is a tantalizing tension of modern scholarship on gift-giving in India that the classical theory of gifts, from Dharmaśāstra and elsewhere, is usually described as explicitly denying the creation of obligation between donor and recipient, while other Dharmaśāstra descriptions of gift place it squarely in the realm of debt and enforceable obligation. In particular, the legal obligation of donors to make gifts only of permissible property (i.e., not stolen, mortgaged, held as deposit, etc.) and of recipients to faithfully and accurately represent themselves as worthy according the definitions of the texts. Failures on either account can result in legal action to void and/or reclaim the gift.

Interestingly, the topic of legal witness usually appears under the Nonpayment of Debts. Its placement under this title occurs in the first presentation of the titles of law in the *Arthaśāstra* (KA 3.11.25–50) and was subsequently followed by Manu and other Dharmaśāstra authors.[19] Later compilers of Dharmaśāstra digests seem to have naturally moved the topic of witness to the general discussion of legal procedure. The root-texts' placement of the discussion of witness in this title of law is most likely a product of its original textual position in the *Arthaśāstra*, but it still begs the question of the connection between debt and witness. As we see in the *Laws of Nārada* quotation above, witnesses are invoked in the context of other legal guarantees for contracts such as sureties and collateral. Like sureties, witnesses accept a certain responsibility for the debt being contracted, though without the obligation to repay the debt themselves. Nevertheless, a witness to a contract or a transaction takes on a kind of promissory debt to testify to the details of the transaction should any dispute about it arise. The act of witnessing in a judicial context then becomes an act of discharging a debt owed to the contracting parties. The connection of witnessing with debt begins to signal the wider ramifications that debt has in the Hindu conception of law.

[18] Though the specifically legal side of *dāna*, gift-giving, in classical and medieval India has not been sufficiently studied, studies on the ethics of gift-giving, not to mention its social, political, and religious implications, are abundant. The best recent work to engage deeply with medieval Dharmaśāstra views of *dāna* is Maria Heim, *Theories of the Gift in South Asia* (New York: Routledge, 2004), whose bibliography points to current work in the field.

[19] The *Arthaśāstra* is a text of perhaps the first century AD that describes rules for statecraft, political economy, and law in an almost exclusively secular manner. The Dharmaśāstra tradition, beginning with Manu, completely co-opted the Arthaśāstra tradition by incorporating it under the *dharma* of the ruler. Separate focus on statecraft, politics, and law outside the boundaries of *dharma*, therefore, ceased after Manu and did not reappear until the late medieval period. See Patrick Olivelle, "Manu and the *Arthaśāstra*: A Study in Śāstric Intertextuality," *Journal of Indian Philosophy* 32:2–3 (2004): 281–91.

In the same discussion, the *Laws of Nārada* also contain a fairly extensive discussion of the question of independence or autonomy (*svatantratva*) and its relationship to legal competence. At first glance, this topic also may seem to have little connection to contractual debts strictly construed. The discussion opens as follows: "In this world there are three who are independent: the king, the teacher, and every householder of every caste in his own home" (NS 1.28). Anticipating a later discussion, Asahāya comments, "These three are autonomous because of the dependence of a specific inferior [group] on a superior [person]."[20] The next verses explain, "All subjects are dependent; the king is independent. The student is dependent; the teacher is independent. Women, sons, slaves, and other retainers are dependent; the householder is independent with regard to that which he has inherited" (NS 1.29–30). Dependence in this sense creates debt relationships between the two categories of persons. Obligations exist in both directions. The succeeding rule (NS 1.32) then links autonomy with full legal competence or majority (*vyavahārajña*). Finally, of course, autonomy and legal competence are set forth as prerequisites for making valid legal transactions or, in other words, for entering into contracts (NS 1.38). Legal dependents are incompetent to make contracts, while any transaction made by a legal autonomous person, who is not abnormal or incapacitated (NS 1.36–7), is legally valid.

Autonomy, therefore, like *dharma* itself, is relative or contextual. To be an autonomous person in Hindu jurisprudence means to be free from the fixed roles of law with respect to a certain group. Autonomy thus brings with it an unlimited and unchallengeable authority over that group, but also a responsibility for it. With the exception of rulers and full-fledged ascetic renouncers, no one is autonomous in all situations, and even this absolute autonomy is sometimes challenged.[21] The issue of autonomy thus relates back to the tendency to minimize choice in Hindu law. For most people, autonomy is at best a right and responsibility that lasts for a limited time and that has a limited range of application. More important and more prominent in human life are the series of non-autonomous roles that are recognized under the law and within which most people lead the majority of their lives.

[20] Asahāya on NS 1.28: *trāyo 'pi svatantrā uttarādharaviśeṣāpekṣayā*.

[21] Patrick Olivelle, "Renouncer and Renunciation in the Dharmaśāstras." In Richard Lariviere (ed.), *Studies in Dharmaśāstra* (Calcutta: Firma KLM, 1984), pp. 81–152.

Table 4. *The eighteen titles of law in Hindu jurisprudence (MDh)*

1. Non-payment of debt
2. Deposits
3. Sale without ownership
4. Partnerships
5. Non-delivery of gifts
6. Non-payment of wages
7. Violation of conventions
8. Cancellation of sale or purchase
9. Disputes between owners and herdsmen
10. Boundary disputes
11. Verbal assault
12. Physical assault
13. Theft
14. Violence
15. Sexual crimes against women
16. Law concerning husband and wife
17. Partition and inheritance
18. Gambling and betting

## DEBTS AND DUTIES IN ORDINARY LIFE

The examination of the Non-payment of Debts as the first of eighteen titles of Hindu law leads now to a investigation of the other titles and their relationship to the overall scheme of *dharma* and to debt in particular. In general, the titles of law are held to be the legally recognized forms of civil and criminal wrongdoing. According to Medhātithi: "The objects of dispute fall with eighteen heads: it is only with regard to these that disputes arise among men ... The various ramifications of these are included under each head; if these ramifications were to be enumerated separately, there would be thousands of them."[22] A Hindu title of law, therefore, is the theoretical form in which a person must bring his or her case to a court,[23] though it was recognized that actual disputes were far more diverse.

This organization separates the legally actionable forms of dispute and crime into the traditional number eighteen.[24] Despite some variation in

[22] Medh on MDh 8.3 (Jha's translation, Vol. 6, p. 17).
[23] One could compare the Hindu titles of law to the old forms of action in English law.
[24] Eighteen is a sacred number in Hindu traditions: eighteen Upaniṣads, eighteen books of the *Mahābhārata* and chapters of its *Bhagavad-Gītā*, eighteen Purāṇas, and then variations on the number eighteen in forms such as 108, 1008, etc.

the number and arrangement of the titles,[25] all Dharmaśāstra texts place the Non-payment of Debt first. A very old practice of textual organization within Dharmaśāstra and other textual genres of Sanskrit calls the first procedure or topic to be described the archetype (*prakṛti*) and the subsequent procedures or topics the ectypes (*vikṛti*). We saw this practice in the placement of the Brahmin as the archetype in the enumeration of the duties of the four castes. The archetype is fully described, while ectypes are only described in terms of their distinction from the archetype as matter of textual concision. The Non-payment of Debts is the archetype for the other titles of law, not only because its description overlaps with and in some respects encompasses the contents of the other titles but also because debt as its thematic content pervades the subsequent titles. In terms of overlap, questions about witness, autonomy, competence, documentation, and contractual securities are all assumed in and carried over to discussions of the later titles. In terms of the theme, the archetypal or paradigmatic quality of debt must be established by examining the other titles.

The entire scheme of the titles of law is the extension of a notion of debt through a series of common points of dispute or conflict that arise between people. The ramifications of the doctrine of congenital debts as applied to situations and practices of ordinary life are seen in the complex mundane contractual debt-situations spelled out in the *dharma* texts. Though all of the titles of law cannot be individually described here,[26] a few examples from them will illustrate how the idea of debt functions as an underlying concept throughout. The *Laws of Nārada* again provide an accessible point of entry into the titles of law because they constitute the main chapters and structure of this work.

An obvious instance of the extension of debt into ordinary life comes in the title of law called Partnership. The cooperative and joint endeavors of a group of people, small or large, depend upon the sharing of risk and the acceptance of mutual obligations. The definition and specification of that risk and those obligations are the subject of this title of law. In the *Laws of Nārada*:

[25] Patrick Olivelle (ed. and trans.), *Manu's Code of Law: a Critical Edition and Translation of the* Mānava-Dharmaśāstra (New York: Oxford University Press, 2005), p. 14, provides a comparative table from major Dharmaśāstra texts.

[26] Ashutosh Dayal Mathur, *Medieval Hindu Law: Historical Evolution and Enlightened Rebellion* (Delhi: Oxford University Press, 2007), provides a solid overview of the titles of law as presented in the medieval texts.

When merchants and the like undertake a joint venture, that is referred to under the title of law called Partnership. They undertake a joint venture to make a profit, and their contributions are the basis of the venture; thus it is on this basis that they share proportionately in the proceeds. The proportion of loss, expenditure, or profit which each partner should bear is directly related to his investment. The proportion contracted for strictly determines his responsibility with regard to merchandise, sustenance, expenditures, payments, freight, and looking after valuables. (NS 3.1–4)

The productive, sharing side of partnerships is tempered by the risks involved in linking one's assets and interests to those of other people:

If any one partner is negligent, or does something which is prohibited, or without the consent of all the other partners, he must pay for the resulting loss . . . If one partner should meet with a calamity, his heir should take over his share. If there is no heir, then one of the others, or, if they are all able, all the other partners. (NS 3.5, 7)

Rules of this sort are what we expect from a "lawbook," namely the specification of wrongdoing in a particular context followed by some account of the sanction involved for contravening the rules and/or legal rearrangement to be made in order to restore order. Interestingly, however, the missing verse from the quote above suggests another side to the law: "One who, through his own efforts, saves the property of the partnership from a predicament brought about by fate, robbers, or the king, is entitled to a share of one tenth" (NS 3.6).

Here, a positive act is both praised and rewarded as a matter of law. Rules that enjoin positive rewards for certain actions are in fact common in legal systems. The most common modern parallels are tax breaks and benefits for charitable donations, for having children, or for owning a home. The point here is that the law often goes beyond defining the legal minimum of acceptable human action. It regularly also specifies and sometimes rewards laudable human action. Law in this case is not simply about what negligent partners do *to* us, but also about what good partners do *for* us.

The range of roles defined in Hindu law is by no means limited to partners, of course. In the title of law Breach of Contract for Services, for instance, employers and laborers of many kinds are described in terms of the legal obligations expected of each. The *Laws of Nārada* lists common contract laborers: "The laborers are: a student, an apprentice, a hired man, and an overseer. The slaves are those born in the house, and the like" (NS 5.3). The corresponding employers are also subsequently described.

The fact that students are included in this group suggests the nature of the relationship between students and teachers. In each case, a set of duties or obligations is enjoined upon both the superior and subordinate. Thus, among other specific things, a student should "do any work asked of him" (NS 5.10), while a master craftsman should "instruct him [the apprentice] and feed him from his own household; he should not make him do any other work, and he should treat him like a son" (NS 5.16).

Similarly, in the title the Non-payment of Wages, rules regarding the payment of merchants, carriers, herdsmen, farm workers, and even prostitutes by their clients or employers define even more roles recognized under the law. In general, "The employer should regularly pay wages to the hired man as agreed: in advance of the work, during the work, or at the end" (NS 6.2). However, "If someone has promised to do a job but does not, he should be paid and then forced to do it. If he takes pay and does not do the job, then he must give back twice the amount of pay" (NS 6.5). General rules of this kind are supplemented by rules such as "A merchant who reserves a conveyance must pay one fourth of the wages if he does not use it and all the wages if he abandons it once it is halfway to its destination" (NS 6.8).

Most titles of law follow this type of elaboration. A definition of the title's scope is followed by one or more generally phrased rules which are in turn followed by exceptions, special rules, or other extensions of the general rules. As the elaboration progresses, more and more specific legal roles are detailed in relation to the special rules. Commentators on these rules and roles will frequently provide more complete lists of the persons intended by an illustrative list in the root-text and give further examples of the often allusive or cryptic legal scenarios presented in the source. It is here that we find occasional intrusions of social history into the scholastic tradition. Local or contemporary legal practices are sometimes incorporated into the commentarial discussions of particular rules of law. However, far more often, the examples given by commentators only *appear* to be actual instances known to the commentator, when they are in fact stock examples used and repeated in many commentaries.

The simplest explanation is this instance is thus probably not the best, or at least not complete. Shared examples and borrowed explanations from one commentator to another demonstrate the inward-looking nature of the Dharmaśāstra tradition. Other examples and explanations, even if unique in the extant textual tradition, may also be part of the stock examples used in this scholastic tradition. In a few instances, however, historical sources external to Dharmaśāstra can be used to argue for the influence of historical circumstance or authorial innovation. This can only be done on a case-by-case basis, however. Presuming, to the contrary, that it was the job of commentators to update texts and make them relevant to their own times has been an all-too-easy characterization for some scholars of Hindu law. It makes sense that they could have been updaters, but the commonalities between commentarial examples and explanation reveal that new rules, examples, and explanations were the exception and not the rule.

The gap between jurisprudential and practical legal concerns, however, does not change the interest on the part of commentators to preserve and protect their theological account of *dharma*'s proper explication, a tradition that insists upon law as central to Hindu identity and Hindu institutions. Moreover, the commentators' interests focus on the ordinary endeavors of persons in a variety of roles acknowledged by the law. The complex legal roles of partners, owners, laborers, corporate leaders, and heads of household are extensively subcategorized and differentiated in the texts to such an extent that almost every imaginable social role and the legal debts or obligations that role entails are at some point discussed in the Dharmaśāstra. As in every legal system, therefore, the law reduces the infinite diversity and flux of social life and social identity into a complex, but still bounded, set of legal roles.

Among these roles, perhaps the most important return us to the roles defined by the congenital triple-debt. Though the focus of this chapter has been on the titles of law, a subject that technically falls under the caste *dharma* of the ruler, the archetypal rules of caste *dharma* for a Brahmin describe an abundance of religious rites, dietary restrictions, rules for marriage, and so on that more directly serve the sages, gods, and ancestors of the triple-debt. In other words, the paradigmatic legal role in Dharmaśāstra is the householder, the observant married Brahmin male. That role serves as a kind of legal minimum for entry into the legal roles protected under the ruler's *dharma* and described under the titles of law. Theoretically, only a householder is entitled to become a partner, owner, laborer, etc.

In a general sense, therefore, the *dharma* for the Brahmin householder is the archetype for the *dharma* of the ruler and of other householders. Within this broad framework, however, the further legal roles of the idealized householder begin from a different archetype, namely the roles of debtor and creditor. The roles of partner, owner, mortgagee, guild member, husband, father, etc. derive from the paradigmatic roles of debtor and creditor. The congenital debts of the householder thus structure the contractual debts in the titles of law, though the two constantly work together.

The caste *dharma* descriptions of the Brahmin set forth the rules and roles for discharging the triple-debt. The same householder described there, however, also becomes responsible for debts to his wife, governed under the title of law Relations between Men and Women, and to his children, governed under the title Partition of Inheritance. In this way, the householder's congenital and contractual debts constantly circle back to the household and the joint family, even as the notion of debt expands into other roles beyond it. Marriage and the joint family are probably the best example of how classical Hindu law brings debt and law together in the realm of ordinary life. Marriage is the first step toward discharging one of the important three religious debts, this one the debt owed to the ancestors which is paid by having a son. However, paying the debt to the ancestors involves assuming new debts to one's wife and then to one's children. Most important in this context is the way in which tacking between a very abstract and a very concrete notion of debt in classical Hindu law unites deeply held religious sentiments and goals with all manner of ordinary financial and other debt-related circumstances through the medium of law and jurisprudence.

## THE ROLES OF LAW AND THE HINDU PERSON

Congenital debt thus structures the overarching trajectory of a person's life and defines the primary roles to be played in a human life. Contracts and the debts or obligations created by them in voluntary, ordinary contexts define the quotidian roles of a person, the structural foundations of ordinary life itself. Contracts create both a relationship and set of roles – debtor/creditor, mortgagor/mortgagee, buyer/seller, etc. – that constitute the simplest and the "ritually" paradigmatic forms for more complex legal roles – head of the household, neighbor, member, witness, owner, husband, etc. The other titles of Hindu law describe and delimit many of the myriad legal roles that one might assume in life. The application of the theology of congenital debts to situations of ordinary life thus results in the formation of the abundance of legal roles that we make for ourselves.

Through such legal roles, debt is connected to the question of legal authority. No person can sustain the constant self-examination and thought it would take to continuously act in life on the basis of rational choices to discharge one's debts. If self-reflections and doubts about debt and obligation were to occur on a day-to-day basis, the authority of the law and the efficacy of the more or less unconscious habits of legal conformity would lose their purchase on people's lives. As we have seen, law cannot function in the presence of constant reflection and choice. Rather, the roles defined in the law structure many of the so-called choices that people make. In fact, these legally defined roles effectively predetermine what may appear to be or to feel like real choices. Law works because people do not really choose all the time. Instead, for various reasons, they take on the choice-reducing roles of law for the benefits they derive or for the exclusions or sanctions they avoid.

With respect to debt, therefore, the purpose of law is not so much to enable the free formation of relationships as it is to order and rectify pre-existing relationships and roles given in the nature of the human condition as defined in the law itself. The individual is rarely treated as such in classical Hindu law, but rather always in relation to a role enmeshed in a host of debts to others. The question that *ṛṇa* as a concept challenges us to consider is: how does the law bridge the gap between what humans can expect or hope for from each other and what they can demand or force upon each other? We are accustomed to thinking of law as governing only the latter case, the imposition of obligation according to a rule of law. However, just as important is the former case in which the law sets up or defines certain roles that govern and prefigure the reasonable expectations that humans may have of one another. Law does not, of course, completely exhaust the cultural roles and concomitant expectations which we take on and make, but it is an important and underestimated factor in how society establishes cultural expectations about proper and acceptable behavior among certain classifications of persons.

A familiar contemporary example is the "deadbeat dad," the divorced or separated father who fails to provide financial and other support to his (ex-) wife and children. The laws surrounding child support and the penalties for being in arrears are framed in terms of the enforceable financial obligations that can be imposed on fathers who do not maintain their families at the legal minimum.[27] Nevertheless, encoded also into the text of such laws and certainly explicit in the legislative debates surrounding the enactment of the statutes are views and visions of what society should expect of fathers. The language of obligation, even calling the parties the "obligee" and "obligor," permeates the legal texts on child support. To say, however, that the law ends at the point of enforcing payments on

[27] For example, the title of 42 U.S.C. §666 is "Requirement of statutorily prescribed procedures to improve effectiveness of child support enforcement." Other sections in this part of the U.S.C. have similar titles. Most legislation specifically targeted at "deadbeat dads" is passed at the state level, however.

"deadbeat dads" mistakes the lowest common denominator of the law for its highest purpose. That baseline statutory rule is, to be sure, necessary and important, but both the motivation for the rule and the expectations created by the rule are hidden from view when the rules of law are emphasized at the expense of the roles of law. The original motivation for "deadbeat dad" legislation was to empower and protect the usually less powerful and less financially stable mother and children. The statute itself in turn created expectations of what a good father who happened to divorce or separate from his family should do. The role of "deadbeat dad" thus opens a man up not only to legal prosecution but also, and just as importantly, to social *and legal* stigmatization. Conversely, the role of "supportive father" both prevents legal trouble and affirms a certain ethical goodness in living up to the expectations of the law. All of this arises despite a different kind of social and legal stigma that might have attached to any "divorced" man, regardless of his support of his family, perhaps a hundred years ago. Whereas older legal rules might have ignored the question of child support and focused instead on making divorce difficult or impossible, today's divorced father who dutifully pays child support receives affirmation for the latter role and little, if any, condemnation for the former.

In Hindu law, as in other religious legal systems, maintenance of one's extended family, especially under conditions of death and divorce, is a central concern. Dharmaśāstra provides elaborate schemes for maintaining a variety of relatives that belong to one's joint family. The extent of the joint family varied from place to place in classical and medieval India, but the idea that a joint family should not be broken up or divided was common.[28] In this respect, maintenance probably preceded inheritance as the preferred mode of intra-familial property arrangements.[29] In general, "the manager of a joint Hindu family is under a legal obligation to maintain all male members of the family, their wives and children."[30] Such obligation also extended to a man's illegitimate sons, concubines, and, to some extent, even to an outcasted wife. Failure to provide such maintenance threatened the cohesion of the joint family. By contrast, providing proper maintenance constituted the central obligation of the head of the joint family. A similar legal role held for the head of the household in Islamic

[28] The best study of the Hindu joint family in its historical contexts remains Günther-Dietz Sontheimer, *The Joint Hindu Family: its Evolution as a Legal Institution* (New Delhi: Munshiram Manoharlal, 1977).

[29] John D. Mayne, *A Treatise on Hindu Law & Usage*, 1st edn (Madras: Higginbotham, 1878), p. 366.

[30] P.V. Kane, *History of Dharmaśāstra* (Poona: BORI, 1962–75), Vol. 3, p. 804.

law.[31] The role of head of the household thus carries with it tremendous legal entailments, especially, in the Hindu view, a set of obligations for maintaining a large range of relatives. Those obligations are effectively debts under the law that are judicially actionable. Hindu law links the legal articulation of certain roles for people to the special debts taken on by assuming that role.

The importance of roles under the law, therefore, opens up questions about what it means to be a person. Whitman wrote long ago that such roles "are not the Me myself/Apart from the pulling and hauling stands what I am."[32] And, in other Hindu traditions and sometimes in Dharmaśāstra too, assertions of a permanent, eternal, unchanging, and indestructible self stand as a centerpiece of Hindu philosophical bulwarks against the competing views of Buddhists and Jains. More prominent in Hindu jurisprudence, however, is the person-in-role, the person whose essential self according to some other views matters little. Without denying the existence or the ultimate importance of the essential self, Hindu jurisprudence nevertheless makes a case for the value of the person-in-role that challenges religious ideas about personhood in Hinduism and elsewhere.

A person's value and their treatment within society is, of course, greatly affected by the acceptability of the social roles or self-presentations that a person assumes or makes. What Goffman calls the various "fronts" that people use to present themselves in everyday life[33] are in part, perhaps great part, defined by and in the law. These "fronts" coalesce in relation to what Goffman calls "teams," social groupings continually recreated according to situation and interaction.[34] Both negative and positive reasons exist for the coordinated efforts of a "team." In some cases, we play along because of the belief that punishment by an "unseen audience" will result if one does not maintain certain standards of behavior.[35] In other cases, the intimacy and rights of "familiarity" that exist within a group act as a positive motivation for maintaining a conformable "front."[36] The dual motivations at the level of everyday social interaction are mirrored in the way that law rhetorically constructs both negative and positive spheres of human action.

[31] Knut Vikør, *Between God and the Sultan: A History of Islamic Law* (New York: Oxford University Press, 2005), pp. 309–18.
[32] Walt Whitman, "Song of Myself." In Jerome Loving (ed.), *Leaves of Grass* (New York: Oxford University Press, 1998 [1855]) p. 32 [sec. 4].
[33] Erving Goffman, *The Presentation of Self in Everyday Life* (New York: Anchor, 1959), pp. 22–30.
[34] *Ibid.*, p. 104. [35] *Ibid.*, p. 81. [36] *Ibid.*, pp. 83, 85.

The tendency, however, is to focus exclusively on the negative sphere, the realm of punishment and sanction. Gramsci, for instance, offered a brilliant critique of hegemony in social life, especially in capitalist societies. When applied to the law, hegemony would mean the power of legal rhetoric to convince people that obedience and conformity to its values is in everyone's best interest, even though the reality may be that many people are in fact being exploited and controlled by force and violence.[37] Without denying the force of legal hegemony in this sense, the "constitutive rhetoric" that the law provides is more than an ideological canopy of exploitation.[38] At least from the Hindu and other religious legal viewpoints, law offers a site for social coordination and ethical self-cultivation, not to mention more abstract goods such as justice and order.[39]

These are useful and insightful explanations of how law constitutively creates the roles that it in turn rewards and protects. However, they do not at the same time give a full explanation for why such roles are important. They explain the mechanism well but not the rationale.

What I am interested in here is the social status of Whitman's "Me myself." Apart from the relatively limited intimate relationships that each person may have in the course of his or her life, the person-out-of-role has hardly any social presence.[40] Put differently, the essential self of a person is of no interest to a stranger. As a result, we all must assume roles in order to establish ourselves as social beings, as persons in the world. Outside of these roles, we matter little to anyone but our closest friends and family, and even there we tend to play roles that obscure the essential self.

Hindu jurisprudence represents a system in which consideration of the essential self becomes secondary to consideration of the person-in-role. In so doing, the authors of Dharmaśāstra articulate a notion of personhood that is closely connected to their notion of law. Under the law, many, but not innumerable, roles are described and bound by rules. Those roles are

[37] For a study of Gramsci and law, see Douglas Litowitz, "Gramsci, Hegemony, and the Law," *Brigham Young University Law Review* 2000:2 (2000): 515–52.

[38] On the idea of law as constitutive rhetoric, see James Boyd White, "Rhetoric and Law: The Arts of Cultural and Communal Life." In *Heracles' Bow: Essays on the Rhetoric and Poetics of the Law* (Madison: University of Wisconsin Press, 1985), pp. 28–48.

[39] I have explored this creative side of the law in Donald R. Davis, Jr., "Before Virtue: Halakhah, Dharmaśāstra, and What Law Can Create," *Law & Contemporary Problems* 71:2 (2008): 99–108.

[40] C.J. Fuller, *The Camphor Flame* (Princeton: Princeton University Press, 2004), pp. 89–99, distinguishes between substantial and relational identity of both humans and deities in his explanation of different forms of connection in religious worship. Law recognizes primarily, sometimes exclusively, relational identity in Fuller's terms.

not mere instruments of control. They are also instruments of recognition. That is to say, the law cannot recognize the individual as such, but rather only specific person-types or roles that are written into the law itself. The law anticipates and acknowledges divergence between the ideal subjects or roles and real persons, but it simultaneously insists upon both the desirability and the legality of the former. As a result, law exerts a pressure on individuals to assume the roles encoded in legal texts and administered through legal institutions. To deny or to escape from these roles opens a person to the anomie of literal lawlessness in which the protections and the restricted sanctions of the law may give way to extra-legal cruelties that may be far worse than what the law itself threatened.

No legal system can practically deal with every possible contingency of personal circumstance and personal history. Though these may in some cases be mitigating factors for judicial decisions or other applications of the law, in general a person must appear before the law in some role. Their essential identity or self is not and cannot be recognized. They are never Joe Smith or Devadatta; they are always Joe Smith the proprietor and Devadatta the merchant. Joe cannot be sanctioned for being Joe, nor Devadatta for being himself as a self, but rather only for being Joe the fraudulent proprietor or Devadatta the crooked merchant. The legal expectations and demands of them derive from the role or roles that they play, not from who they are as people, as individual selves.

The assumption of certain legal roles does more than influence one's social persona. It is also the price of entry into the protections afforded by law's punishments. Law tells us not only that we should behave but also how we can expect and demand that others behave. The roles defined in law predict to some extent how other people will act as farmers, workers, corporate leaders, and so on. The predictions are in some measure guaranteed by the sanctions imposed on those who contravene the rules of the role. So, there are good reasons to accept the roles defined under the law. Without them, not only law but also social life itself becomes terribly uncertain. Law provides the coordination of expectation and demand necessary for a productive and flourishing society. The personal price for such coordination, for "law and order," is, from one point of view, the suppression of one's essential self. From another perspective, however, the self or one's personhood is in fact a collection of roles. If one lives up to the expectations set forth in those roles, then the law provides both benefits and protections. Conversely, if one enacts roles in a way that contravenes the definition of those roles under the law, then one is open to punishment and sanction. Furthermore, if one enacts roles that are not even defined under the law, then one runs the even greater risk of being outside the law. In such a position, the limits on punishment are few and the outcry against atrocities is only silence.[41]

In the final analysis, the rules of law only operate in conjunction with the roles of law. In the Hindu case, the connection is developed very explicitly in that rules link with specific caste-statuses, life-stages, as well as with the myriad roles detailed in the ramifications of debt through human life described in this chapter. The authors of Dharmaśāstra proffer the idea that different statuses and different roles entail unique debts, those debts defining what it means to be a particular kind of person. Debt thus structures the entire Hindu jurisprudential view of the law of persons. The specific theology of the triple-debt puts the Hindu spin on the Hindu case, but the larger truth about law's creation of and dependence upon the development of extensive, but not unlimited, legally recognized roles puts the value of legal rules into a different light. Legal rules do not apply to legally or socially unmarked persons; they apply to persons-in-role. The spirit of Hindu law calls into question any ideal of the autonomous, unmarked individual as the normal or standard subject of the law. Instead, in order to understand law's effects, we must consider not only its rules, but also its roles.

[41] For further comments on the horrors of being outside the law, see my critical remarks on Hindu law in the Conclusion to this book.

CHAPTER 4

# *Persons and things* (svatva)

The social person is fractured in Hindu jurisprudence. The integrity of the individual is not defined through assertions of basic rights or strict boundaries of body and spirit. Individuals act, but they act in social roles that only collectively define their worldly persona. The fractured nature of people's relationship to things signals and in part creates the fractured state of the social self in Hindu jurisprudence. Here, as before, the higher self, the famous *ātman* of Hindu philosophy, is not in question, nor is it understood to be anything but whole and eternal. Rather, Dharmaśāstra recognizes a social self (cf. *bhūtātman* in MDh 12.12) as a kind of legal fiction that promotes a multiplicity of *dharma*s that tend to fragment a person into differing and distinct roles. *Svatva*, property or ownership, concerns the way in which our interactions with material objects define us socially and legally, and in some views theologically as well. As in Christianity, therefore, "Property is an analogy for the human condition theologically understood ... because the nature of being human reflects, refracts, and refines the nature and function of property."[1]

In this chapter, I explore Dharmaśāstra views on the law of things, the substantive complement to the law of persons discussed in the previous chapter. After surveying some important theoretical opinions about the nature of property and ownership in the long history of Hindu jurisprudence, I look at the ways in which owning particular things corresponds to the projection of certain social persona. Interest in this correspondence is at least as old as Marx and I essentially assume his insights into the way ownership connects to class and stratification. At the same time, the Hindu legal view of property as inherently fractured or fracturable challenges Marxist ideas that take absolute ownership for granted. While ownership is still linked closely to social status and class in Hindu law in

[1] Frank S. Alexander, "Property and Christian Theology." In J. Witte, Jr. and F.S. Alexander (eds.), *Christianity and Law: An Introduction* (Cambridge: Cambridge University Press, 2008), p. 205.

a way that can justifiably be called exploitative, the emphasis in the texts is rather on the guarantees provided by the fundamental recognition of multiple ownership. The familiar strategy in Hindu jurisprudence is to connect ordinary ownership with a theological framework that pulls the many different kinds of relationship that people have with things into the ambit of what is now a juridical or legal view of those relationships.

## THEORIES OF PROPERTY IN HINDU JURISPRUDENCE

The earliest and most significant debate concerning property in the Hindu law tradition[2] revolves around the question of how property arises, whether from the legitimate means of acquisition identified in the Dharmaśāstra or by non-textual, worldly means of obtaining things. One of the earliest rules that gave rise to this question reads as follows, "Ownership is established by inheritance, purchase, partition, possession and discovery; additionally, acceptance for Brahmins, conquest for Kṣatriyas, and wages for Vaiśyas and Śūdras" (GDh 10.39–42).[3] The question in the texts is whether or not a person can legally own property if he or she acquires it in a way not specifically stated in the texts themselves. In Hindu law terms, is property a worldly (*laukika*) matter or a scriptural (*śāstrika*) matter?

The early Dharmaśāstra position seems to have been that property and the closely related act of acquisition became legal only if they arose through one of the textual means of acquisition described above. The position became known technically as "acquisition only according to the *śāstra*" (*śāstraikasamadhigamyatva*). The early *dharma* texts implied, but did not fully develop this doctrine, which was defended only later in the medieval commentaries.[4] Derrett says, "Gautama does not hint that his enumeration is anything other than a careful study of instances of Property-creation ... Property was required for every daily transaction, and even to the ritualist

[2] Any study of property in Hindu law necessarily depends upon the seminal article of J. Duncan M. Derrett, "The Development of the Concept of Property in India." In *Essays in Classical and Modern Hindu Law*, Vol. 2 (Leiden: Brill, 1977), pp. 8–130. Ethan Kroll's forthcoming dissertation, "The Sanskrit Philosophy of Property" (University of Chicago), on the philosophical history of property in India, and especially on the extensive debates over property in early modern Bengal, promises finally to surpass Derrett's foundational effort. I have benefited from significant excerpts of Kroll's work.

[3] Compare MDh 10:115: "Seven means of acquiring wealth are in accordance with the Law: inheritance, finding, purchase, conquest, investment, work, and acceptance of gifts from good people."

[4] Julius Jolly, *Hindu Law and Custom*, trans. Batakrishna Ghosh (Calcutta: Greater India Society, 1928), p. 198, cites the *Smṛtisaṃgraha*: "the right of ownership is to be ascertained not through mere natural observation but only by means of science (*śāstra*) for otherwise it cannot be said reasonably that the property of one has been taken away by another."

it was essential to know how exactly Property in goods and land *could* be acquired, apart from how it might morally be acquired."[5] In other words, the later characterizations of this view of property may be caricatures of a rather pragmatic, unsystematized early view of property that ignored philosophical justifications of property as such.

The philosophical interest in property originates in the Mīmāṃsā tradition, specifically in its discussions of the wealth to be used for performing ritual sacrifices. At this point, the doctrine that property may be acquired only according to the *śāstra* was intertwined with the idea that "all property is meant for ritual."[6] From the earliest Mīmāṃsā commentator, Śabara (at PMS 4.1.2), onward, the technical hermeneutic distinction between acts that subserve the person (*puruṣārtha*) and acts that subserve the ritual (*kratvartha*) was used to categorize and effectively promote property with the former label.[7] The rules for acts of the ritual are extensively and meticulously specified in the Vedic texts focused on by the Mīmāṃsā, while the rules for acts of the person are both much less numerous and less well-defined, making worldly discretion and substitution increase significantly in this area. If it subserved the ritual, not the person, then property would be both relatively unimportant for the life of the individual and bound for its definition and legal existence to the rules of ritual procedure, making it nonexistent outside that limited context. Since property is needed and used constantly in life, the basic philosophical importance of property cannot be limited to the ritual. Furthermore, since the scriptures require the sacrificer to use his own wealth to perform the rites, ownership of property cannot be created by and in the rite itself, but must exist outside of and prior to the ritual act.

Medieval Dharmaśāstra texts rely extensively on this Mīmāṃsā argument, while changing the terms of the debate slightly. In the *Mitākṣarā* (preface to YS 2.114) for instance, Vijñāneśvara makes it clear that "property is a worldly matter" (*laukikam eva svatvam*).[8] What this means in terms of *dharma* is that property is not in the first instance connected to Vedic or śāstric precepts. It is a worldly matter and its incidents are determined socially. Nevertheless, property is essential to *dharma* because it

[5] J. Duncan M. Derrett, *Religion, Law and the State in India* (London: Faber, 1968), p. 127.

[6] P.V. Kane, *History of Dharmaśāstra* (Poona: BORI, 1962–75), Vol. 3, p. 609: "*yajñārtham dravyam utpannam, yajñārthaṃ vihitaṃ vittaṃ*" (quoting *Mitākṣarā* on YS 2.135).

[7] See Derrett, *Religion, Law and the State*, pp. 130–8, for a thorough discussion of the impact of the Mīmāṃsaka views of property on Hindu law.

[8] Vijñāneśvara's entire discussion is translated in Ludo Rocher and Rosane Rocher, "Ownership by Birth: The *Mitākṣarā* Stand," *Journal of Indian Philosophy* 29 (2001): 241–55.

enables the performance of rituals, the maintenance of the household, the giving of gifts, and other proprietary outlays of *dharma*. Property is thus an instrument of *dharma* but is not created through it; property enables *dharma*, not vice versa.

Vijñāneśvara presents four arguments made in favor of viewing property as derived from the *śāstra*, the most interesting of which is the objection that discarding the textual means of acquisition erases the distinction between possession and property, making a thief's possession equivalent to an owner's.[9] In his counter-arguments to the interlocutor's case, Vijñāneśvara cites an unsourced Mīmāṃsā text,

> "If the restrictions imposed on the ways of gaining ownership affected the ritual, the ritual would be valid only when it is performed with property acquired by means of one of the restricted ways ... [S]ince the final opinion maintains that the restrictions on ways to acquire property affect the individual, the ritual is valid even if it's performed with property acquired in defiance of the restrictions." [10]

The centrality of the ritual within Mīmāṃsā is vividly captured in this statement. More important than the negative consequences for the individual is the sanctity and efficacy of the ritual. Once material wealth dedicated for the ritual has made it into the ritual context, its legal or illegal origins no longer matter. The individual may still have sinned, but that sin does not taint the ritual accomplished by means of potentially tainted wealth. The dislocation and marginalization of the individual here is remarkable.

Taken to a broader level, Vijñāneśvara's arguments collectively acknowledge a diverse and conventional concept of property that makes its legal effects and incidents bound to local definitions of legal acquisition. The concern throughout seems to be to protect the validity and legal inviolability of transactions in property, that what is important is safeguarding propertied transaction, not property itself, much less the owner's status.

More technical and more philosophically subtle definitions of property also exist in Hindu jurisprudence, though the great bulk of interest in property happened outside the Dharmaśāstra tradition.[11] First, as we have

[9] See Priyanath Sen, *The General Principles of Hindu Jurisprudence* (Calcutta: University of Calcutta, 1918), pp. 43–4, for the argument aligning theft with possession in the absence of textual dictates.

[10] Rocher and Rocher, "Ownership by Birth," pp. 244–5.

[11] I rely on Kroll, "Sanskrit Philosophy of Property," Chapter 1, here for the basic historical development of ideas concerning property in Indic intellectual traditions.

seen, the Mīmāṃsā tradition, especially beginning with Śabara, but with important contributions by Prabhākara in his *Bṛhatī* and tenth-century commentator Pārthasarathi Miśra in his *Tantraratna*, makes the first key intervention into a theory of property. Second, at least with Raghunātha Śiromaṇi's early sixteenth-century *Padārthatattvanirūpaṇaṃ*, if not before, the school of New Logic (Navyanyāya) inaugurated by Gaṅgeśa in the late thirteenth century came to dominate the philosophical discourse around property. Dharmaśāstra's interest in property accelerated greatly after the extensive discussion in Vijñāneśvara's *Mitākṣarā*, though all Dharmaśāstra discussions of property rely heavily on ideas developed in these two other scholarly traditions.

The earliest legal formulation of property is "the fact of using something as one desires" (*yatheṣṭaviniyogatva*). As Derrett points out, this definition suffers from two fatal problems, namely that "the thing might be used unlawfully" and that "the thing, while owned, may not be used at all."[12] A subtle modification of this early definition addressed both of these concerns, "the fact that something is suitable to be used as one desires" (*yatheṣṭaviniyogayogyatva*).[13] This reformulation, however, also suffered from the fact that a person may have a practical and legal capacity to use something even without owning it, for example when borrowing something.[14] The definition was criticized, therefore, for being insufficiently precise. Both of these definitions presume a cardinal principle of the Mīmāṃsā view of property as inhering in a relationship between an owner and a thing (*svasvāmisaṃbandha*).

Later authors, beginning with Raghunātha Śiromaṇi, asserted that such definitions simply begged the question of how to define that relationship or connection. In response, both subjective and objective definitions of property were put forth. The subjective versions focused on a person's cognition that "this is mine" (*mamedam*) and attempted to analyze property in terms of legitimate or correct epistemological knowledge.[15] If the cognition/impression (*saṃskāra*) or the knowledge (*jñāna*) that something "is mine" could be justified epistemologically, then property might be defined in subjective terms. The difficulties in convincingly demonstrating correct cognitions as a legal matter led to efforts to define property objectively as

[12] Derrett, "Development of the Concept of Property," p. 107.

[13] Derrett, *ibid.*, attributes this formulation to the *Madanaratnapradīpa*, but Ethan Kroll informs me that the first attested instance of this formulation is in the older Vācaspati Miśra's *Nyāyavārttikatātparyaṭīkā* from the ninth century.

[14] *Ibid.*, p. 108. [15] *Ibid.*, pp. 113–15.

an ontological category (*padārtha*) of its own.[16] Like other inherent qualities of objects, in this view, property arises as a quality or characteristic of certain objects and may be destroyed through the intervention or application of acts such as selling or gift.

Most scholars rejected the idea that property could exist only as a quality of the thing owned, but one final formulation of property brought together subjective and objective considerations. In this view, found in the anonymous *Svatvarahasya*, both property and ownership arise simultaneously as part of a single ontological category that is brought about through concurrent "practical observations" or cognitions by several people, including the owner, that a certain thing is property and that a certain person is its owner.[17] The combination of subjective and objective elements in this definition assuages weaknesses in more exclusive formulations, but it also results in a rather complicated and highly theoretical formulation of property that may not have served practical legal interests in any meaningful way.

Nevertheless, this brief survey of theories of property in Hindu jurisprudence demonstrates, first, that a deep philosophical interest in the nature of property originated in a concern to integrate the real wealth to be used for religious rites into a larger view of how a person may own that wealth to begin with. The broadened perspective on property as something affecting the person, not the ritual, was incorporated into Dharmaśāstra as a justification for seeing all property as a worldly matter, determined and defined in local communities as a matter of law. The worldly interest, however, extended also into the dizzying philosophical discourse of the New Logic school, which combined an interest in philosophy with an interest in law. For the greater part of the Hindu law tradition, however, the intricate justifications of property at a philosophical level took a back seat to determining what one can do with property once it is so identified. It is to the more practical effects of a recognition of property in Hindu jurisprudence that we now turn.

## THE JOINT FAMILY AND FRACTURED PROPERTY

*Svatva*, of course, did not exist in a theoretical vacuum and the interest in property was of immense practical concern because it had very real effects. The first practical division of property distinguished moveable (*jaṅgama*) and immoveable (*sthāvara*) property. This corresponds in many ways to

[16] *Ibid.*, pp. 108–12.
[17] *Ibid.*, p. 117.

the legally more salient division of property into personal, self-acquired property (*svayaṃ prāptaṃ dhanam*, *svayam arjitam*) and ancestral property (*riktha*, *dāya*). Myriad further specifications of the types of property are also given in the Dharmaśāstras.

More important than categories is context. In Hindu law, as in Islamic law, "preservation of a person's life and progeny ... is provided by the institution of property ... the individual proprietor is the prototype of the legal person."[18] Thus, while the ideal legal subject is the individual proprietor, the theologically ideal context for the existence of property is the joint family (*kula*). The individual's capacity and right to ownership is never denied, but it is almost always subordinated to the claims and the goals of the joint family to which that individual belongs. Sontheimer describes the joint family in Hindu law as "a property-acquiring, – managing and – enjoying unit centering around the relationship between father and son."[19] The centrality of that relationship, however, then leads to a much longer list of members of the joint family related to these two key figures, including:

1 coparceners, other male descendants who share ownership;
2 mothers and step-mothers;
3 wives;
4 unmarried daughters;
5 widows;
6 sons by permanent mistresses;
7 daughters of the same, if consented to; and
8 married daughters in matrilocal communities.[20]

The inherence of debt, discussed in the previous chapter, also grounds the theological justifications of foundational principles of property within the joint family. Mutual obligations between father and son are premised upon the idea that a father and son are really identical, that the father is, at least in part, reborn in the son. From this premise arises both the idea of mutual maintenance – a father providing for his son in youth, and the son providing for the father in old age – and the liability of sons,

[18] Bernard G. Weiss, *The Spirit of Islamic Law* (Athens: University of Georgia Press, 1998), pp. 158–9. See also Baber Johansen, "Secular and Religious Elements in Hanafite Law: Function and Limits of the Absolute Character of Government Authoity." In E. Gellner and J. Vatin (eds.), *Islam et Politique au Maghreb* (Paris: Centre National de la Recherche Scientifique, 1981), pp. 283–9.

[19] G.-D. Sontheimer, *The Joint Hindu Family: its Evolution as a Legal Institution* (New Delhi: Munshiram Manoharlal, 1977), p. xx.

[20] *Ibid.*, p. xxi.

grandsons, and great-grandsons for the debts of a deceased ancestor.[21] This legal relationship over several generations is expressed religiously in the rites of ancestor worship (*śrāddha*) that are among the oldest in Hinduism and are exclusively associated with it among the South Asian religions.[22] According to Sontheimer, "the purpose of the ancestral cult … was to ensure the continuity of the line and adherence of the property to one's own descendants in spite of the claims of other relatives."[23] In other words, recognition of a right to perform the ancestral ritual was the essential discriminating factor in the partition and allocation of inherited property. This is the so-called principle of "spiritual benefit" (discussed below, pp. 98–99). The more closely related to the male performing this rite for the family, the larger one's share of property and control.

Women, too, held specific rights to property, even beyond basic claims to maintenance. Dowry (*strīdhana*) was an ancient practice in India and rules guaranteeing and specifying it are found throughout Dharmaśāstra. Manu states, for example,

> Tradition presents six types of women's property: what a woman receives at the nuptial fire, what she receives when she is taken away, what she is given as a token of love, and what she receives from her brothers, mother, and father. What she receives subsequent to the marriage and what her husband gives her out of affection – upon her death that property goes to her children even if her husband is alive. (MDh 9.194–5)

Later texts, however, also began to include wives, daughters, and even widows in the extended lists of potential heirs to joint family property.[24]

The most discussed topic in Dharmaśāstra concerning property, however, is the question of inheritance and the related question of the nature of the joint family. Perhaps the most famous fact about Hindu law known to casual students of the tradition is that there are two "schools" of Hindu law, the *Mitākṣarā* and the *Dāyabhāga*, that derive from two influential and roughly contemporaneous (twelfth-century) commentators from Southern India and Bengal, respectively, and that present radically different interpretations of inheritance. It is ironic, therefore, that this fact is both incorrect and misleading, being rather an invention of the colonial period and applicable in Anglo-Hindu and modern Hindu law only after the time of Colebrooke, the great Orientalist and judge on the Superior Court of Calcutta. The

[21] *Ibid.*, pp. 26–34.

[22] For a reliable description of ancestral rites in Hinduism and their central role as distinctively Hindu rites, see Axel Michaels, *Hinduism: Past and Present* (Princeton: Princeton University Press, 2004), pp. 144–9.

[23] Sontheimer, *Hindu Joint Family*, p. 32.

[24] *Ibid.*, pp. 50–5.

characterization of the jurisprudential distinction between ownership by birth (*janmasvatvavāda*) and ownership by the father's death (*uparamasvatvavāda*) as a debate between the *Mitākṣarā* and *Dāyabhāga* "schools of Hindu law" is a phony, artificial creation of Colebrooke, as Rocher has clearly shown.[25] I state this so boldly primarily to encourage future scholars of Hindu law to stop repeating this mischaracterization of the classical Hindu law. There were no schools of Hindu law until Colebrooke invented them in a letter to Thomas Strange, printed in 1825, as an appendix to the first volume of the latter's *Elements of Hindu Law*.[26]

Of course, both of these texts articulated their own versions of these two legal positions, and they remain the most cogent and extensive discussions of them, but both positions also had earlier advocates and later critics. Ownership by birth was advocated in similar terms by Viśvarūpa and Asahāya in the ninth century, while ownership by the father's death had prior supporters in Bhāruci, Dhāreśvara and Medhātithi.[27] Pratāparūdra in the sixteenth century found fault with both views.

The distinction between the two broad views of inheritance still demands our attention, however, because behind them lies an important insight into the Hindu understanding of property. Briefly, advocates of ownership by birth contend that a son's property rights begin at and by virtue of his birth in the world. Vijñāneśvara, as we saw above, circumvents the list of śāstric means of acquiring property by arguing that property has a worldly basis, which in this context would include birth. He then focuses on the word "partition" (*vibhāga*) and states that, in normal worldly parlance, it refers to "dividing property which several individuals own jointly," that is including both the father and the sons. Finally, he cites a passage attributed to Gautama, "The teachers say that one becomes an owner right from birth."[28]

[25] Ludo Rocher, "Schools of Hindu Law." In J. Ensink and Peter Gaeffke (eds.), *India Maior: Congratulatory Volume Presented to J. Gonda* (Leiden: Brill, 1972).

[26] J.H. Nelson, *A View of the Hindu Law as Administered by the High Court of Judicature at Madras* (Madras: Higginbotham, 1877), pp. 20–2, railed against the "false principles" of Hindu law including the idea of schools of Hindu law, relying on the opinion of the great Sanskritist A.C. Burnell who called it "unnecessary and foreign to the original texts." Nelson himself says, "it is to be observed that the extraordinary doctrine of 'Schools of Hindu law' seems to have been invented by English lawyers in very early times, unhesitatingly accepted by Sir Thomas Strange" (p. 20).

[27] See Ludo Rocher, *Jīmūtavāhana's* Dāyabhāga*: The Hindu Law of Inheritance in Bengal* (New York: Oxford University Press, 2002), pp. 28–32, and Sontheimer, *Hindu Joint Family*, pp. 92–5.

[28] Rocher and Rocher, "Ownership by Birth," pp. 248–9. The citation from Gautama is not attested in the extant *sūtra* text, but is widely cited in other Dharmaśāstra commentaries. The possibility that Vijñāneśvara fabricated the quote has been suggested by Jolly and others.

Underlying these arguments is Vijñāneśvara's controversial interpretation (on YS 1.52) of the word *piṇḍa* in the *Laws of Manu*: "The closest relative of a person belonging to the same ancestry (*anantaraḥ sapiṇḍād yas*) shall take his property" (MDh 9.187). *Piṇḍa*, according to Vijñāneśvara means a part of the body or particles of the body shared between father and son. In other words, "in the *Mitākṣarā* inheritance and the order of succession are based on the degree of consanguinity."[29]

In contrast, Jīmūtavāhana interprets *piṇḍa* in the perhaps more natural way as the rice-balls offered as part of the ancestral *śrāddha* rites (as is clear in the immediately preceding verse of MDh 9.186).[30] Ignoring the possibly made-up textual foundation for ownership by birth from Gautama, Jīmūtavāhana finds no textual or śāstric basis for birth as a means of acquiring wealth, implicitly advocating some version of a śāstric basis for property.[31] He thus focuses on the implications of this term *piṇḍa*, in which he finds the key to the notion of ownership by death of the father. Here we return to the notion of "spiritual benefit," often associated, incorrectly, only with Jīmūtavāhana.[32] "Spiritual benefit" refers to the religious sustenance provided by a son's ritual offering of rice-balls to the previous three generations of his male ancestors. With the fourth generation, a permanent religious ascent to a heavenly status is effected. *Piṇḍa*s, therefore, are "shared" for three generations prior to and after the offerer. Jīmūtavāhana's view of inheritance derives from his view of *śrāddha*'s importance, particularly the notion that property rights derive through the "service" of the *piṇḍa*s for the father and other ancestors and, therefore, only began at the death of the father. No death, no *piṇḍa*s; no *piṇḍa*s, no service; no service, no right to inherit property. Death, in its connection to ancestral worship, marks the beginning of a legal claim to joint family property and one's kinship proximity to the offerer of a family's *piṇḍa*s determines the amount of one's claim to inheritance and the order of succession.

[29] Rocher, *Jīmūtavāhana's* Dāyabhāga, p. 27.

[30] *Dāyabhāga* 11.6.17.

[31] *Dāyabhāga* 1.19: "There are no grounds to accept that birth in and of itself bring abour propietary rights, for birth does not appear in any Text as a form of acquisition [*janmanāiva svatvam ity pramāṇābhāvac ca arjanarūpatayā janmanaḥ smṛtāv anadhigamāt*]."

[32] Ludo Rocher, "Inheritance and *Śrāddha*: The Principle of 'Spiritual Benefit.'" In A.W. Van den Hoek, D.A. Kolff, and M.S. Oort (eds.), *Ritual, State and History in South Asia. Essays in Honour of J.C. Heesterman* (Leiden: Brill, 1992), pp. 637–49. There Rocher shows that "spiritual benefit" (Jīmūtavāhana's *upakāraka*) was neither invented by Jīmūtavāhana nor exclusive to the region of Bengal.

In sum, there are two contrasting elements of the spirit of the Hindu law of inheritance. First, joint family property is sacrosanct and it must be preserved and transmitted through generations intact. Second, rights to inheritance derive from the "spiritual benefit" offered by male descendants to their ancestors in the *śrāddha* rites. Ownership by birth emphasizes the first element and the integrity of joint family property seems to have been a very powerful legal principle or goal in practice, so much so that it took British administrators nearly a hundred years to even begin to concede that private property outside the joint family even existed in India.[33] Ownership by death emphasizes the religious foundations of inheritance in ancestral worship. The tremendous power of the heads or managers of joint families in practice suggest that this principle, too, affected real inheritance allocations, though apparently not to the extent of contravening the basic integrity of the family's wealth.[34]

Both Kane and Derrett were of the opinion that the "principle of spiritual benefit 'was more true to the Hindu tradition'" and that "'one cannot help feeling on a careful study of the Dharmasūtras that the ancient *sūtra* writers saw an intimate connection between taking the inheritance and the offering of *Piṇḍa*s and laid little emphasis on mere relationship by blood.'"[35] From the perspective of Dharmaśāstra interpretation alone, this may be correct, but the other principle of protecting the joint family also finds a crucial place in the overall scheme of *dharma*, even if ownership by birth may have been a kind of legal fiction intended to support this goal. Both principles, however, suggest a broader truth about property.

Property is always an extension of relationships.[36] Though its philosophical justification depends upon an objectively demonstrable assertion of exclusiveness, "this is mine" (*mamedam*), property is the material symbol of human relationships of various kinds, but especially those relating to the household and to corporate groups. This is why the debate between the supporters of the ownership-by-birth and ownership-by-death forms

[33] William Logan, *Malabar*, 2 Vols. (New Delhi: Asian Educational Service, 1995 [1887]); Dharma Kumar, "Private Property in South Asia? The Case of Medieval South India," *Comparative Studies in Society and History* 27:2 (1985): 340–66.

[34] See Sontheimer, *Joint Hindu Family*, pp. 206–14, though the influence of the doctrine of ownership by death is insufficiently recognized.

[35] Both cited approvingly in Rocher, *Jīmūtavāhana's* Dāyabhāga, p. 30.

[36] Alexander, "Property and Christian Theology," pp. 207–8: "Property is identity, power, and control; property is that which defines relationships between persons with respect to a thing . . . Every delineation of property right is a normative conclusion about the relationship between the actors, the activity, and the thing in question."

of inheritance became so heated. They concerned more than the best way to transfer property across generations. They represented fundamentally different views of the nature of the household or joint family.

Property had to serve simultaneously the old Indic adage that "the purpose of wealth was to conduct rituals"[37] and the idea that property was essential both to the transactions of ordinary life and to the individual and corporate bodies that engaged in them. The tension between these ideals manifested textually in the two views of inheritance, but also in contrasting views of the joint family. On the one hand, we have an inviolable, inseparable joint family in which the father had very restricted rights of alienation. On the other, we have a separable, but ritually integrated joint family in which the father had strong rights to divide family property at his discretion, even if inheritance proper only occurred with his death. The further implications of these views of the household will be considered shortly, but we must first look at another important aspect of the Hindu view of property, namely the nature of property not only within, but also outside the context of the joint family.

According to Derrett, "The distinctive feature of the Indian concept of Property, therefore, is the capacity of *svatva* to exist in favour of several persons simultaneously, not only identical *adhikāras* being shared, as in the case of co-owners, but especially where the *adhikāras* are inconsistent, and mutually exclusive."[38] It was thus characteristic of the Hindu jurisprudential view of property to admit that there could be several owners of a thing, especially when it came to land. Within the joint family, the multiple and concurrent claims of sons to a portion of the family estate typify this idea of co-existent *svatva*s. Outside the joint family, the easiest example of this fractured sense of property is land tenure.

Essentially, what we find in historically attested instances of medieval land tenure are very close parallels to Dharmaśāstra descriptions of the different ownership claims to a single piece of land. Social status/caste and type of landholding match up quite neatly between text and historical archive. For example, Brahmins in Kerala always held the *janmaṃ/aṭṭipēṟ* dominion rights to land and Puḷaya Untouchables always held *kuṭimalaṭima* occupancy (or slavery) rights. In between, other castes

[37] In addition to the common definitions cited by Kane above (*yajñārtham dravyam utpannam*, etc.), there are also broader formulations such as NS 1.39: "all transactions are rooted in wealth" (*dhanamūlāḥ kriyāḥ sarvāḥ* ) where Asahāya glosses *kriyāḥ* (perhaps originally meaning "rituals") as *dharmārthakāmakriyāḥ*, suggesting a totality of human transactions in property.

[38] Derrett, "Development of the Concept of Property," p. 86. Compare, Sen, *General Principles*, pp. 49–51. *Adhikāra* means both the rights and responsibilities of ownership in this case.

held rights as mortgagees (*veppu*, etc.), renters (*pāṭṭaṃ*), or cultivators (*kāṇaṃ*). But, only people of specific social status/caste seem to have held the corresponding forms of land tenure.[39] The correspondence is striking because it means that India's famous system of social stratification, especially in the form of castes, manifested materially in the types of property available to be owned by particular castes. Obviously, the exceptions to this correspondence historically must be numerous, but the general pattern remains: higher status meant greater control over and extent of property; lower status meant derivative forms of ownership without alienation rights, though with legal guarantees.

As a modern parallel, we might look to the mp3 revolution and file-sharing in the music industry. The sense of fractured ownership is very well revealed when we begin to explore not only a lawyerly understanding of the copyright issues involved in downloading music, but also the ordinary understandings of what people themselves think they own. Among the various owners of an mp3 file are the artist, the label, the download host/provider, the consumer, and her friend who liked the song, too. Nimmer shows, for instance how a website offering 10,000 songs might eventually have over 500,000 claimants to some level of ownership in those songs.[40]

The law tries to define the legitimate ownership rights of all these parties. More than that, the law creates new language and ways of understanding how each party has a claim to this commodity. "Intellectual property," "fair use," "substantial similarity," and so forth have entered into the day-to-day vocabulary of many regular users of mp3 files. Like the various claims to ownership of an mp3 file, *svatva* is an operative ownership that rarely requires formal legalization to be recognized in practice. And, conversely, just as various *svatva*s mark and, in some measure, determine the social status and power of various owners of a thing, so also are the various owners of an mp3 file socially marked and managed in terms of the type of property claim they make on the file. The teenage file-sharer, the multinational corporate record label, and the artists who wrote and sang the song are very different persons legally and socially and it is law that, to a great extent, encodes the different social roles of these "persons." We have fairly fixed ideas about which has power, which integrity, and which is just trying, usually without malice, to get something for nothing.

[39] See Donald R. Davis, Jr., *The Boundaries of Hindu Law: Tradition, Custom, and Politics in Medieval Kerala* (Torino: CESMEO, 2004), pp. 41–78, for a complete discussion of the Kerala case.

[40] David Nimmer, "'Fairest of them All' and Other Fairy Tales of Fair Use," *Law & Contemporary Problems* 66:1–2 (2003): 265–6.

The overall point in the context of property, of people and things, is the need for scholars to reflect on how humans' relationships to objects they own affects both their position in everyday life and their position in the law. In fact, on this issue, law tends to reproduce entrenched social forms through the language of ownership. Part of dismantling such entrenched forms, especially of course inequitable or discriminatory forms, may mean legal allowance for border-crossing between different statuses and different forms of ownership.[41] Outside of such legal reservation, one cannot think of such boundary jumping. Here again, an instrumental use of the law is intended to have a constitutive effect on the community, one that takes ordinary objects of ownership, music and apartments, and redefines the ethical goods associated with such ownership.

## OWNING AN ORDINARY LIFE AND OWNING A SPECIAL LIFE

In his famous discussion of property, Hegel writes:

> The person must give himself an external *sphere of freedom* in order to have being as Idea ... What is immediately different from the free spirit is, for the latter and in itself, the external and in general – a *thing*, something unfree, impersonal, without rights ... A person has the right to place his will in any thing. The thing thereby becomes *mine* and acquires my will as its substantial end (since it has no such end in itself), its determination, and its soul ... [M] y will, as personal and hence the will of an individual, becomes objective in property.[42]

Hegel's concept of property begins with the will and the appropriation of a lifeless, meaningless material object. That appropriation converts the object into a thing of value because it is an externalized form of, in Hegel's terms, a personality. Property has meaning in life and becomes a legal entity due to its origins and foundation in an individual's will. Hegel's theology of the freedom of the Spirit thus imparts significance to material objects.

In the Hindu view, by contrast, property is a token of relationships, while for Hegel relationships are tokens of property and contract, the objectification of the will and the freedom to transact those objects

[41] Here, I think of recent housing projects in downtown Chicago in which a certain percentage of condominiums now being built in the old Cabrini Green neighborhood are being reserved for low- and middle-income families who meet certain income criteria. Whether it will have the desired effect remains to be seen.

[42] G.W.F. Hegel, *Elements of the Philsophy of Right*, trans. H.B. Nisbet, ed. A.W. Wood (New York: Cambridge University Press, 1991), pp. 73–7 (§41-§46).

through agreements. For Hegel, property as an act of personal will comes first and leads to higher-order relational institutions, first civil society, then the state. In Hindu law, relationships come first and are materially expressed and rigidified by property.

The priority of relationships is signaled everywhere in Dharmaśāstra. Household relationships form the core of the much-discussed issues of inheritance, marriage, and adoption. Corporate relationships beyond the family stand behind contracts and gifts. The relationships of households and corporate groups to a ruler constitute the basis for taxation and largesse. The paradigm here again mirrors the idealized view of Hegel: "The *family* is the first ethical root of the state; the *corporation* is the second, and it is based in civil society."[43] The key difference lies in the final goal or telos of Hindu jurisprudence. Instead of the state being the final aim of ethical development, the system of castes and life-stages lies above even the ruler, though the ruler has the primary responsibility for protecting it (see Table 5). Moreover, the Hindu scheme is circular in its movement, beginning in the household as the first site of ethical development, but also returning to it as the pinnacle of the fully realized ethical practice of caste and life-stage. Throughout the process, which is both synchronic and diachronic, property is the material manifestation of ethical observance and accomplishment at each social level.

Property under the law allows us to express our pleasures and aspirations of who we want to be, but it also expresses us as persons marked by the material tokens of particular social statuses that culturally correspond to what we own. The same is true whether we think of positive or negative cases. Whatever we may think of the proverbial poor man stealing bread to feed his hungry family, the truth is people usually steal tokens of who they want to be or who they think they should be. If "property is theft" in Proudhon's famous quip and theft is about perceived or desired status, then property, too, is intimately tied to social status. The nature of the physical things with which one comes in contact greatly affects one's status.[44] Ownership may be viewed as an extension of this problematic, by thinking of it as things that one habitually or regularly comes into contact with because they are one's property. The properties of the person are in part determined by the properties of their property. Cognitively, we

[43] *Ibid.*, p. 272 (§255).

[44] The view of persons and things as transmitting substances to each other is particularly strong in India and the phenomenon has been explored in great detail in the field of ethnosociology, especially by McKim Marriott and his students. See, for example, McKim Marriott (ed.), *India through Hindu Categories* (New Delhi: Sage, 1990).

Table 5. *Property and the dharma of castes and life-stages*

| Social institution | Form of property as a material manifestation of that institution's relationships |
|---|---|
| 1) household | 1) inheritance, marriage |
| 2) corporate group | 2) contract, gift |
| 3) ruler | 3) taxation, largesse |
| 4) system of caste and life-stage | 4) property of the a) household as supported by b) corporate groups and c) the ruler |

may say that the key thought of property *mamedam*, "this is mine," shades quickly into "this is a part of me."

To have a life, therefore, is in great measure to own a life. To use Radin's influential categories, law must be concerned about both "fungible" and "personal" property, but it must be especially vigilant in protecting the latter.[45] In Hindu terms, both fungible and personal property should support the overarching goal of securing the flourishing of the system of castes and life-stages.[46] Put differently, fungible property connotes ownership of an ordinary life in Hindu law, while personal property signifies ownership of a special life. Brahmins, rulers, and renouncers[47] all have special lives and special concerns with ownership that are extensively discussed in Dharmaśāstra, but all persons have their *svadharma*, their personal duty and its material manifestations in property, that grounds their ordinary lives but also extends beyond the ordinary to define them socially and individually.

Above and beyond the individual person, however, corporate entities from household to state also express their "personalities" through property,[48] even as their social status is similarly expressed by the cultural ranking of their property. One need only think of how houses are

[45] Margaret Radin, *Reinterpreting Property* (Chicago: University of Chicago Press, 1993): "I used the label 'personal' to denote the kind of property that individuals are attached to as persons, and I used the label 'fungible' to denote the kind of property that individuals are not attached to except as a source of money" (p. 2); "I gave the example of a wedding ring. It is fungible when owned by a jewelry store for resale, but it may be personal when owned by someone who feels it has symbolic emotional significance" (p. 16).

[46] J.E. Penner, *The Idea of Property in Law* (Oxford: Clarendon, 1997), p. 206, criticizes Radin for being "blind to the constitutive value of fungible property, in particular, property we just consume. Some people shape their lives very largely around the delights of the table."

[47] Even Hindu deities are thought to own property as legal persons. See Günther-Dietz Sontheimer, "Religious Endowments in India: The Juristic Personality of Hindu Deities." In H. Brückner, A. Feldhaus, and A. Malik (eds.), *Essays on Religion, Literature and Law* (New Delhi: Manohar, 2004).

[48] Hegel, *Philosophy of Right*, p. 208 (§169): "The family, as a person, has its external reality in *property*; and only in the latter, in the shape of *resources*, does its substantial personality have its existence."

decorated by owners inside and out to begin to imagine the differences in social status expressed by both the wherewithal and the inclination to have expensive original paintings, handloomed rugs, manicured gardens and lawns, and elaborate outdoor decks. The contrast with the mass-produced posters, carpet remnants, "concrete" gardens or untended lots, and mini-balconies of student apartments is striking. The students' *svatva* as renters limits their legal ability to make changes. To have a different form of property, they must also or first change status by becoming "higher" owners of some sort. Conversely, it is in part by obtaining that different form of property that they change their status.

The law both protects and restricts the range of property differences allowed within a given social status. Zoning regulations may require houses to be of brick and their roofs of wood shingles. They may limit the square footage of any house in a given neighborhood and prohibit unsightly or potentially dangerous items from being placed in the front of homes. Social status is guarded by the circumscription of legally allowable property in corporate institutions of all kinds.

The ideal human relationships encoded in property laws have also fascinated political philosophers for a long time.[49] Property for Locke was the expression of a democratic principle of individual liberty in which property, material appropriation with which "man hath mixed his Labour," forged a bulwark against the state. For Marx, socialism abolishes private property and expresses the complete equalization of the individual through a standardized relation to collective property. The list could go on, but the point is that larger questions of political philosophy are intimately linked to underlying views of property. Most often, a view of polity informs and structures a view of property in a tautological manner. "Proper" property is the material evidence for the success of a political vision.

The state, however, as the pinnacle of most political visions, also expresses its status and nature through the types of property it possesses and restricts itself to. The distribution of appropriations and allocations for defense, social services, infrastructure, and so forth signal both the political power and status of a state and its internal self-understanding. Hindu jurisprudence also saw a close connection between the existence of the state, its protection of property, and its oversight of theologically stipulated social statuses.[50]

[49] For an overview, see Jeremy Waldron, "Property Law." In Dennis Patterson (ed.), *A Companion to Philosophy of Law and Legal Theory* (Malden, MA: Blackwell, 1996).

[50] Benoy Kumar Sarkar, "The Theory of Property, Law, and Social Order in Hindu Political Philosophy," *International Journal of Ethics* 30:3 (1920): 311–25, and J.N.C. Ganguly, "Hindu Theory of Property," *Indian Historical Quarterly* 1 (1925): 265–79.

This brings us to an ugly side of Hindu law, specifically its view of property. One must acknowledge that the system of castes and life-stages (*varṇāśramadharma*), the notion of *dharma* that underlies all Hindu law, is an inherently hierarchical and exploitative system of social stratification by birth. Since the system also undergirds and materially manifests in a differential ownership of property, it is worth pausing to point out the, from a modern perspective, plainly unjust and unequal notion of inherent status that theoretically and practically produces particular relationships to property. Modern Hindus rightly often deny that this view of caste difference *must* continue as part of their religion today, but it would be both disingenuous and incorrect to suggest that the system of castes and life-stages never typified Hindu theologies or was never defended by them. Theological defenses of human inequality are by no means exclusive to Hinduism, but we must forthrightly state the form which this theology takes in the Hindu tradition in order to understand a crucial part of the spirit of Hindu law.[51] Backreading of Hindu texts that tries to deny through selective interpretation the critical role of caste and life-stage in Hindu theologies does a disservice to both scholars and practitioners.

This critical remark, from which we may learn something negatively, does not, however, prevent us from learning something positively from the Hindu view of property as well. Penner proposes a conceptual analogy between "beauty" and "property." Our interest should, he claims, lie rather in why we consider some things beautiful or as property and not others instead of fussing about a Platonic definition of either.[52] What the Hindu view of property contributes to this analogy is a drastically expanded idea of what counts as property. The distinctive idea of co-existing *svatva*s in a single material object suggests that jurisprudence would benefit from recognizing a wider view of property-claims. Even though, as we have seen, the foundation and telos of Hindu notions of property in the system of castes and life-stages produces an unabashedly exploitative and unequal distribution of property and status, the flipside of that problem points to the legal guarantees offered by co-existing properties. Further legal recognition and valuing of the multiple statues and forms of property that may co-exist in a building, a piece of land, or a corporation may actually increase efforts toward equitable distributions of wealth and equal access to property and status. Beyond distribution, however, the Hindu system suggests another way to overcome "the bias in an income society against

[51] For a thematically related, but broader criticism of Hindu law, see the Conclusion to this work.
[52] Penner, *Idea of Property*, pp. 5–6.

the use of property which generates value only when we actively participate in *creating* something with it. Rather we have an interest in 'participating' in our property only in so far as we can *consume* it."[53]

The idea is to overcome the rigidities and theological fixities of the Hindu system without losing the protections and recognition of real proprietary rights in entities that currently find little or no real acknowledgement under the law. Expanding the language of property into new conceptions of ownership is more than a mere rhetorical shift. It is legal provision for a potential theological acceptance of statuses and persons currently relegated to the margins in the legal "theology" of the day.

In this way, owning not only an ordinary life, but also a special life becomes a viable possibility for all of humanity. Dharmaśāstra singles out certain ideal-types of people (Brahmins, rulers, and renouncers, most commonly) for extensive discussion and connects their ideal life situations to specific *svatva*s that define who they are in material terms. In these discussions, property is the material artifact of both personal emotion and social status, as theologically defined. A very old passage from the *Bṛhadāraṇyaka Upaniṣad* evocatively captures the spirit of property and its relation to the context of family:

> In the beginning this world was only the self (*ātman*), only one. He had this desire: "I wish I had a wife so I could father offspring. I wish I had wealth so I could perform rites." That is the full extent of desire; one does not get anything more, even if one desires it. So even today when one is single, one has the desire: "I wish I had a wife so I could father offspring. I wish I had wealth so I could perform rites." As long as someone has not obtained either of these, he considers himself to be utterly incomplete. (1.4.17)

To have the cognition that something is mine and to secure it for use at one's pleasure is to begin to appropriate an ordinary life for oneself, to become complete. When the law works to limit or to encourage the kinds of property one may have, the material objects of ordinary life become transformed into legal property, that is property that has legally assigned theological value. To say that property has only socially determined value neglects the more purposive, expressly transcendental value imparted to property through conscious theological agendas, broadly defined.

[53] *Ibid.*, p. 217. Penner relies here on Arendt's distinction of wealth and property in modern society.

CHAPTER 5

# *Doubts and disputes* (vyavahāra)

An essential element beyond how one knows *dharma* and what constitutes *dharma* substantively is the question of how to remove doubts about it and resolve disputes that may arise over it. Doubts and disputes fall under the category of *vyavahāra*. There are two basic meanings of *vyavahāra*. The first is a general sense of practice, business, or everyday transactions. The other, specific sense is legal procedure, the processes of litigation including a trial. The two senses productively interplay in that legal procedure must take account of legal precedents both about what people have generally done in ordinary life and about what judges have specifically done in court.[1] Day-to-day practice, likewise, is judged to be good or bad in relation to the decisions emerging from legal procedures.

In this chapter, legal procedure is described on the basis of the many definitions offered within Hindu legal texts,[2] but is also set in the context of larger discussions of *dharma*. The larger issue raised, however, draws inspiration from a new wave in legal anthropology. In recent studies on such diverse places and times as contemporary Africa, nineteenth-century Corsica, and classical Athens, several authors have rethought the once axiomatic truth of legal anthropology that social harmony was at the root of all dispute settlement, i.e., the restoration of social peace through negotiation, giving each party a little of what they claim, etc.[3] In the new wave,

[1] For an account of precedent in Hindu law, see Davis, "Maxims & Precedent in Classical Hindu Law," *Indologica Taurinensia* 33 (2007): 33–55.

[2] For a litany of traditional definitions of *vyavahāra*, see P.V. Kane, *History of Dharmaśāstra* (Poona: BORI, 1962–75), Vol. 3, pp. 245–8.

[3] John L. Comaroff and Simon Roberts, *Rules and Processes: the Cultural Logic of Dispute in an African Context* (Chicago: University of Chicago Press, 1981): "[T]he processual paradigm envisions dispute as normal and inevitable rather than pathological or dysfunctional" (p. 5). See also Stephen Wilson, *Feuding, Conflict, and Banditry in Nineteenth-century Corsica* (New York: Cambridge University Press, 1988); David Cohen, *Law, Violence and Community in Classical Athens* (New York: Cambridge University Press, 1995).

by contrast, conflict is seen not only as normal but as essential to the delivery of justice. Law in this view is the fair management of necessary social conflict. Justice meanwhile consists, socially, of developing the capacity and the fora for people to make conflicting claims and, psychologically, of cultivating the sensibility that should one have a claim or problem, a fair procedure exists to deal with it. From this inspiration, I examine the place of conflict in Hindu jurisprudence and its place in relation to Hindu legal procedure.

## THE NATURE OF HINDU LEGAL PROCEDURE

The opening passage of the Hindu legal text called the *Laws of Nārada* provides the backdrop for the specific problem of relating *dharma* to legal procedure:

> When men had *dharma* as their only focus and were speakers of the truth, there was no legal procedure, no enmity, and no (selfish) conflict. Legal procedure came into being when *dharma* was lost among men. The overseer of legal procedures is the ruler; he bears the rod of punishment. (NS Mā 1.1–2, adapted from Lariviere)

The principal commentator on this text, Asahāya, considers the possibility that the first sentence means that *dharma* and legal procedure, along with its attendant enmity and conflict, are mutually exclusive – like shade and light, to use his metaphor. He immediately rejects this argument, however, as that of a straw man and, instead, declares that Nārada's view is represented by the second sentence. "Legal procedure," argues Asahāya, "was created in order to reestablish *dharma* itself – it is not the enemy of *dharma*."[4]

The question raised here is: what is the relationship of legal procedure and *dharma*? The question is familiar and yet distinctive to Hindu jurisprudence. It is familiar because it parallels arguments in Western philosophy around the concept of justice, particularly the much-discussed "procedural justice" of Rawls. At the same time, the parallel is only partly appropriate because *dharma* is not justice and *vyavahāra* is not merely procedure, legal or otherwise. We will return to the comparative point in due course, but we must first look at the nature of Hindu legal procedure and its relationship to *dharma*.

[4] Asahāya on NS Mā 1.1–2: *tasyaiva dharmasyābhyuddharaṇārthaṃ vyavahāraḥ pravartitaḥ na dharmapratipakṣabhūta*

Hindu legal procedure is subdivided in two different ways. In the first division, legal procedure consists of the four stages of a trial – plaint, reply, evidence, and decision – with lots of description of each stage.[5] This is the processual division of *vyavahāra*. This division includes extensive discussions of the qualification and examination of witnesses, modes of evidence from witness, documents, and possession to oaths and ordeals, as well as description of the highly restricted, but permissible forms of legal representation.[6]

In the second division, legal procedure is categorized under the eighteen titles of law described earlier in the chapter on debt. Some titles are civil in nature and some criminal, though it is not completely clear that the distinction made in Sanskrit is precisely the same.[7] This is the substantial division of *vyavahāra*, the sacred number eighteen being further subdivided into hundreds and thousands of judiciable causes for litigation.

Several texts yield the further impression that legal procedure is principally intended to produce a decision (*nirṇaya*) about *dharma* that takes into account both collective memory or tradition and political interventions or exigencies. It can do this, however, because its authority has been guaranteed by the experts of old (see *Vyavahāra-Nirṇaya*, DhK 4), i.e., by persons who were able to perform *dharma* correctly and fully without problem or doubt. This again is a theological move. The Veda is the guarantee of *dharma* itself but the human knowers and transmitters of the Veda, the impersonal persons, are the guarantee that legal procedure accords with *dharma*, is *dharma*, and produces *dharma*. In this way, the theological focus of *dharma* in Dharmaśāstra, the Veda, remains intact and unassailable, but a conflictual paradigm (*vivāda*) co-exists as the present means for the determination and execution of *dharma*. The deflection of authority from Veda to Vedic people enables the holding together of seemingly incommensurable paradigms of legal and ethical action.

[5] For a thorough description of the stages of trial as described in Dharmaśāstra, see Ludo Rocher (ed. and trans.), *Vyavahāracintāmaṇi by Vācaspati Miśra: A Digest of Hindu Legal Procedure* (Gent, 1956) and Part Three of Rocher, *Studies in Hindu Law and Dharmaśāstra*, ed. Donald R. Davis, Jr. (Torino: CESMEO, forthcoming)

[6] On witness in Hindu law, see Richard W. Lariviere, "Witness as the Basis for all Other Modes of Proof in Hindu Law," *Adyar Library Bulletin* 51 (1987): 60–70. On the special understanding of legal representation or substitution in Hindu law, see Ludo Rocher, "'Lawyers' in Classical Hindu Law," *Law and Society Review* 3 (1969): 383–402.

[7] The technical distinction is between *dhana-/artha-mūla* and *hiṃsāmūla* offenses. See Ludo Rocher, "Ancient Hindu Criminal Law," *Journal of Oriental Research Madras* 24 (1954–5): 15–34.

Legal procedure, or *vyavahāra*, is also defined in the *dharma* texts both through folk etymology and through an analysis of conventional usage. The folk etymology derives *vyavahāra* as meaning the removal (*hāra*) of various (*vi*) doubts (*ava*). Though linguistically spurious, the etymology does reveal a common understanding of legal procedure as a means for assuring and fixing one's knowledge of what *dharma* is. The definition based on conventional usage is given in the *Laws of Kātyāyana* (25, SC 1) as follows:

> When the detailed enumeration of traditional reason (*nyāya*) that is called *dharma* and that can be proven [only] with effort is transgressed/contradicted, the dispute that is based on what is to be proven is called a legal procedure.

In one commentary to this verse, Devaṇṇabhaṭṭa suggests that disputes arise for two reasons, either to "acquire some good(s)" to which one feels entitled under one of the eighteen titles of law or to "avoid the *dharma* of another person with respect to conventional *dharmas*" (SC 2). Devaṇṇabhaṭṭa elaborates this point: "Legal procedure refers to a dispute about the concealment or denial of property as well as a dispute over [legal] conventions or personal *dharma*. Therefore, legal procedure certainly cannot refer to disputes arising from thievery or violence" (SC 2).[8]

Another commentary states,

> Traditional reason (*nyāya*) is that which is collectively agreed upon by learned persons (*śiṣṭasaṃpratipanna*), the normative practice in worldly affairs. Its enumeration means a decision (*nirṇaya*) the instigation of which is a claim in the form "That is my property; another has stolen it" or "This field, property, etc., may be used for this but not for something else" … The word *vyavahāra* refers conventionally to a dispute that is based on proving something and whose result is a decision based on *nyāya*. (PMādh, DhK 5)[9]

The commentator Mādhava here gives to the term *nyāya* the abstract meaning of traditional reason, bordering perhaps even on justice. He interprets the goal or fruit of legal procedure to be a decision that both establishes and enacts reason handed down through tradition.

Interestingly, Mādhava's interpretation is strongly criticized by Mitramiśra who states, "In Madanaratna, however, *nyāya* means a way

[8] Devaṇṇabhaṭṭa, SC 2, on KS above: [citing Hārīta:] *svadhanasya yathā prāptiḥ paradharmasya varjanam … dhanāpahnavavivādaḥ pāṣaṇḍādīnāṃ svadharmasamayavivādo 'pi vyavahāra ity arthāḥ | na caivaṃ cauryapāruṣyādivivādo na vyavahāra iti śaṅkanīyam.*

[9] Mādhava, *Parāśaramādhavīya*, on KS above: *nyāyaḥ śiṣṭasaṃpratipannaṃ laukikam ācaraṇaṃ tasya vistaraḥ 'idam madīyaṃ dhanam anyenāpahṛtam' 'tat kṣetradhanādikaṃ etasya yuktaṃ nānyasya' ity upapattipuraḥsaro nirṇayaḥ…tatpravartako 'rthipratyarthinor yo vivādaḥ sa vyavahāra ucyate.*

of knowing, i.e., legal evidence; its enumeration means setting it forth" (*Vyavahāra-Prakāśa*, DhK 5).[10] Relying on several other texts, Mitramiśra argues that *nyāya* does not have the abstract meaning of reason given to it by Mādhava, but rather it means simply evidence in court. Thus, the whole verse would mean that legal procedure is a dispute rooted in something to be proven with the first half-verse describing the procedure of that proof, namely an adducing of evidence to prove a claim that is then contradicted by the respondent. On grammatical grounds, Mitramiśra's interpretation of the verse does seem to me more likely, but Mādhava is not the only commentator to invoke abstract reason in connection with legal procedure.

Varadarāja elaborates on the earlier verse from the *Laws of Nārada* by saying:

> Because of the sinfulness of the times in the Kali era, because of the predominance of *adharma*, and in order to eliminate the disorder/injustice (*anyāya*) connected to this, Manu and the other disciplined sages (*śiṣṭa*) promulgated, i.e., set forth order/justice (*nyāya*) in the form of legal procedure and the like. Manu and the others have made the ruler the overseer of order/justice and the punisher of those who oversee disorder/injustice. (*Vyavahāranirṇaya*, DhK 4)[11]

Varadarāja's use of the negative term *anyāya* seems at first to force an abstract interpretation of *nyāya*, because *anyāya* cannot mean "lack of evidence" here. However, injustice is always concrete in a way that justice need not be. This is why our sensitivity to and our sensibility about what constitutes injustice is always sharper than our ability to see and define justice.[12] Moreover, there are two other possible concrete meanings for *anyāya*, either procedural disorder or injustice as a specific violation of moral law. Other commentaries on the same verse confirm, though not definitively, that *nyāya* should be connected primarily to the ruler's role as punisher in the context of legal procedure. The threat here is that in our degenerate age, the substantial results of bad actions, remember that *adharma* is a substance too, threaten to wreak chaos in the human world and usher in a kind of entropic dissolution of the supports of the cosmos provided by human beings. The sages set the ruler, the king, in place in

[10] Mitramiśra, *Vyavahāraprakāśa*, on PMādh above: *madanaratne tu nyāyaḥ pramāṇaṃ tasya vistaraḥ pravṛttir yasmin viṣaya iti sādhyamūla ityādi tulyam.*

[11] Varadarāja, *Vyavahāranirṇaya*, on NS Mā 1.1–2 above: *kaliyuge kāladoṣān manuṣyāṇāṃ adharmaprādhānyāt tannibandhanānyāyanivṛttyarthaṃ manvādibhiḥ śiṣṭaiḥ vyavahārādinyāyaḥ pravartitaḥ pradarśitaḥ | tasya nyāyasya draṣṭā anyāyadraṣṭṝṇāṃ ca daṇḍayitā manvādibhiḥ rājā kṛtaḥ.*

[12] Paul Ricoeur, *The Just*, trans. David Pellauer (Chicago: University of Chicago Press, 2003), p. 54.

order to fend off this chaos by punishing those who do not follow their proper *dharma*s and/or perpetrate *adharma*s. While it is thus possible to see an abstract sense of justice in *nyāya* here, the commentators seem to view the matter in more concrete terms: legal procedure and the ruler's control of it has been promulgated within the tradition as a way to preserve order and stability in the face of an unavoidably destabilizing time. *Nyāya* then refers to the concrete institutions of tradition, including legal procedures, legal maxims, and legal education to be used by the ruler and his appointees or substitutes to resolve doubts and disputes about *dharma*.[13] Legal procedure, in this view, is part of a set of concrete elements that indirectly support *dharma*.

The differing valuation of legal procedure in relation to *dharma* may also be examined in yet another way. If we look again to the initial quote from the *Laws of Nārada*, "legal procedure came into being when *dharma* was lost among men," we see a different relationship of *vyavahāra* and *dharma*. Theologically, we could say that legal procedure is the ritual substitute for *dharma* that arises because of the incapacity to perform *dharma* sufficiently from one's own ability in the present age. The treatment of legal procedure as a kind of ritual substitute for *dharma* serves two purposes, both crucial to religious law. On the one hand, a legitimated substitute carries the theological justification and authority necessary to bring legal procedure into accord with an eternal standard in the form of the Veda. On the other, the possibility of substitution opens the door for context-driven solutions to legal problems in the contemporary moment. As with all substitutes, legal procedure is equally efficacious in the appropriate context, so long as it conforms to the collective will of the tradition indicated by a plethora of terms that refer to the intellectual heritage of Sanskritic disciplines.[14] Legal procedure, informed by the weight of tradition, functions as a proxy for *dharma*. Put another way, an inherently conflictual process produces an ethical good – but this anticipates the argument to come.

Medhātithi makes a crucial distinction in regard to *vyavahāra* and its place in the overall scheme of *dharma*. At *Laws of Manu* 8.3 and 5.110, Medhātithi states that *vyavahāra*, as its meaning of "daily business" would indicate, deals with factual events (*siddhārtha*) and the perceptible lessons or courses of action to be learned from those facts (*pratyakṣādyavagamyatva*). Therefore, the texts, specifically the *smṛti*s, concerning *vyavahāra* cannot

[13] For further discussion of *nyāya* in the context of Hindu law, see Davis, "Maxims & Precedent."

[14] Common terms for this intellectual heritage or tradition include *nyāya*, *vyutpatti*, *vṛddhavyavahāra*, *śiṣṭācāra*, etc.

be based upon the Veda (*vedamūla*) because the Veda only concerns things that "should be done" (*kārya*, *sādhya*). Medhātithi wants immediately to argue that Dharmaśāstra contains rules that derive not only from an assumed authority in some Vedic text, but also rules that derive from "daily business." The important passages read:

> In every situation, a *smṛti* text is a source for understanding *dharma*. But, people still have to determine what *dharma* is, and it would be wrong to think only of *smṛti* texts as authorities. For one cannot say that *smṛti* texts dealing with *vyavahāra* are based on the Veda, because they deal with factual events (*siddhārtha*, lit. "purposeful actions that have been accomplished") and with matters learned through perception, etc., such as winning and losing. (MDh 8.3)[15]
>
> Who ever said that the statements of Manu and the others are exclusively based on what should be done? One should assent to something according to the nature of whatever source one may learn it from. In regard to the Aṣṭaka rite and so forth, which pertain to what should be done, a statement of that sort must be the source; but, in regard to an action already accomplished, the source must be one that pertains to accomplished actions. (MDh 5.110)[16]

For Medhātithi, a clear distinction exists between Veda and Dharmaśāstra. Veda deals exclusively with things that should be done and all of its statements must be interpreted as supporting the injunction of certain actions. Dharmaśāstra, by contrast, deals both with things that should be done, that is Vedic actions whose direct source may or may not be known but is always presumed, and things that concern empirical facts and the knowledge gained from that empiricism.

Medhātithi's simple example is the difference between a purified pot and a clean pot. A pot becomes pure through mantras and rites enjoined in the Vedas, but a pot, even the same pot, becomes clean though water and scrubbing, and one needs no textual authority to know the latter. *Vyavahāra* for Medhātithi is like a clean pot, something we do not learn from the Veda but rather from experience and tradition. Like the clean pot, however, *vyavahāra* is used in the performance of duties enjoined in the Veda, namely the duties of a ruler, the *rājadharma*s. Medhātithi sets forth a common transitive principle whereby the investigation of legal disputes

[15] Medh on MDh 8.3: *sarvathā pramāṇamūlāni smṛtikāraṇam | vyavasthā tu kartavyeti | na ca smṛter eva pramāṇakalpanā yuktā | na hi vyavahārasmṛtir vedamūlā śakyate vaktum siddhārtharūpatvāt pratyakṣādyavagamyatvāj jayaparājayaprakārāṇām.*

[16] Medh on MDh 5.110: *yat tu kāryamūlatvaṃ manvādivākyānām iti kenaitad uktam | yatra yādṛśaṃ mūlatvena śakyate 'vagantuṃ tatra tad evābhyupagamyate | aṣṭakādau kāryarūpe tādṛśam eva vākyaṃ mūlam | siddhe tv arthe siddhārthaviṣayam eva.*

is held to be part of the ruler's duty to protect and is therefore among the textually ordained *dharma*s of the ruler. "For everyone," however, "the investigation of legal disputes results only in the removal of doubt" (MDh 8.2).[17] In other words, what is basically a worldly matter for most people is a special, Vedic duty of the ruler. The result for ordinary people occurs in this world; for the ruler, the result is also transcendent. One final statement of Medhātithi completes the point. In his commentary on the first substantive verse of the Law for Rulers section of the *Laws of Manu*, he states:

> It is said that the word *dharma* means a statement of what should be done ... A ruler should do both things with visible effects, such as the six means of statecraft, and things with unseen effects such as the Agnihotra rite. In this text, we teach primarily things with visible effects. And it is this that is known as the ruler's *dharma* anyway ... In this case, the *dharma*s that are taught have their source in other means of knowledge; they are not all based upon the Veda. But, though based on other sources, in this text we only state what does not contradict the Dharmaśāstra. (MDh 7.2)[18]

So, following this statement, we may say that Medhātithi recognizes a duty, something that "should be done" (*kartavya*), and even calls that duty *dharma*, even though it has no connection, even putative, to the Veda. But, to be *dharma*, it must not contradict the Dharmaśāstra. Taken together with the statements above, we see Dharmaśāstra being presented as a distinct, independent source of *dharma* beyond the Veda. This pertains especially to the *dharma* of the ruler, but extends to anything commonly known even by empirical means. Medhātithi thus separates the *dharma* of the Veda and the *dharma* of the Dharmaśāstra, without denying some links between the two.[19] With respect to *vyavahāra*, the ruler, and to some extent Brahmins of his court, possess the only right (*adhikāra*, see MDh 7.2) to investigate legal disputes as a matter of their personal *dharma* as sanctioned by the Veda and Vedic tradition. But, for the ruler and his Brahmins, and for everyone else, legal procedure is also a *dharma* derived

[17] Medh on MDh 8.2: *sarveṣāṃ saṃśayacchedamātraphalaṃ tu vyavahāradarśanam.*

[18] Medh on MDh 7.2: *dharmaśabdaḥ kartavyatāvacana ity uktam | rājñā ... kartavyaṃ ca dṛṣṭārthaṃ ṣaḍguṇyādi adṛṣṭārtham agnihotrādi | tatreha prādhānyena dṛṣṭārtham upadiśyate | tatraiva ca rājadharmaprasiddhiḥ ... pramāṇāntaramūlā hy atra dharmā ucyante na sarve vedamūlāḥ | anyamūlatve ca yad atra dharmaśāstrāviruddhaṃ tad ucyate.*

[19] Wezler's essay, "Dharma in the Vedas and in the Dharmaśāstras," makes a similar distinction on the basis of earlier textual evidence, perhaps signaling that Medhātithi's understanding was already part of the tradition.

from the worldly experience and tradition of people and set forth in broad terms in Dharmaśāstra.

Vijñāneśvara makes a similar transitive argument, but he is more explicit about the religious or ritual duty involved in legal procedure for a ruler and his Brahmins. At *Laws of Yājñavalkya* 1.359, he follows the root-text in saying that properly punishing criminals is for a ruler like offering a sacrifice with abundant gifts. So, punishment is for a ruler a personal *dharma*.[20] The next verse then incorporates legal procedure into the picture, "A ruler, knowing well that each instance of punishment brings a reward equal to a sacrifice, should along with his judges conduct legal procedures everyday" (YS 1.360). Legal procedure, according to Vijñāneśvara, is "for the purpose of discerning who is a criminal and who is not" and this is an essential preliminary in the primary duty of punishing the appropriate persons, without which "one loses heaven." So, protection of his subjects is the highest duty of a ruler, and punishment, which is equal to a sacrifice (*kratutulyaphalam*), protects the people from interference in their personal *dharma*s. Legal procedure in turn is necessary for punishment. Once again, *vyavahāra* is a kind of instrument necessary for the performance of primary *dharma*s, the clean pot needed for the royal rituals of protection and punishment.

In summary, we see that legal procedure in Hindu jurisprudence is, first of all, intimately connected to the figure of the ruler, under whose personal *dharma* the responsibility for legal procedure falls. It is also one of several institutional tools that collectively preserve and transmit the substantive and procedural traditions of Hindu law. For the ruler and the Brahmins directly enjoined to conduct and adjudicate legal procedures, *vyavahāra* is a direct *dharma* in the usual sense. For these two and for others, however, legal procedure is additionally held to be an indirect necessity for *dharma* because its efficacy and internal processes are all derived through experience and empirical observation.

Interestingly, one thing we do not find in the jurisprudence of Hindu legal procedure is a sense that communal or social harmony is the goal of *vyavahāra* and that the negotiated dispute settlement familiar from the old wave of legal anthropology is preferable to clear victory and knowledge of

[20] Compare Mādhava's opening discussion of *vyavahāra*: "And so, protection of the land and of the people is a [virtuous] quality of the ruler. The investigation of legal procedures is the *dharma* connected to that [quality] ... The *dharma* of the ruler is characterized by the investigation of legal procedure that are connected to this quality of rulership [*tathā ca rājño bhūpālakatvaṃ mānuṣyapālatvaṃ ca guṇaḥ | tatprayuktadharmo vyavahāravicāraḥ ... ataḥ paraṃ bhūpatvaguṇaprayukta-vyavahāravicārātmako rājadharmo 'bhidhīyate*]" (PMādh, VyK, 6–7).

what is good. As Medhātihi states, "in a legal procedure, one person wins and the other loses."[21] In other words, although it is often claimed that classical Hindu law gave primacy to equity over legality, the jurisprudential texts at least advocate a balance of the two during a legal procedure itself, while acknowledging in no uncertain terms that a legal process and its final decision can legitimately go against the demands of equity, no matter how unfortunate.[22]

## LEGAL PROCEDURE IN RELATION TO THE *DHARMA* OF THE RULER

With this basic understanding of the nature of Hindu legal procedure in mind, we turn now to the place of legal procedure within the broader notion of *dharma* in or of the ruler. Once again legal procedure is categorized in two different ways. The commentator Mādhava explains the first point of relation, "The thorough consideration (*vicāra*) of those [legal procedures] is the normative duty (*ācāra*) of the ruler that takes the form of his proper *dharma*" (PMādh, DhK 6). In other words, as before, we see that legal procedure is the special provenance of the ruler or the king. In the language of Dharmaśāstra, legal procedure is a personal or special *dharma* of the ruler, on par with the many other personal *dharma*s of ritual performance, diet, etc., and special *dharma*s such as military protection and taxation. On this view, legal procedure finds its place in the greater scheme of *dharma* through the taxonomy of *dharma*s peculiar to different castes and life-stages (*varṇāśramadharma*). This categorization is important because it signals a subordination of legal procedure to a more significant understanding of the structure of *dharma* in human communities that emphasizes the ritual effects, the embedded hierarchies, and the contextuality of *dharma* in all times and places.

In the second categorization, legal procedure is classified as one of three major topical headings of Dharmaśāstra, the others being customary laws (*ācāra*) and penances (*prāyaścitta*). Basically, customary law (the subject of Chapter 7) provides the essential substance of *dharma*, the rules for what should be done, legal procedure provides a mechanism for resolving doubts and conflicts about what the substance of *dharma* actually is,

[21] Medh on MDh 8.3: *vyavahāre jīyata itara itaro jayatīti*.

[22] For example, *Laws of Nārada*: "Even an innocent man may be convicted of theft, and a thief may go free" (NS Mā 1.36) and "When lawsuits have been resolved, evidence becomes useless ... As the benefits of rain are useless for ripe grain, so evidence is useless for resolved lawsuits" (NS Mā 1.53–5).

and penances serve as a technique for rectifying and repairing violations or transgressions of the *dharmas*' substantive provisions. One may heuristically think of this three-fold classification in the following terms: *ācāra* approximates substantive law, the primary rules of injunction and prohibition; *vyavahāra* constitutes procedural law, the secondary rules defining litigation procedures and legal institutions intended to interpret and implement the substantive rules; and *prāyaścitta*, together with the ruler's punishment (*daṇḍa* in Chapter 6), resembles penal law, the retributive and rehabilitative means to respond to violations of the substantive rules as determined through the procedural law. This division is not at all rigid, however, especially because many substantive legal rules are spelled out in the descriptions of legal procedure's eighteen titles of law. Nevertheless, a limited set of standard topics becomes popular among the digest writers of medieval India and these include the three mentioned here as well as a few others. In other words, legal procedure becomes one of several *isolatable* topics within Dharmaśāstra and one that is squarely attributed to the responsibility of the ruler.

The two categorizations produce somewhat different effects in terms of the relative importance of legal procedure in the overall system of *dharma*. In the first categorization, legal procedure is merely a subcategory of the ruler's *dharma*, which in turn is a subcategory of the *dharma*-system of castes and life-stages. In the second, by contrast, legal procedure assumes an important role as one of the major topics of Dharmaśāstra. More importantly, it (and a select few other topics) take on an almost independent existence as scholarly topics, no longer necessarily subsumed under the heading of *dharma*. The fact that several digests of medieval India, and indeed the important *Laws of Nārada*, dealt with only one of these major topics, and not all, is a deviation from the integrated vision entailed in *varṇāśramadharma*. Many authors produced digest-commentaries that dealt exclusively with legal procedure and nothing else, e.g., *Vyavahāranirṇaya*, *Vyavahāramāla*, *Vyavahārasaukhya*, etc., though many other single-focus digests on other topics were also written.

What links these two classifications, however, is the figure of the ruler. Much has been written about kingship and the state in ancient and medieval India, and any full consideration of the topic must of necessity extend well beyond the texts of Hindu law.[23] At the same time, there

[23] See, among many others, U.N. Ghoshal, *A History of Indian Political Ideas* (Bombay: Oxford University Press, 1959), J.W. Spellman, *Political Theory of Ancient India* (Oxford, Clarendon Press, 1964), and Hartmut Scharfe, *The State in Indian Tradition* (Leiden: Brill, 1989).

is an important reason to restrict our consideration of the ruler to the Dharmaśāstra. As we have seen, rulership forms part of a larger systematic presentation of *dharma* and to introduce other textual sources concerning political life and theory might put the larger system out of focus.

A still pervasive and insightful formulation of the relationship of rulers and law contends that "the classical legal system of India substitutes the notion of *authority* for that of legality."[24] As a result, the ruler was "an administrator and not a legislator."[25] The important point captured by these concise characterizations is the primacy given to non-legislative sources of legal authority in Hindu jurisprudence. Recognition of a royal power to legislate is limited at best in Dharmaśāstra, but to draw a stark contrast between systems based on authority and others based on legality mistakes legislation for law and badly underestimates the power of Indic rulers in legal situations.

The criterion of legality should rightly not be equated with legislation, which is itself misconstrued as "positive law." The notion of legality suggests that legal rules have a significance independent of any particular personal authority who can back them up with force. Moreover, legality implies that rules are held to determine what is legal and illegal, or even right and wrong, in a system, and not the potentially variable judgments of a person. Hindu jurisprudence certainly recognized a concept of legality in this sense. In fact, we have already seen an excellent example of such recognition in Medhātithi's assertion that what makes killing in general wrong is not that it is inherently evil morally speaking but rather the fact that there is a prohibition against it.[26] Conversely, what makes killing in the specific context of animal sacrifice permissible is the fact that there are rules commanding it. Here, as everywhere in Dharmaśāstra, textual and traditional authority and legality go hand in hand. To suggest that Hindu legal thought failed to acknowledge the criterion of legality ignores the absolutely central place of rules or commands in the legal imagination of the Hindu tradition. Human actions must conform to such rules for the benefit and flourishing of the system of castes and life-stages and of the individual – in that order. More relevant to the present discussion, a ruler's

[24] Robert Lingat, *The Classical Law of India*, trans. J.D.M. Derrett (Berkeley: University of California Press, 1973), p. 258. See also Oliver Mendelsohn, "How Indian is Indian Law?" In M. John and S. Kakarala (eds.), *Enculturing Law: New Agendas for Legal Pedagogy* (New Delhi: Tullika, 2007), pp. 132–57.

[25] Lingat, *Classical Law*, p. 256.

[26] See the earlier discussion in Chapter 1 and Donald R. Davis, Jr., "A Realist View of Hindu Law," *Ratio Juris* 19:3 (2006): 307–8.

punishments, appointment of judges, administration of the state, military endeavors, and fiscal appropriations must all conform to the express dictates of the Dharmaśāstra. The flourishing of the ruler's *dharma* is what enables or makes possible the flourishing of the entire system of *dharma* and of the *dharma*s of individuals.

Furthermore, although no specific scope is created by the *dharma* texts for the legislative acts of a ruler, the edict or decree of a ruler is regularly discussed in the texts and is occasionally declared to be a source of *dharma* for the restricted circumstances in which it was produced. The most famous statement to this effect comes from the *Laws of Nārada*: "The power of kings is the edict. It is based on their word: whatever they say, right or wrong, is the *dharma* for litigants" (NS 18.19). One might call this the protection clause for Hindu rulers in that rulers are theoretically insulated from any second-guessing of their judicial decisions on the grounds that the decisions were right or wrong according to an independent standard or interpretation. Theirs is the final jurisdiction on legal disputes. In the context of a trial, therefore, a ruler's decree refers to the ruler's judgment and it imposes the specific acts now called *dharma* upon the litigants. From the litigants' perspective, the verdict is a command specifically directed toward them. In the language of the text, it is a binding determination (*nirṇaya*, *vyavasthā*). It is not merely the ruler's authority at work in this scenario, for this suggests judgments based on caprice and open-endedness, as though the ruler simply decides as he pleases. What is at issue here, however, is a guarantee that no higher appeal can be made than to the ruler; in other words, a safeguarding of the institution of the litigation process itself. Its results must be obeyed by the disputing parties not only because the decision can be enforced by the ruler, but also because the legal procedure itself serves to legalize the specifically formulated removal of doubt surrounding a particular matter of law. In this way, the ruler's authority and the legality generated by the *vyavahāra* process work together to recognize a legal resolution that ideally conforms to the dictates of Dharmaśāstra and customary law. However, that resolution is still acknowledged as an irrefutable declaration of *dharma*, even if it does contradict other legal rules. To interpret Nārada's statement to mean that the king can do as he pleases misses the point.

The larger problem with any denial of legality in Hindu legal thought is the misidentification of legislation with law. Lingat contrasted Indic authority to Western legality and, in so doing, revealed his own bias in favor of a Civil law view that "primacy belongs always to the positive law and in particular to statute."[27] He further claims that "law is understood to express the will of all."[28] Both claims are questionable historically and theoretically.[29] It does not follow that because Hindu law gave primacy to scholastic textual sources and customary law it, therefore, lacked a notion of legality. Nor, of course, even if we grant Lingat's claim that legislation has become the paramount source of law in the West, does it mean that European legal systems lacked a notion of authority. Myriad instances could be cited of legality constraining authority in India and of authority overwhelming legality in Europe. In the end, what remains of Lingat's insight is the need to recognize the very small role given to legislation in Hindu jurisprudence. That small role makes Hindu law look more like Islamic law than either Common or Civil law or other legal systems such as those in China.[30] The real distinction between Hindu law and European law, then, is the incorporation of a theory of universal legislation into the jurisprudence of the latter. Hindu law did recognize a lawmaking capacity in the ruler and historical examples of that capacity are in evidence,[31] but did not universalize that capacity to an extent that we could plausibly or usefully call legislative.

In spite of the influence of Lingat's formulation of the Indic ruler as mere administrator, he also – almost in the same breath – provided the counterpoint to his own argument:

> If we wanted to find a near counterpart to this conception [of legality and rule of law] in the traditional system of India we should probably find it in the regulations and "statutes" of corporate bodies and others such as we have mentioned which, established by the interested parties themselves or declaring their customs, fixed everyone's rights and obligations. No doubt there was positive law there.[32]

[27] Lingat, *Classical Law*, p. 258. [28] *Ibid.*

[29] For a related critique of Lingat's view of positive law, see Richard W. Lariviere, "Dharmaśāstra, Custom, 'Real Law,' and 'Apocryphal' Smṛtis," *Journal of Indian Philosophy* 32 (2004): 613–15.

[30] Lingat in fact recognizes exactly the same resemblance of Islamic and Hindu law, "In either case the authority of law rested not on the will of those who were governed by it, but on divine revelation, on the one hand the *Koran* and the *Sunna*, and on the other hand the *Vedas* and *smṛti* ... In either system interpretation has the same importance and custom holds a significant (if not the same) role, even though in principle it could not contradict a revealed text" (*Classical Law*, pp. 260–1).

[31] For examples, see J. Duncan M. Derrett, *Religion, Law, and the State in India* (London: Faber, 1968), pp. 169, 188–95; J. Duncan M. Derrett, *History of Indian Law (Dharmaśāstra)*, Handbuch der Orientalistik Vol. 2. Part 1. ed. J. Gonda (Leiden/Köln: Brill, 1973), pp. 21–3; and Donald R. Davis, Jr., "Intermediate Realms of Law: Corporate Groups and Rulers in Medieval India," *Journal of the Economic and Social History of the Orient* 48:1 (2005): 104–6.

[32] Lingat, *Classical Law*, pp. 257–8.

In this allusive, but revealing, part of Lingat's conclusion, we find an acknowledgment of the existence of another practical source of lawmaking in classical and medieval India. Above the level of the family, joint and quite large as it may have been in some cases, and below the level of the state, there were many intermediate corporate groups in pre-modern India that probably constituted the primary stabilizing and direct force of law.[33] A complete list of such groups would be very long but would include, for example, religious groups (both monastic and temple-centered institutions), military associations, craft guilds, trading communities, pastoral and farming groups, caste associations, and sectarian movements. It is the immediacy, specificity, and promulgation of law in these groups that undoubtedly led Lingat to see in them a closer approximation to law in a legislative context than elsewhere in Hindu jurisprudence. In terms of law's practicability, corporate groups were the main social institutions in medieval India to establish laws and enforce them on their members. We must imagine here that an individual could quite easily have belonged to several corporate groups simultaneously.

The *dharma* texts primarily take note of such groups under the title of law known variously as the Transgression of Compacts or the Non-observance of Conventions.[34] As a title of law, the jurisprudence of these intermediate legal communities still falls under the ultimate purview of the ruler. It is not surprising, therefore, that the ruler is frequently mentioned in Dharmaśāstra discussions of corporate groups and their laws. Despite textual statements against anyone but the ruler or his appointees conducting legal procedures or meting out punishment, corporate groups are authorized to carry out their own trials and to administer punishments.[35] Nevertheless, corporate groups are at the same time mandated to seek out the ruler's help when the group's internal processes and punishments are not heeded. In such cases, the texts tell us, rulers should issue decrees that either rectify and reinstantiate the pre-existing rules of the group or, in rarer cases, proclaim a new set of regulations to be followed by the group.

[33] For an examination of the role of corporate groups in Hindu law in historical context, see Davis, "Intermediate Realms of Law."

[34] For a translation of an extensive Dharmaśāstra discussion of this title, see Donald R. Davis, Jr., "The Non-Observance of Conventions: A Title of Hindu Law in the *Smṛticandrikā*," *Zeitschrift der Deutschen Morgenländischen Gesellschaft* 157:1 (2007): 103–24. The ideas of this paragraph all restate arguments made in this article.

[35] Textual statements regularly enjoin corporate groups to adjudicate their own disputes. See, for example, *Laws of Bṛhaspati* 1.73, 92–94, 75 (trans. at Jolly 1.25–31) and NS Mā 1.7, 1.135.

The general picture of law that emerges from these discussions places the ruler in a position of ultimate responsibility for both adjudication and punishment as the two principal focal points of Hindu legal procedure. The ruler's authority and responsibility is linked both to the theologically articulated paradigm of castes and life-stages and to the pragmatically focused discussions of statecraft and politics that form a significant part of the ruler's *dharma*. Within the ruler's *dharma*, a textually limited but practically enormous space is created in the texts for the laws of corporate groups who are in many ways legally autonomous, but whose authority and power sometimes comes to depend on the ruler, both in the texts and in other historical sources. The nature of these corporate groups again affirms the impact of law on ordinary life because people's identities and often a great deal of their labor would have been invested in these communities. Law, like politics, is always local, and the concerns of ordinary activities as carried out in the framework of corporate communities were a central focus of law on the ground and a clear, if limited, focus of the textual reflections of law found in the Dharmaśāstra.

## HINDU LEGAL PROCEDURE AND THE NECESSARY LIMINALITY OF JUSTICE

Having discussed both the nature of Hindu legal procedure itself and its relationship, or variously conceived relationships, to *dharma*, I want to reflect on the implications of its philosophy or jurisprudence for the more general question of law's relation to justice. The repeated emphasis on conflict in the discussions of Hindu legal procedure is striking. Over and over again, *vyavahāra* is called the dispute between a plaintiff and defendant, a claimant and respondent. It is worth mentioning parenthetically that legal representation is not well-developed so that litigants must present their own cases and have their own knowledge of the procedural rules.[36] Still, the emphasis on conflict, on adversarial argument and the adducing of evidence, is difficult to fit within an idea that what is intended to result from the trial is social harmony, or even justice as I understand it. At the same time, the conceptual and ethical pre-eminence of the system of castes and life-stages is an undeniable and harmonious order which jurisprudence is made to support. Comaroff and Roberts describe this tension as one between "rules and processes" in the anthropology of law, with

[36] See Ludo Rocher, "'Lawyers' in Classical Hindu Law," *Law and Society Review* 3 (1969).

rules representing a fixed normative standard and processes depending upon conflict and strategy.[37] Where is justice to be found in this tension? It is clear, for instance, that the legal decision and the just decision in our own adversarial system are not always the same. So, what sort of justice, if any, can a conflictual legal procedure produce?

The most famous answer pertinent to this question is the procedural justice of John Rawls. Through his famous fable of the "veil of ignorance," Rawls postulates the realization of his well-known two principles of justice:

> First: each person is to have an equal right to the most extensive basic liberty compatible with a similar liberty for others. Second: social and economic inequalities are to be arranged so that they are both (a) reasonably expected to be to everyone's advantage, and (b) attached to positions and offices open to all.[38]

On the one hand, Rawls falls in the lineage of Kant because his procedural justice, or justice as fairness, lacks any guiding foundation and is, therefore, deontological in nature. On the other hand, despite his commitment to avoid prejudgments about what constitutes justice outside the framework of the hypothetical "original situation," Rawls occasionally reintroduces certain teleological presuppositions through his invocation of "considered convictions of justice"[39] and generally agreed upon ideals of moral judgment. The attraction of Rawls is not, of course, totally undercut by such problematic appeals to ethical standards of justice in a resolutely non-ethical work, but we might ask with Ricoeur whether ethics can be avoided entirely by means of a purely procedural justice. Ricoeur's own position is no: "a procedural conception of justice at best provides a rationalization of a sense of justice that is always presupposed."[40] Ricoeur's assessment is persuasive, so we must follow his own argument a bit further.

Ricoeur is interested in the nature of justice, but he also presupposes its existence as a philosophical matter, a point to which we will return. He makes a crucial point when he writes, "When the just is subordinated to the good, it has to be discovered; when it is engendered by purely procedural means, it has to be constructed."[41] For Ricoeur, both ethics and fair procedures produce a kind of justice, although as he shows, in procedural forms, the process of determining procedures also entails the construction of the sense of justice at the same time. For this reason, Ricoeur finds it impossible to avoid ethical considerations at some

[37] Comaroff and Roberts, *Rules and Processes*, pp. 5–17.

[38] John Rawls, *A Theory of Justice* (Cambridge: Belknap/Harvard University Press, 1971), p. 60.

[39] *Ibid.*, p. 19. [40] Ricoeur, *The Just*, p. 50. [41] *Ibid.*, p. 40.

point, even though procedural fairness in Rawls' sense may in fact be a most desirable situation. In line with his hermeneutic approach to ethics, Ricoeur suggests that a mediation between ethical and procedural tendencies in the sense of justice is possible not through an appeal to intuitive convictions alone, but rather through a critical appreciation of the *Bildung*, or humanistic cultivation, that informs our present sense of justice.[42] In other words, there can be a balance between holding fast to a non-negotiable standard and allowing for a fair process in which people may fight about what is right. And, we find that balance not through intuition or pure reason, but rather through the character, perspective, and prejudices – what Germans call *Bildung* – we build up over the course of our lives.[43] Essentially, then, Ricoeur offers a reinterpretation of Rawls' "reflective equilibrium," the point of dynamic balance between conviction and theory. The nuance of Ricoeur, however, is to emphasize the necessary liminality demanded by the two pulls of justice – a reflective, but critical, appropriation of tradition and a logical, deontological, and empirical construction of theory.

It is precisely in the construction of a necessary liminality, which is my phrase not Ricoeur's, that we may have a parallel to the discussions of Hindu legal procedure. What makes the Hindu law solution similar is that it too posits that the individual, or better the householder, must look back and forth between at least two opposing horizons, one in which justice, for which I find no clear term in Sanskrit, is subsumed under the teleological good of *dharma* (or Veda) and one in which justice is subordinated to a procedural substitute that constructs the *dharma* it promotes. In terms of Hindu jurisprudence, legal procedure operates both *in accordance with dharma* and *to produce dharma*. The dichotomy in Hindu law mirrors in several ways the liminal position suggested by Ricoeur, because it postulates only empirical sources for a knowledge or discovery of the teleological end of *dharma* – "intuition," "considered conviction," and "moral judgment" being understood as the products or effects of *Bildung*. If we learn *dharma* and put it into practice through the process of *Bildung*, we nevertheless also construct or create it through our efforts to bring its empirical sources to bear on the circumstances of our everyday lives. In this way, we live in between a "rule" outside of ourselves and a "process"

[42] *Ibid.*, p. 56.

[43] Still the best account of the central role of *Bildung* in human life is Hans-Georg Gadamer, *Truth and method*, 2nd rev. edn, trans. J. Weinsheimer and D.G. Marshall (New York: Continuum, 1989), pp. 9–18.

in which we participate. Moreover, the "rule" is constantly renegotiated in history and changes processually, while the "process" is intended to produce new rules in new contexts. *Vyavahāra* is the Hindu legal concept that denotes this in-between position.

This necessary liminality demanded in situations of doubt and dispute about *dharma* opens up the philosophical possibilities entailed in finding a point of reconciliation, oscillation, or other juxtaposition of a notion of justice as fair conflict with a notion of justice as an ethical virtue. Even more interestingly, by looking at Hindu law, it becomes possible to ask whether justice must always be the superior category, something presupposed by both Rawls and Ricoeur. In other words, Hindu jurisprudence is presenting a model for a way to assuage the debate, perhaps a way of living in the middle, so to speak.

There is a sense of justice in Hindu jurisprudence, but it is embedded within other concepts such as *dharma* and *vyavahāra*. The embeddedness, however, raises an important question: is there value in not isolating justice for philosophical reflection? To be clear, Hindu jurisprudence speaks constantly of *dharma* as the teleological end of human life, but *dharma* is simultaneously the reflection of the Veda, the result of legal procedure, and the primary political good to be protected by a ruler. Legal procedure plays a necessary intervening role between an ultimate ethical end and a worldly fairness. Moreover, *dharma* as law is the point of mediation between a life of transcendental pursuit and discovery and a humanly constructed justice. Law tacks between these two and must in order to find both validity and applicability. Following Berman, we may extend the list and say that *dharma* as law implies an "integrative jurisprudence" combining an appropriation of three elements: the transcendental, the historical, and the political.[44] In Hindu law terms, *dharma* is *veda*, *śiṣṭācāra*, and *rājavicāra*. The collapsing of these three elements may in fact be definitive of a system of religious law. The key point, however, is to remember that law or *dharma* simultaneously partakes of all three. Through legal procedures, each of the elements comes to have representation in practical human affairs. On this view, legal procedure is the worldly substitute for a perfect *dharma* and it is, therefore, the encompassing category, the point of contact and, most importantly, the liminal world within which humans must sort out the balancing of the three elements.

[44] Harold J. Berman, "Toward an Integrative Jurisprudence: Politics, Morality, and History," *California Law Review* 76 (1988): 779–801.

Table 6. Dharma *as the integration of the transcendental, historical, and political*

| | |
|---|---|
| *Dharma* = law as the integration of: | 1) *veda* = transcendental, natural, moral<br>2) *śiṣṭācāra* = historical, constructed, procedural<br>3) *rājavicāra* = political, contingent, exigent |

Recognizing that the notion of justice and the debate surrounding it are far more extensive and nuanced than could be addressed here, I will instead simply summarize the potential contribution that Hindu law might make to the larger consideration of law and justice. The Hindu jurisprudence on legal procedure depicts an inherently, indeed necessarily, conflictual paradigm for the discovery and performance of *dharma* in the present age. Legal procedure is a ritual substitute for other kinds of *dharma*-performance that have become difficult or impossible to maintain. This procedural solution by means of law actually effects an ethical process, the discovery and performance of duty, whose goal is theologically tied back to the Veda through *dharma*. The highest concept of the system is, of course, *dharma* and everything is subordinated to it. Justice, however, does not appear even among the constituent concepts of *dharma*, which would include legal procedure. Instead, the teleological movement toward *dharma* is constructed on the basis of an ethically, institutionally, and socially necessary liminality, positioning oneself in between three main horizons of *dharma*, represented graphically in Table 6.

Dharmaśāstra combines all three concerns or horizons and legal procedure is the practical context for their balancing. In the end, the liminal space of *dharma* imagined as both theory and practice holds together both the apparently directionless and deontological idea of fair conflict and the purposeful ethics of becoming more and more Vedic, not to mention certain political exigencies that might arise. And all of this is accomplished or, at least, imagined without any clear sense of justice or philosophical postulation of justice as an overarching end.

CHAPTER 6

# *Rectitude and rehabilitation* (daṇḍa)

Punishment is the practical tool for bringing law into the world. Theologically, but also theoretically, *dharma* enters the world through the Veda and the unbroken transmission of its *dharma* down to the present in the learned tradition. However, via an indirect theological route, *dharma* enters the world of practice through the punishments of a ruler. The importance of the ruler thus extends well beyond responsibility for the legal procedures discussed in Chapter 5. In fact, there is little doubt that Hindu law viewed protection of the people and the promotion of the system of castes and life-stages as the ruler's main duties. Punishment is the root and the means of such protection and promotion.

The elaboration and specification of punishments for specific crimes is extraordinarily detailed in the Hindu legal texts. To examine the spirit of the Hindu legal view of punishment, however, we must first examine the general description and theories of punishment presented in the texts. The relationship of the general theories to the system of *dharma* and to political ideas will then reveal a view of punishment that supports both religious and political ends. Rather than focusing on the effects of punishment only at the level of the state, however, we will also examine its role in the system of castes and life-stages. Of all the usual elements of law, punishment is the one that connects most obviously to what a legal system can do to us, but the Hindu tradition emphasizes the fact that punishment does a great deal for us as well. Punishment functions as the necessary complement of all other elements of law.

## CRIME, PUNISHMENT, AND RECTITUDE

*Daṇḍa* is crucial to the scheme of *dharma* presented in Hindu law.[1] In the first place, punishment is, like legal procedure, one of the special

[1] I am indebted in the following description of *daṇḍa* to the seminal study of crime in Hindu jurisprudence in Ludo Rocher, "Ancient Hindu Criminal Law," *Journal of Oriental Research Madras* 24 (1954–5): 15–34.

responsibilities of a ruler. Beyond this, however, *daṇḍa* is the check on all transgressions or violations of *dharma* by any person. Hindu jurisprudence often personifies punishment as a deity. The following passage from the *Laws of Manu* highlights the central importance of punishment both for the king's personal *dharma* and for the wider system of castes and life-stages:

For the king's sake, the Lord formerly created Punishment, his son – the Law and protector of all beings – made from the energy of Brahman. It is the fear of him that makes all beings, both the mobile and immobile, accede to being used and to not deviate from the Law proper to them … Punishment is the king; he is the male; he is the leader, he is the ruler; and, tradition tells us, he stands as the surety for the Law with respect to the four orders of life. Punishment disciplines all the subjects, Punishment alone protects them, and Punishment watches over them as they sleep – Punishment is the Law, the wise declare. (MDh 7.14–15, 17–18)

This poetic identification of *daṇḍa* and *dharma* in these verses expresses well the overarching view of punishment in the spirit of Hindu law. It is bound to and identified with the ruler and, more importantly, guarantees the flourishing of the castes and life-stages. Punishment imposes a discipline that ensures the movement of the social world toward the theologically defined ends of Hindu law. This grand vision, however, is supplemented with very detailed studies of the nuances of crime and punishment. The most thorough digest of Dharmaśāstra views of punishment is the sixteenth-century *Discrimination about Punishment* (*Daṇḍaviveka*) of Vardhamāna, which serves as the primary basis for the following description of crime and punishment in Hindu law.

Punishment in criminal cases is classified under six headings:

1 murder;
2 theft;
3 rape;
4 slander;
5 assault; and
6 miscellaneous.[2]

Vardhamāna distinguishes criminal and civil punishments and justifies his focus on the former:

All kinds of *civil* disputes originate either from greed or from ignorance and so either of the parties must be guilty of false assertion of right or concealment of facts, for which offences they become liable to punishments, in civil cases also.

[2] *Daṇḍaviveka*, pp. 23–4.

That is right. (But [this work] … is not at all concerned with such punishments, following incidentally from civil disputes.) The present treatise is, however, concerned with crimes proper, which are those that are reported to the king by spies and in which offenders are hauled up (before courts of justice) by the king's men and then tried, *not from any private complaint.* [3]

This statement connects punishment proper, that is *daṇḍa*, to crime proper, that is those cases that are brought before the ruler through the policing efforts of his functionaries. Other punishments, especially pecuniary or other asset-related fines, resulting from civil litigation are bracketed off as emerging from the legal procedure itself, and thus not directly part of the ruler's *dharma* to punish.[4]

The distinction is important for understanding the spirit of punishment in Hindu law. Punishment is intended for violations of the law of castes and life-stages, both social and private. Punishment only indirectly or incidentally relates to civil infractions classified under most (usually the first fourteen) of the eighteen titles of law that cover private disputes. A judicial decision to compensate a loss, or transfer property back to an owner, or reallocate inheritance is not classified as punishment proper when implemented. Rather, civil litigation and its attendant wealth transfers are more like assisted self-help, a legal form of personally prosecuting a claim that is guaranteed by a ruler. In its main sense, therefore, *daṇḍa* pertains to crime and to sin, but not to civil wrongs, whether contractual or tortious.

The forms of *daṇḍa* are traditionally divided into four categories:

1 warning;
2 censure;
3 fine; and
4 corporal punishment.[5]

These four categories are in turn subdivided into more specific forms: for example, fixed and variable fines or the ten/fourteen places on the body where physical punishment may be inflicted.[6] Very typically for Dharmaśāstra, therefore, the tradition creates a branching tree of categorization

[3] *Daṇḍaviveka*, p. 24.

[4] For further discussion of Vardhamāna's definition of crime and its distinction from other legal offenses, see Ludo Rocher, "Ancient Hindu Criminal Law," pp. 31–2. Rocher also discusses the technical terms for "crime proper," *kevalasāhasa* and "punishment proper," *kevalasāhase daṇḍaḥ* (pp. 30–1).

[5] *Bṛhaspati* 29.2 (Rang. ed.), 27.4 (Jolly)

[6] *Daṇḍaviveka*, pp. 16–17.

and subcategorization that progressively enumerates both the legal causes and forms of punishment. This scholastic practice of listing continues further to the enumeration of factors affecting the type and level of punishment to be administered.

Vardhamāna lists the following eleven categories of circumstantial factors affecting the determination and administration of punishment:

> The caste (of the offender), the thing (involved in the offense), the quantity (of that thing), the utility (of that thing), the person, concerning whom the offence has been committed (*parigrahaḥ*), the age (of the offender), power (i.e., the pecuniary condition of the offender), qualifications (of the offender), the place (of the commission of the offense), the time (of such commission) and the specific offense are the several factors (to be considered, while inflicting punishment).[7]

The meting out of punishment is famously constrained in Hindu law by the plethora of factors impinging on the determination of proper punishment for specific cases. Though all legal systems acknowledge mitigating circumstances in the fixing of punishment, Hindu jurisprudence assumes from the outset that every case is specific and, therefore, that the textually stated punishments for various crimes are always affected by intervening circumstances of the case at hand. In other words, there is no sense of automatically applied punishments for certain crimes, in which the crime itself fixes or predetermines the appropriate punishment regardless of the circumstances.

Vardhamāna's very long discussion of the factors affecting punishment signals the profound importance of a realist approach to penal law in Hindu jurisprudence.[8] A few examples will provide the gist of such factors. Certain people are categorically exempt from capital punishment, principally various kinds of Brahmins but sometimes rulers as well. The punishment for illicit sex with a woman who willingly consents is half that prescribed for rape. Only corporal, not pecuniary, punishments should be administered to persons of low or untouchable castes. Traders and artisans should not be punished by confiscating the tools of their trade, since this promotes intolerable poverty and leads to anger, resentment, and more criminal activity. Recidivist criminals should be punished more harshly than first-time offenders. Corporal punishments can be commuted to fines in the case of Brahmin offenders, persons of good family, or those who diligently perform religious rites.

[7] *Daṇḍaviveka*, pp. 26–7.

[8] *Daṇḍaviveka*, pp. 26–56; the ensuing examples are all drawn from this discussion.

Despite the clear preference for extensive, if not exhaustive, enumeration as the best method for communicating the penal law, Dharmaśāstra texts also rank the severity of legal infractions. The most heinous of all crimes is called *sāhasa*, usually translated as violence but, as Rocher has shown, also intimately connected with and sometimes coextensive with *steya*, theft.[9] Aggravated theft, or robbery, committed against the owner is the paradigmatic crime in Hindu jurisprudence. The title of law dealing with robbery is held to be more serious than the other three titles dealing with crime proper (slander, assault, and theft), which are in turn more serious than the remaining fourteen titles dealing with civil infraction.[10]

The four standard titles of Hindu criminal law would seem to be insufficient to cover all the possible criminal actions that might be perpetrated. Dharmaśāstra commentators, therefore, made deft use of a title of Hindu law found in most texts and known consistently as Miscellaneous (*prakīrṇaka*).[11] This title points to practical workings of criminal and penal law that remain unspecified and little analyzed in other sections of Dharmaśāstra. As we have seen, it is a well-known rule of Dharmaśāstra that: "Neither the king nor any official of his shall initiate a lawsuit independently" (MDh 8.43). Under the Miscellaneous title, however, we find reference to many instances in which a ruler may himself initiate a legal procedure, because they are *nṛpāśraya*, literally "dependent on the ruler" (NS 18.1). Such instances include "violations of his edicts, the performance of his work, granting villages, [and] the disposition of the constituents of his kingdom" (NS 18.1–2). Interestingly, they also include "deviations from their duties by heretics, adherents of the Veda, guilds, and corporations" (NS 18.2). In other words, Dharmaśāstra texts grant the ruler the right to initiate investigations and to administer punishment for certain kinds of criminal offense.

As usual, the texts enumerate exactly which categories of crime may be prosecuted through the ruler's own initiative:

The title of Miscellaneous includes disputes connected with the king, violations of his edicts, the performance of his work, granting villages, the disposition of the constituents of the kingdom, deviations from their duties by heretics, adherents of the Veda, guilds, and corporations, disputes between father and son, violations of penances, the suspension of donations, the anger of monks, the sin of

[9] Rocher, "Ancient Hindu Criminal Law," pp. 27–8.

[10] *Ibid.*, p. 27.

[11] *Ibid.*, pp. 32–3: "It was the chapter on *prakirṇaka* or 'Miscellaneous' which made it possible for the author of the *Daṇḍaviveka* to cover many types of crimes which could not find their place under the traditional headings."

mixing castes, restrictions on their livelihoods, and whatever has not been covered thus far. All this is to be found under Miscellaneous. (NS 18.1–4, also quoted in *Daṇḍaviveka*, p. 220)

Obviously, crimes in violation of the ruler's decrees or against other formal actions of the state may be prosecuted by the ruler without outside prompting because the ruler himself is in some sense the aggrieved party. Also interesting, however, is the meta-structure of legal administration that the ruler provides to corporate groups of various kinds. When their respective efforts to promulgate and enforce their group laws within the group fail, the ruler is called upon to intervene and rectify the violations through his own punishment.

Through this purposefully open-ended title of law, Dharmaśāstra authors and commentators were able to find an expandable and flexible traditional category under which to consider a host of penal and criminal laws, especially those relating to a ruler and brought into the Dharmaśāstra scholastic tradition from the parallel, though largely usurped, tradition of Arthaśāstra, the science of statecraft.[12] This title, in addition to the other criminal titles, gave the Hindu law tradition an excellent framework for defining both crime and punishment in considerable detail. The details, of course, served the larger vision alluded to in the opening quotation from Manu in this section, but they also attest to a truly sophisticated jurisprudential tradition in this area. The wider functions of punishment in Hindu law, however, still remain to be discussed.

## THE DETERRENCE AND EDUCATION OF BOTH SIN AND CRIME

Punishment in Hindu law actually takes two forms: *daṇḍa* and *prāyaścitta*. Both are important to the spirit of Hindu law. The first, *daṇḍa*, refers to the punishments meted out by legal authorities, usually a ruler, for criminal and civil offenses. The second, *prāyaścitta*, denotes the self-imposed penances or expiations that are generally undertaken voluntarily by a person who has committed a legal or religious transgression. A third, more famous, concept, that of *karma*, is very often lumped together with other forms of Hindu punishment, but *karma* is in a special sense unimportant in Hindu law. Before considering *daṇḍa* and *prāyaścitta*, I must explain how and why I think *karma* is unimportant.

[12] On the relation of these two scholastic traditions and the co-opting of Arthaśāstra into Dharmaśāstra, see Patrick Olivelle, "Manu and the *Arthaśāstra*: A Study in Śāstric Intertextuality," *Journal of Indian Philosophy* 32:2–3 (2004): 281–91.

The most widely cited study of punishment in Hindu law argues that "the higher principle of retribution" unifies a diversity of punishment schemes in early Indian texts.[13] More specifically, "punishments are retribution of acts (rather than of persons)."[14] With retribution of acts at the center, *karma* appears prominently as well. The idea of a cosmic moral causation that preconditions human life and determines the bodily form of the eternal soul is the most widely known idea from ancient India, and one shared by almost all ancient Indic systems of thought. Actions have consequences. Pleasurable results are rewards and painful results are punishments. Dharmaśāstras confirm this idea in no uncertain terms: "Action produces good and bad results and originates from the mind, speech, and the body. Action produces the human condition – the highest, the middling, and the lowest" (MDh 12.3).

The study of *karma*'s effects, however, focuses solely on bad action and is considered an ancillary subject to the larger question of penance.[15] The fourteenth-century commentator Mādhava explains that the consequences (*vipāka*) of bad *karma* affect three aspects of life, namely birth, health, and happiness.[16] The objecting straw man interrupts as follows:

> The consequences (of actions) can be neither enjoined nor prohibited because one can neither put them into practice nor prevent them. Therefore, a discussion of this topic is improper in this text because it is a treatise that puts injunctions and prohibitions first.[17]

The interlocutor relies here on the Mīmāṃsā tradition's claim that *dharma* concerns only positive and negative rules of action. Mādhava's response to this argument invokes in turn two other principles of Mīmāṃsā to justify the discussion, but also to place it in proper perspective:

> This is not a flaw, because the usefulness of the discussion derives from the fact that it is praise and explanation (*arthavāda*) with respect to penance. And, praise or explanation shares in the singularity (of expression, *aikyatā*) with regard to both injunction or prohibition because it, respectively, promotes what is enjoined

[13] Terence P. Day, *The Conception of Punishment in Early Indian Literature* (Waterloo: Wilfred Laurier University Press, 1982), p. 241.

[14] *Ibid.*, p. 242.

[15] The commentator Mādhava states this directly: "Even though in ordinary speech the word *dharma* is common to discuss both good and bad actions, nevertheless here it refers only to bad action because given the nature of penance, what is brought to mind is only bad action and its cessation [*yady api loke dharmaśābdaḥ sukṛtaduṣkṛtayoḥ sādhāraṇaḥ tathāpy atra prāyaścittasya prakṛtatvāt tannivarttyatayā duṣkṛtasyaiva buddhisthatvāt tatraiva paryavasyati*]" PMādh, p. 480.

[16] PMādh, p. 481: *jātyāyurbhogalakṣaṇaṃ vipākaṃ*.

[17] *Ibid.*: *nanu nāyaṃ vipāko vidhātuṃ pratiṣeddhum vā śakyate ananuṣṭheyatvād avarjanīyatvāc ca | ata eva tasmin vidhipratiṣedhapareṇa śāstreṇa tannirūpaṇam ayuktam.*

and turns people away from what is prohibited. This is the rule (*maryādā*) among those who know the tradition. [18]

Mādhava accepts the objector's premise that the consequences of *karma* have no direct connection to positive or negative rules, but he also makes use of the Mīmāṃsā category of praise and explanation to assert an important, but secondary, link between the discussion of *karma* and the main thrust of *dharma* rules. That link is the final unity of expression between any given injunction or prohibition and the supportive praises, discouragements, and/or explanations that might relate to one of these. Again, this is a Mīmāṃsā principle called *ekavākyatā*, in which all textual statements are understood to express one and only one idea, namely to command or to prohibit a specific action. Other ancillary statements, including those in the category of praise and explanation, have value and relevance only in connection to and in support of some singular command or prohibition.

Mādhava's statement places bad *karma*'s consequences, i.e., the effects or results of *adharma*, at the theological margins of *dharma*. As praise and explanation, the consequences of bad *karma* are not something a person can do anything about. As a result, considerations of bad *karma* and its effects cannot form part of the all-important question of *dharma* and law: what is mandatory, what is required of me as either an act or a restraint of *dharma*? *Karma*'s effects have an important supporting role to play in relation to *dharma*, especially penance, but they are not structurally necessary to the systematic presentation of *dharma* in terms of caste and life-stage.[19] The horrible portents of bad *karma* are called the inspiration (*prarocana*) for voluntary penance. The Dharmaśāstra authors do not discuss *karma*'s consequences at all in connection with *daṇḍa* and only secondarily in connection with *prāyaścitta* because the so-called punishments of *karma* lack a true agent.[20] Karmic punishment occurs impersonally, not through the action of an agent whose punishing actions might be

[18] *Ibid.*: *nāyaṃ doṣaḥ | prāyaścittārthavādatvena tadupayogāt | arthavādas tu vihite pravarttakatvena pratiṣiddhān nivarttakatvena ca vidhipratiṣedhaikyatāṃ bhajate iti nyāyavidāṃ maryādā.*

[19] Dharmaśāstra assigns *karma* to a significant place, but one that must be considered separately from the central systematic concern of the *dharma* of castes and life-stages. An early glimpse of this distinction appears in the transitional verse from the discussion of the law of castes and life-stages to the discussion of *karma* in the *Laws of Manu*: "'You have described the Law for the four classes in its entirety, O Sinless One! Teach us accurately the ultimate consummation of the fruits of actions'" (MDh 12.1).

[20] P.V. Kane, *History of Dharmaśāstra* (Poona: BORI, 1962–75), Vol. 4, p. 177: "The teaching of the works on Karmavipāka, though dismal and terrifying, comes to this that no soul need be without hope provided it is prepared to wait and undergo torments for its misdeeds."

constrained by *dharma*. The emphasis in both *dharma*- and *karma*-talk is on positive duty rather than negative consequence.

The speculations about actions and their immediate and dilatory effects reached incredible complexity in Indic traditions, only a part of which is reflected in Dharmaśāstra. Instead, the Hindu law tradition tends to assume or accept much about *karma*'s workings without investigating or elaborating a clear theory of its own. As a result, we find many different views of *karma* expressed in one and the same text.[21] More often, we find that *dharma* authors and commentators tended not to engage in *karma* speculation to the extent seen in other Indic intellectual traditions, being concerned simply to enumerate various systems of *karma* and rebirth without much theoretical consideration.[22]

Notably, the sixteenth-century *Discrimination about Punishment* (*Daṇḍaviveka*) of Vardhamāna lacks any substantive discussion of *karma* or *karma* theory. It has been too easy to connect *karma* and *daṇḍa* as something like cosmic and earthly punishments, respectively. Within the main exposition of the law of castes and life-stages, however, *karma* is mostly presumed as a theoretical backdrop, a remote truth that does not impinge much upon either the determination or the performance of *dharma*. As Hacker and others have reminded us, all *dharma* is *karma*. In other words, all lawful action is a part of action generally, but the analysis of what is lawful and good must be distinguished from the analysis of the material and spiritual effects of keeping the law and doing good, or their opposite.

Finally, if the central argument of this book is correct, *karma vipāka* does not fit into the center of Hindu law because it deals with an invisible process that is otherworldly, not ordinary. It, therefore, does not fit into the scheme of law because its theology is directed toward supramundane processes and substances. It, of course, forms a backdrop for all human action, but cannot become the central focus of Dharmaśāstra because of its lack of focus on ordinary life. The karmic implications of ordinary acts are the subject of Dharmaśāstra, namely that *dharma* equals law in positive *karma* while *adharma* equals negative *karma* and its consequences. In this way, the "ripening" (*vipāka*) of *karma* fits in only indirectly as a part of *dharma*.

[21] See Ludo Rocher, "Karma and Rebirth in the Dharmaśāstras." In Wendy Doniger O'Flaherty (ed.), *Karma and Rebirth in Classical Indian Traditions* (Berkeley: University of California Press, 1980), pp. 61–90, for a thorough review of the plural and sometimes contradictory views of *karma* within the *Laws of Manu*.

[22] *Ibid.*, p. 77.

For these reasons of theological marginalization, ambiguity, disinterest, and incongruity, I want to suggest that *karma* in general is not a significant element in the spirit of Hindu law. *Karma*'s effects (*karmavipāka*) are the fineprint in the *dharma* contract set forth in Dharmaśāstra. The effects are given in some detail but no one reads them and their purpose, in any case, is to present collectively a horrible imagined scenario for doing what is bad in order to encourage doing what is good. Instead, only good *karma*, another name for *dharma*, is really crucial to the tradition. As a result, we may leave *karma* behind and turn to the forms of punishment that are important for Hindu law. More importantly, we may leave behind the idea that retribution is the only key to understanding the role of punishment in Hindu law. Retribution in the form of *karma*'s consequences takes care of itself.

Punishment in Hindu jurisprudence is rather about prevention and deterrence, in the first place. A frequent refrain in Dharmaśāstra is the use of legal procedure and punishment by a ruler to "check" or "thwart" criminals (*duṣṭanigraha*). As a sixteenth-century digest states, "Criminals are suppressed by [the ruler] carrying out legal procedures against them. And when criminals are suppressed, the law of castes and life-stages is established. And only when that is established can people perform the duties enjoined by that law."[23] The sequence here also links legal procedure (*vyavahāra*) and normative practice (*ācāra*) as mutually constitutive institutions. Stated simply, procedural and substantive law mutually reinforce one another. In terms of prevention and deterrence, a key link in this mutual relationship is to suppress criminals by bringing them before the law and punishing them. At the social level and from the perspective of the ruler or state, this preventive aspect of punishment predominates.

At the personal level, by contrast, penance (*prāyaścitta*) is the form of punishment that, according to the texts, deters future infractions or crimes. Penance corrects the offender's mindset and, if mandated as a public ceremony, can send a public message about the seriousness of the transgression. According to the commentator Vijñāneśvara, "The enumeration of the marks [of sin] such as consumption and other diseases is made in order to generate a sense of urgent fear (*udvega*) in Brahmin-murderers and the like such that they become focused on penance" (YS 3.216).[24]

[23] *Sarasvatīvilāsa*, p. 15: *vyavahāradarśanāddhi duṣṭanigrahaḥ | duṣṭanigrahe sati varṇāśramadharmāvasthitiḥ | tadavasthitau satyām eva tadvihitadharmānuṣṭhānam.*

[24] Vijñāneśvara on YS 3.216: *etac ca kṣayitvādilakṣaṇakathanaṃ prāyaścittonmukhībhūtabrahmahād yudvegajananārthaṃ.*

Both *daṇḍa* and *prāyaścitta* are punishments. *Daṇḍa* is a form of punishment that is a mandatory duty for a ruler, while *prāyaścitta* is voluntary (*kāmya*) according to the contrition of the offender.[25] Ultimately, however, worldly punishment and penance merge as in the following passage: "When men who have committed sins are punished by kings, they go to heaven immaculate, like virtuous men who have done good deeds" (MDh 8.318; VaDh 19.45). The commentator Kullūka affirms, "In this way, what is stated is the fact that, like penance, punishment too causes the destruction of sin."[26] Together, they work initially to establish a baseline of social order and personal restraint that allows the law of castes and life-stages to flourish. That order is premised on the deterrent effect of these imposed and voluntary punishments. Such deterrence negatively attempts to prevent or restrain criminal action at both a social and personal level.

Though this view of punishment as a negative reaction to normative transgression is significant within Hindu jurisprudence, it can also mislead us about the more prominent positive presentation of punishment in the *dharma* texts. A negative cast on punishment tends to misrepresent the way in which Hindu legal punishments serve to support and, in fact, make possible the functioning of the system of castes and life-stages. In other words, punishment has a positive character and purpose that complements the preventive or deterrent effect it may have, overshadowing any retributive function. Punishment in Hindu law thus emphasizes rectitude and deterrence over retribution. In fact, punishment in the Hindu view is what makes law possible at all, a point which we must now examine in more detail.

## PUNISHMENT AS LAW'S VEHICLE

Punishment contains a recognition of human imperfection and fallibility. Law in its fullest sense can only exist in the world if punishment is there to redress the inevitable failings of human beings, their unavoidable deviation from an ideal path of perfection. Without punishment, law remains an elusive ideal to which no one can aspire. With punishment,

[25] Robert Lingat, *The Classical Law of India*, trans. J.D.M. Derrett (Berkeley: University of California Press, 1973), p. 63: "It is true that penance, as distinguished from punishment, is voluntary ... Penance is thus not simply expiatory. It is also deterrent."

[26] Kullūka on MDh 8.318: *evaṃ prāyaścittavad daṇḍasyāpi pāpakṣayahetutvam uktam*. See also *Daṇḍaviveka*, p. 9, where this passage and several others are cited to demonstrate that punishment ameliorates sin as well.

law becomes the training ground for a whole variety of religiously aimed actions. Punishment simultaneously guarantees the overall stability of the system and enables transgressors to be readmitted into it.

The year 1921 saw the publication of two rather different studies of the relationship of punishment or violence and law. Both investigate how the creation of the law of the state requires punishment, especially in the form of state violence. The first study, Benjamin's "Critique of Violence," is well known for its provocative thesis about the possibility of non-instrumental political means to achieve a functioning social order without the law of the state.[27] The second is a little-known essay by Sarkar, "The Hindu Theory of the State," which advances an apologetic account of Hindu statecraft by arguing that behind the two pillars of the state, property (*svatva*) and law (*dharma*), lies punishment (*daṇḍa*).[28]

Benjamin's essay is famously complex, some would say opaque, but he states the argument most relevant to this discussion as follows: "All violence as a means is either lawmaking or law-preserving. If it lays claim to neither of these predicates, it forfeits all validity. It follows, however, that all violence as a means, even in the most favorable case, is implicated in the problematic nature of law."[29] Further, he writes, "Lawmaking is power making, and, to that extent, an immediate manifestation of violence."[30] Benjamin uses his critique of the seemingly inevitable connection of law and violence to sketch out a program of revolution achieved through non-violent, non-instrumental means that would shatter what he sees as the pernicious mythology of violence that keeps law in place in the world. Throughout, Benjamin's focus is violence, not punishment, but his word choice purposefully provokes a reorientation toward the state's actions against individuals by selecting a different term. Nevertheless, he very often means punishment, even though he considers other forms of state violence that would not qualify as punishment, for example military and some police violence.

The profundity of Benjamin's claim that law depends upon violence for its existence is, from one perspective, difficult to fathom, because it appears to reduce law to so many manifestations of violence for "legal ends." This leaves little place for law to serve any other purpose. Indeed, Benjamin

27 Walter Benjamin, "Critique of Violence." In *Reflections: Essays, Aphorism, Autobiographical Writings*, trans. Edmund Jephcott, ed. with an intro. Peter Demetz (New York: Harcourt, Brace, and Jovanovich, 1978), pp. 277–300.

28 Benoy Kumar Sarkar, "The Hindu Theory of the State," *Political Science Quarterly* 36:1 (1921): 83.

29 Benjamin, "Critique of Violence," p. 287.

30 *Ibid.*, p. 295.

seems quite prepared to discard law as a social institution altogether for "the coming age is not so unimaginably remote that an attack on law is altogether futile."[31] Ignoring the important and explanatory context of post-World War I Europe in which Benjamin wrote, what remains clear from this essay is the power of violence to create law and to preserve it.[32] We need not follow Benjamin into the nettlesome critique of the ideology of law in order to profit from his insightful reflections on law's great dependence on violence and punishment. Still, Benjamin's conclusion is obviously a negative one: the intimate, perhaps inextricable, relation of law and violence necessitates a rejection of law and violence in favor of a wholly different, revolutionary program of social ordering.[33]

By contrast, Sarkar, while also finding a deep and necessary connection between law and violent punishment in Hindu jurisprudence, argues the positive case that law's essentially educative function depends upon the existence of a ruler's punishments. Sarkar's focus is not law and violence as such, but rather a larger overview of Hindu statecraft. Though his remarks on the narrower point are accordingly not as extensive as Benjamin's, his central point mirrors Benjamin's in important ways.

> Two "inseparable accidents" of the Hindu theory of the state are, first, the doctrine of *mamatva* ("mine"-ness) or *svatva* (*suum*), i.e. "one's own"-ness, *proprium* or property, and secondly, the doctrine of *dharma* (i.e. law, justice, and duty). And behind them both lies the doctrine of *daṇḍa* (punishment, restraint, or sanction). Herein is to be sought the nucleus of the whole Hindu philosophy of sovereignty. A state is a state because it can coerce, restrain, compel. Eliminate control or the coercive element from social life, and the state as an entity vanishes. *Daṇḍa* is *überhaupt* the very essence of statal relations. No *daṇḍa*, no state. A *daṇḍa*-less, i.e. sanctionless, state is a contradiction in terms. [34]

Sarkar summarizes this in outline:

I. No *daṇḍa*, no state.
II. (a) No state, no *dharma*.
    (b) No state, no property.[35]

[31] *Ibid.*, p. 300.

[32] Robert M. Cover, "Violence and the Word," *Yale Law Journal* 95 (1985–6): 1601–29, argues that legal interpretation itself is the process in which law and violence meet. Cover trenchantly exposes the often hidden ways in which violence is endemic to law's agendas.

[33] The order imagined by Benjamin, aside from being unbearably inefficient and tedious, denies individuals their need to be wrong, to make mistakes, and to learn from punishments, both light and heavy. In a world where diplomatic negotiation and consensual, compromising discourse are the only models for social ordering (*Ibid.*, p. 293), only an exclusively relativist or pluralist truth and understanding can emerge.

[34] Sarkar, "Hindu Theory of the State," pp. 83–4. [35] *Ibid.*

He then proceeds to discuss the prevalent image of punishment in Hindu texts as creating the orderly world by destroying the rule of anarchy, or in Sanskrit parlance, the "logic of the fishes" (*matsyanyāya*). At the heart of punishment's efficacy is fear, according to Sarkar, and its effect is deterrence.[36] In this respect, the Hindu view congrues well with classic European formulations of the origins of and right to punish. Beccaria's 1764 treatise, for example, contends that punishment originates in the "despotic spirit of every man" and the "universal principle of anarchy" and that the right to punish, therefore, protects the law "from the private usurpations of each individual."[37] As a consequence, law's purpose is "nothing other than to prevent the offender from doing fresh harm to his fellows and to deter others from doing likewise."[38] In addition to fear, however, Sarkar intersperses clear references to the educative function of punishment. In fact, he concludes his essay by claiming, "In accordance with the doctrine of *daṇḍa*, then, the state is conceived as a pedagogic institution or moral laboratory, so to speak. It is an organization in and through which men's natural vices are purged, and it thereby becomes an effective means to the general uplifting of mankind."[39]

Benjamin would no doubt scoff at Sarkar's positive characterization of punishment as the work of a Pollyanna. After all, if the texts are any indication, real people in classical and medieval India must have been executed, banished, beaten, and mutilated in the name of the law, and abstractions to the "moral laboratory" of the state as a teacher of virtues seem to soften and excuse the cold realities of punishment. However, instead of taking sides in the debate over whether law's connection to violence and punishment should be judged positively or negatively, I want to look further into some of the Hindu views of punishment in order to find perhaps a way of, if not reconciling the two views, at least making use of the insights of both.

To do this, we should examine one of Rocher's important points in his study of Hindu criminal law. His survey of Dharmaśāstra revealed that the term *sāhasa*, violence generally or robbery specifically, is often a cover term of sorts for the whole gamut of crimes. Moreover, he asserts, "*Sāhasa* is not only more serious than all of them, but the fact that it is dangerous to law and order is one of the fundamental characteristics ascribed to it."[40] The

[36] *Ibid.*, pp. 88–9. Compare, Kane, *History of Dharmaśāstra*, Vol. 3, p. 22: "These eulogies of *daṇḍa* presuppose the theory that people obey the law and the dictates of the *śāstra* through the fear of force or punishment."

[37] Beccaria, *On Crimes and Punishments and Other Writings*, trans. Richard Davies, ed. Richard Bellamy (New York: Cambridge University Press, 1995), p. 9.

[38] *Ibid.*, p. 31. [39] Sarkar, "Hindu Theory of the State," p. 90.

[40] Rocher, "Ancient Hindu Criminal Law," p. 27.

latter part of this assertion echoes a key point made by Benjamin that "law sees violence in the hands of individuals as a danger undermining the legal system."[41] The general violence of criminal activity in Hindu jurisprudence is thus similarly seen as the most insidious threat to the order of law. The main problem with violence then is less the injury it causes to some person or group than the threat it poses to the state or other legal authority.

For Benjamin, this is still the view from the world of law and thus of an ideology of inevitable violence. Nevertheless, Rocher's observation confirms the fact that Hindu scholiasts, too, worried about the dangers of non-legalized violence and, like legal thinkers almost everywhere, postulated legal punishment as the only legitimate response. Benjamin himself begins to suggest a way out of the purely negative characterization of law's dependence on violence when he asserts "the necessity of seeking the reason for the commandment [against immoral action] no longer in what the deed does to the victim, but in what it does to God and the doer."[42] For Benjamin, law and its violence must be eliminated in order to cease the physical torment of the legally condemned, but immoral action must still be condemned instead by a rhetorical and institutional focus on the negative consequences of that action for the individual and for God as an ahistorical, transcendent entity.

The shift of focus in punishment's purpose away from protecting or avenging the victim toward convicting the perpetrator psychologically and morally would at first seem to be little more than rehabilitation. Here Benjamin seems implicitly to deny what the Hindu tradition would assert, that self-imposed penance and correction is also a form of punishment and violence, though surely outside the realm of legal means in Benjamin's terms. At this point, the Hindu law tradition offers a metaphor for law – already invoked several times in this work – that allows us to see a positive aspect to punishment that neither denies its often ugly connection to violence nor sees it as the state's glorious instrument of ethical formation.

Punishment, like all other elements of Hindu law, is part of the ritual of *dharma*. In ordinary life, say a family, punishment serves all of the purposes already described. It balances inequities through retribution; it instills fear and deters future transgressions; it rehabilitates transgressors and permits them to re-enter the social order in good standing; it educates individuals about how to be and to know in society. Through all of this, however, punishment also makes the overarching ritual of society

[41] Benjamin, "Critique of Violence," p. 280. [42] *Ibid.*, pp. 298–9.

effective and productive of its final goals. When those goals are defined through theological reflection on the processes of ordinary life, as they are in Hindu jurisprudence, the workings of punishment simultaneously establish and support a legal regime modeled on ritual.

When the ritual context is not the family, but society, more specifically the theologically constructed social order of castes and life-stages, the ritual becomes coextensive with life itself for anyone who is part of that legal world. At this level, punishment is the vehicle of law, the means by which law's processes dynamically affect people's lives. In the rhetorical world created by this idea of law as ritual is an implicit promise that both along the way, and at the end, of law's journey through a person's life, ritual benefits will accrue. Punishment and penance correct ritual mistakes made by the individual that threaten to take him or her off the proverbial path of righteousness. Punishment and penance are the steering wheels guiding one through the ritual of law. So, yes, they are rehabilitative, but, more importantly, they are ritually efficacious.

To make it to the end of law's ritual and to achieve its benefits, one has to make mistakes and experience punishments. Mistakes, missteps, and outright wrongs are inevitable, but the only thing worse than a wrong is an unpunished wrong. Uncorrected ritual errors, mistaken or intentional, undermine the efficacy of the whole procedure. At this level of abstraction, punishment and penance do suffer from an unsustainable distancing from harsh practical realities, but there are two justifications for the abstraction. First, both punishment and penance exist on a continuum from severe and violent to mild and non-violent. Second, whether severe or mild, punishment, contrary to Benjamin's claim that "the expiatory power of violence is not visible to men,"[43] can, at least in the Hindu view, expiate mistakes and wrongs in such a way that the ritual of law can proceed effectively.

Life in the world of legal rhetoric consists of a ritual comprised primarily of obedient, law-abiding actions and secondarily of mistaken, evil, law-threatening actions. The *Laws of Manu* captures this essential combination well: "If he acts righteously for the most part and unrighteously to a small degree, enveloped in those very elements, he enjoys happiness in heaven" (MDh 12.20). Thus, for Manu, the ambiguous, but still beautiful, teleological end of the ritual of law elevates punishment from being a means to a merely political end to being also a means to accomplish the flourishing of society itself.

[43] Benjamin, "Critique of Violence," p. 300.

CHAPTER 7

# *Law and practice* (ācāra)

In a study such as this, the chapter on practice and history inevitably does the work of an apology. Some readers will have been bothered by the cavalier treatment of historical context evinced in this work thus far. In fact, perhaps the most important trend in recent academia has been the near universal insistence to "always historicize."[1] Nevertheless, the boundaries of what constitutes history are sometimes drawn too narrowly, especially when it comes to India.[2] I am convinced that studies attempting to reveal presuppositions of thought, practices of interpretation, and scholarly generalizations about real-world affairs are necessary and important for historical work. Indeed, they form part of history itself.

In the first chapter of this survey, we examined the authoritative sources of law as expressed in the Hindu law texts. In this final chapter, I return to the question of law's authority, this time in the context of legal practice and customary law. In other words, I want to investigate both the conjunctions and disjunctions of how legal authority is represented and implemented between the Dharmaśāstra tradition and other historical sources. The concept of *ācāra* is both the conceptual and practical link between scholastic norms, ideas, and presuppositions and the rules and institutions of law in practice. It is important in this context because the relative dearth, indeed the striking rarity, of historical references to the Veda and Dharmaśāstra in legal contexts outside Sanskrit texts puts

[1] Frederic Jameson's famous opening slogan in the Preface to *The Political Unconscious: Narrative as a Socially Symbolic Act* (Ithaca: Cornell University Press, 1981) has been widely cited and debated.

[2] On the problem of history in India, see, recently, Velcheru Narayana Rao, David Shulman, and Sanjay Subrahmanyam, *Textures of Time: Writing History in South India 1600–1800* (New York: Other Press, 2003). Compare Patrick Olivelle, *The Āśrama System: the History and Hermeneutics of a Religious Institution* (New York: Oxford University Press, 1993), p. 33: "It is simplistic to assume that only 'events' are historical. Attempts at theoretical and theological self-understanding are as much a part of the history of culture as wars and dynasties."

the signal importance of *ācāra* into relief. We begin by examining the nature of *ācāra* in the *dharma* texts.

### *ĀCĀRA* GENERAL AND *ĀCĀRAS* SPECIFIC

There are two related senses of *ācāra* in Dharmaśāstra. The first, introduced in Chapter 1, refers to customary law as a source of law. To be more precise about the problematic category of custom and customary law, *ācāra* always possesses a normative and obligatory quality that is not necessarily implied by custom alone.[3] For this reason, I usually gloss *ācāra* as "local law" or "community standards" in an attempt to indicate its normative character, but also its restricted applicability. It is difficult to follow the usual characterizations of *ācāra*'s authority as resting on the "*observed* conduct of 'good people.'"[4] How do we imagine this scene? Can we believe that anything we observe "good people" doing is *dharma*? Certainly not. Even Medhātithi anticipated this straw man: "When there are no statements in the revealed or traditional texts, but learned people perform [it] considering it to be *dharma*, then even that [act] should be understood as Vedic only, just like the previous[ly mentioned sources]."[5]

Nevertheless, to speak of "conduct" suggests that one need only witness or observe the behavior of "good people" in order to determine *dharma*. It is this focus on conduct and behavior that, I believe, leads us astray in understanding *ācāra*. If we focus instead on the "good people" element, i.e., the idea that *ācāra* must always be restricted to a particular context or at least the general context of respected people, then we can imagine a different picture of *ācāra*'s authority. Here, *ācāra* would refer to declared norms that are actually practiced and put into practice by people with power over a delimited group. The ideal within Dharmaśāstra is, of course, the learned male Brahmin, the Veda-knower, but the theologically necessary ideal of people with Vedic knowledge slips easily and regularly within

[3] See Donald R. Davis, Jr., *The Boundaries of Hindu Law: Tradition, Custom, and Politics in Medieval Kerala*. Corpus Iuris Sanscriticum et Fontes Iuris Asiae Meridianae et Centralis. Vol. 5. Ed. Oscar Botto (Torino: CESMEO, 2004), pp. 128–44, for a more substantial critique of the labels "custom" and "customary law" for *ācāra*.

[4] Adam Bowles, *Dharma, Disorder, and the Political in Ancient India: The Āpaddharmaparvan of the Mahābhārata* (Leiden: Brill, 2007), p. 197 (emphasis added).

[5] Medh on MDh 2.6: *yatra śrutismṛtivākyāni na santi śiṣṭāś ca dharmabuddhyānutiṣṭhanti tad api vaidikam eva pūrvavat pratipattavyam*. Compare Kumārila on PMS 1.3.7: "It is only those actions that are held by good people to be *dharma*, and are performed as such, that are accepted as *dharma*; because the persons that perform these are the same as those that perform the sacrifices enjoined in the Veda" (Ganganatha Jha, trans., *Tantravārttika*, p. 184).

Dharmaśāstra itself into contextually defined "good people," most often identified with the leaders of a particular community.

The contextually unmarked good (*sad-*) in "standards of the good (people)" (*sadācāra*) is actually marked by default as the archetypal and presumed ideal of a Vedic Brahmin. When the first element is replaced, as it regularly is, with other contextual markers, the theological connection to the Veda is also weakened or lost. Texts speak freely of the *ācāra* of particular places, families, castes, and various corporate groups. When pushed beyond the boundaries of its archetype, therefore, *ācāra* appears to be nothing but the norms accepted and imposed by the leaders of various social institutions. This slippage is very important for understanding how the famous recognition of the customary laws of various social groups in Hindu jurisprudence came to be incorporated into the texts.

Here's how I think we should imagine the textual history involved.[6] A solid consensus of scholars now suggests that Dharmaśāstra is a record of *ācāra* written in a specialized scholastic idiom.[7] If *ācāra* were conduct to be observed, then Dharmaśāstra would be a kind of ethnographic report, an observer's journal. *Dharma* texts were likely not produced observationally, but rather discursively, in the sense that authors composed in dialogue with their peers, their students, their memories, their knowledge of prior texts, and their own agendas (see Table 7). Once the texts were constituted, however, they became the sources for education about law and even for its administration in some cases. New texts and commentaries incorporated both the wisdom of the old texts and, to some extent, the *ācāra* of new places and times. The primary intention of all scholars in the tradition was to set forth the *ācāra*s of the Brahmin caste in textual form. From the *Laws of Manu* onward, the scope of the intention expanded to include the *ācāra*s of the Kṣatriya caste as well. The bulk of Dharmaśāstra is concerned with one of these two textualized expositions of *ācāra*. These two ideal subjects of law dominate the discourse of Dharmaśāstra and together they serve as paradigms for the explanation of any *dharma* that might pertain to other kinds of people.

[6] For a more descriptive account of the cycle of composition, transmission, and reception of Dharmaśāstra, see Donald R. Davis, Jr., "Recovering the Indigenous Legal Traditions of India: Classical Hindu Law in Practice in Late Medieval Kerala," *Journal of Indian Philosophy* 27:3 (1999): 166–7.

[7] Richard W. Lariviere, "Dharmaśāstra, Custom, 'Real Law,' and 'Apocryphal' Smṛtis," *Journal of Indian Philosophy* 32:5–6 (2004): 611–27; Patrick Olivelle, "The Semantic History of Dharma: The Middle and Late Vedic Periods," *Journal of Indian Philosophy* 32 (2004): 491–511; Albrecht Wezler, "Dharma in the Vedas and in the Dharmaśāstras," *Journal of Indian Philosophy* 32 (2004): 629–54.

Table 7. *Relationship of text and practice in Hindu law*

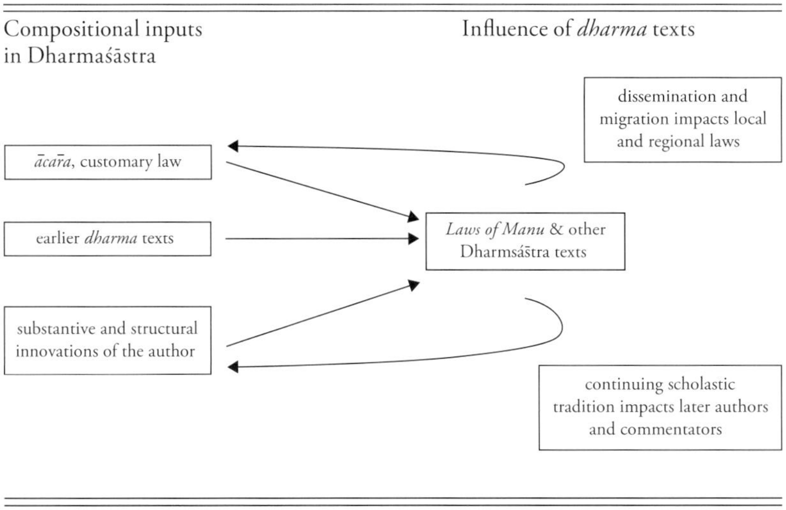


In the general notion of *ācāra*, therefore, the texts are concerned with delineating all the various substantive rules for the two ideal person-types in classical Sanskrit texts, the Brahmin and the Kṣatriya. When the texts take notice of *ācāra* beyond these two, however, the references are invariably brief and allusive, even as the customary laws mentioned are also fully recognized as *dharma*.

In the end, therefore, the difference between *ācāra* and *dharma* is very slight.[8] In fact, by definition all *ācāra* is *dharma*. In the tripartite scheme outlined by Hacker,[9] *ācāra* is first *dharma* during its performance but also *dharma* as the norm before its performance. However, *ācāra* is never to my knowledge likened to *dharma* as merit after its performance. The slender difference between the two, however, is one good reason not to assimilate *ācāra* too quickly to the category of custom or customary law,[10] because those categories tend to drive a wedge between *dharma* and *ācāra* that

[8] Donald R. Davis, Jr., "*Dharma* in Practice: *Ācāra* and Authority in Medieval Dharmaśāstra." *Journal of Indian Philosophy* 32:5 (2004) especially pp. 818, 824.

[9] See Paul Hacker, "Dharma in Hinduism," *Journal of Indian Philosophy* 34 (2006): 490, quoted in the Introduction to this book.

[10] For example, Robert Lingat, *The Classical Law of India*, trans. J.D.M. Derrett (Berkeley: University of California Press, 1973), pp. 176–206, overemphasizes the differences between *ācāra* and *dharma* in his chapter on "Dharma and Custom."

does not exist in the spirit of Hindu law. *Ācāra* is not only a source of *dharma*; it is also its highest form or mode, because it is *dharma* done.

In another tripartite scheme, *dharma* is divided into *ācāra*, *vyavahāra*, and *prāyaścitta*, a classification that I earlier compared to substantive, procedural, and penal law, respectively. While both the procedures of *vyavahāra* and the punishments and penances of *prāyaścitta* (and *daṇḍa*) are forms of *dharma*, they are *dharma*s for when things are wrong. *Ācāra*, by contrast, is the form *dharma* takes when things are right. In the normal, ideal world, people are habituated to perform the normative actions spelled out in the *ācāra* division of *dharma*. This is the division that describes sacramentary and household rites, marriage, eating, bathing, and all the other personal *dharma*s, especially those of Brahmins. These are the rites of law that form the central core of *dharma* – actions that, when appropriated and carried out in conformity to tradition, produce ritual-like results, both in this world and the next. Ordinary actions of human life are thus placed in a theological context whereby a lawful performance of those actions in the particular manner described by the texts and tradition will bring great merit to the person and order to the system.

A favorite example among students comes from the *Laws of Yājñavalkya*: "Holding his penis, he should stand up and, with earth and water that has been drawn up, clean himself thoroughly until the smell and filth are removed" (YS 1.17). The commentary of Vijñāneśvara explains that "the cleansing described in the phrase 'until the smell and filth are removed' is common to people of all life-stages, but the restrictive rule concerning the number of times earth should be used is for an unseen purpose."[11] The question always comes up, do we really need a text to tell us how to clean ourselves or to teach us not to piss into the wind as we learn from the *Laws of Manu* (MDh 4.48)? Not only is the basic act described, but Vijñāneśvara's commentary points to other texts that prescribe a precise number of applications of earth for proper purification.[12] The specificity of the applications of earth already points to what Vijñāneśvara states plainly: the purpose of cleansing is common, but the purpose of detailed purification is unseen, unknown to us through any ordinary means of knowledge.

[11] Vijñāneśvara on YS 1.17: *atra gandhalepakṣayakaram iti sarvāśramiṇāṃ sādhāraṇam idaṃ śaucam | mṛtsaṃkhyāniyamas tu adṛṣṭārthaḥ.*

[12] See, for example, VaDh 6.18–19: "Tradition lays down one application of earth on the penis, three on the left hand, and two on both hands; and five applications on the anus, ten on the left hand, and seven on both hands. This is the purification for householders. It is twice that much for students, three times for forest hermits, and four times for ascetics."

Almost every quotidian act described in the Dharmaśāstra root-texts and commentaries could come with this same disclaimer. The transcendent, unseen effects of cleaning oneself in a particular manner are accepted as unchallengeable truths. The application of a theological framework onto a circumstance of ordinary life thus results in an only partially explainable set of legal rules, the benefits of which are imprecise but certain nonetheless. To explain these rules on the grounds of hygiene alone not only crassly reduces the import of the text to an allegedly scientific basis but also misses the important theological point of any such rule. One way of stating that theological point is to say that no human action is beyond the pale of *dharma* and that everything we do as people matters in ways that we cannot always immediately comprehend. To accomplish the theological (and ethical) goal of such ordinary actions demands the acceptance of an authority in the form of hard-to-justify legal rules.

The second, specific notion of *ācāra* refers precisely to the caste, life-stage, and community-bound rules that together constitute the substantive rules of law pertinent to an individual and to the groups to which he or she belongs. Unlike *ācāra* generally, however, the specific *ācāra*s are described and discussed as part of the ruler's *dharma* and not as part of the general exposition of the authoritative sources of *dharma*. The *Laws of Manu* provides a summary statement: "He who knows the Law should examine the Laws of castes, regions, guilds, and families, and only then settle the Law specific to each … He should ratify the acknowledged practices of virtuous men and righteous twice-born individuals, if such practices do not conflict with those of a particular region, family, or caste" (MDh 8.41, 46). Though the root-text uses the word *dharma* for "Law" in this passage, it is telling that Medhātithi switches freely between *dharma* and *ācāra* when discussing them – a good example of the slight, not great, difference between them. Moreover, such rules are covered under the Vedic umbrella, and some texts take time to justify these specific *ācāra*s in terms of the larger theology.[13]

The rules referred to by Manu are acknowledged to differ from one another and to be distinct from the textual rules (so long as they do not contradict them). However, what I am calling the specific *ācāra*s are in fact never specified in detail within the texts, and this is precisely the point. Hindu jurisprudence leaves ample room for the creation of law outside its own strictures. Theological and legal reasons are given for accommodating

[13] See Medh on MDh 8.41, 46.

the customary laws of various groups, but the enumeration of those laws is not made within the texts themselves. Saying this does not alter the fact that many rules of Dharmaśāstra likely originated from precisely the specific *ācāra*s of Brahmin communities at the time when the texts were composed or compiled. One way to think about this is to say that the texts represent systematized customary laws of the past, while at the same time maintaining the legitimacy and legality of other unspecified customary laws in the present.

To assess the spirit of Hindu law on the role of customary law, we must examine further the tension that occasionally arises within the texts on the relative strength of Dharmaśāstra and customary law in legal contexts.[14] As we saw in Chapter 2, theologically in terms of *dharma*, there is no doubt whatsoever that Dharmaśāstra is superior. Time and again, commentators emphasize that no worldly rule or practice can trump the authority and the claim on human action found in the textual tradition. At the same time, we also find many texts and authors that insist upon the greater authority of customary law in practice. Whether it is Viśvarūpa insisting that texts must be interpreted so as to conform with customary law and not vice versa (YS 3.250), Asahāya saying "when there is contradiction between Dharmaśāstra and customary law (*lokavyavahāra*), one should ignore the Dharmaśāstra and do what is established as customary law" (NS Mā 1.38), or Medhātithi claiming that customary law is really just another form of tradition, no different from the texts (MDh 2.10), the superiority or at least equality of *ācāra* in practical contexts has been regularly defended.

In some cases, the boldness of the claim that *ācāra* is the superior source of law is surprising. For example, the commentator Mitramiśra reads into the Sanskrit particle *ca* "and" in the *pramāṇa* verse (MDh 2.6) from the *Laws of Manu* a huge scope for customary law: "And, thus, even the *ācāra* of those who do not know the Veda, i.e., the poor and vile people, is authoritative. In same way, the *ācāra* of good Śūdras and others with regard to their sons is also authoritative."[15] The surprising element here is whose *ācāra* is being recognized. "Veda-knowers" is a common gloss for "good people" in almost every commentary on this verse. To parallel "veda-knowers" and "non-veda-knowers" (*avedavidām*), as Mitramiśra

[14] Still the best discussion of the tension between Hindu legal texts and customary law within Dharmaśāstra is P.V. Kane, *History of Dharmaśāstra* (Poona: BORI, 1962–75), Vol. 3, pp. 856–84.

[15] *Paribhāṣāprakāśa*, p. 9, quoted in Kane, *History of Dharmaśāstra*, Vol. 3, p. 881, fn. 1722: *evaṃ cāvedavidām api kṣīṇadoṣapuruṣāṇām ācāraḥ pramāṇam | tathā ca sacchūdrādyācāras tatputrādīn prati bhavati pramāṇam*.

explicitly does, undercuts the usual arguments for the Vedic connection to customary law. To specify then that the *ācāra* of Śūdras is also legitimate, when Śūdra in most texts is synonymous with despicable and unworthy, further reverses the expectations set up in most texts. How do we reconcile such views with the usual hierarchy of legal sources?

The solution is one that is found in probably every legal system, even if not recognized as such. When the law is clear and when one's legal duties, obligations, and rights are not confused, questioned, or endangered, then the normal epistemological hierarchy of law's sources applies. Explicit ritual practices, contractual agreements, and mandatory penances must all be carried out in order to obtain the benefits that the law enables. The problem arises when there are doubts or disputes about what the nature of one's legal obligations or rights is in specific instances. In this case, the normal hierarchy of legal sources has already failed and another method for discerning the law is required. In such cases, local law or *ācāra* is one of the main factors for determining the relevant solution or for making a judgment in the context of a formal legal procedure.[16] In the case of the Śūdras mentioned by Mitramiśra, the problem is that the texts say very little about the *dharma* of low caste groups or any other local corporate groups. The resulting ignorance leads to doubt in practice about what to do in the case of people, groups, or institutions that are hardly discussed in the Dharmaśāstra. That doubt requires an extra-textual means to determine the law. In other words, there is little in the Vedas or *smṛti* texts to help Śūdras do *dharma*, but they do have *ācāra*, a suitable substitute. In most situations, *ācāra* is held to be the sufficient source for determining and/or adjudging the relevant law. Stated plainly, under normal circumstances, the normal hierarchy prevails, but in cases of doubt or dispute, non-textualized sources of law must be consulted.

## THE PRACTICABILITY OF HINDU JURISPRUDENCE

Mitramiśra's legitimation of the customary law of even the lowest social groups and Śūdras suggests that the world of legal practice in classical and medieval India was much more complex than was acknowledged in

[16] The ruler's edict is another source of lawmaking outside the texts. This is how we should understand the often misinterpreted rules in the *Arthaśāstra* and *Laws of Nārada* about the four feet of legal procedure. In the context of a trial or other formal legal procedure, customary law and the edict or decision of the ruler can override other means of judicial decision. See Robert Lingat, "Les Quatre Pieds du Procés," *Journal Asiatique* 250 (1962): 489–503.

the Dharmaśāstra. Indeed, we should not expect a scholastic tradition to produce nuanced histories of local legal practice and the whole structure of this study has avoided this problem accordingly. Nevertheless, readers may be justifiably curious about both the Dharmaśāstra's own views of the practicability of its religious jurisprudence and the historical evidence for Hindu law in practice.

The internal evidence for practical law within the Dharmaśāstra begins from the somewhat rare instances in which the textual tradition points beyond itself. What we are looking for are places at which the texts either recognize the independent validity of certain laws outside the purview of the scholastic tradition or employ examples that deviate from the stock, historically unmarked examples used in most commentarial discussions. In the previous chapter, several examples of how Dharmaśāstra accorded rulers limited lawmaking capacity were cited. In addition to the ruler, and probably more important, however, we find the externally pointing discussion in the title of law known as the Non-observance of Conventions. A few further remarks on this title beyond those already given will provide a good summary of the Dharmaśāstra view of how law is administered in practice.

Though a title of law, the content of the Non-observance of Conventions connects notionally with *ācāra*.[17] The conventional rules made by the myriad corporate groups in classical and medieval India acted as one of the prime sources of practical law at the time. It should also be noted that in Dharmaśāstra discussions of *dharmādhikaraṇa*, or trial courts, corporate groups were charged with conducting their own legal procedures as well.[18] The commentator Vācaspati Miśra is quite clear on this issue:

> The words of experts should, however, be respected in all cases. Thus Nārada says: "In the case of merchants, artisans, farmers, and stage-players, a decision is not possible; here persons who themselves know the nature (of these trades) should be charged with it." This is an illustrative statement; it means that each and every case must be decided in association with persons who are experts in that field.[19]

By its very nature, therefore, this title of law displays a concern on the part of Dharmaśāstra authors for practical influence and an incorporation

[17] The following discussion is adapted from Donald R. Davis, Jr., "The Non-observance of Conventions: A Title of Hindu Law in the Smṛticandrikā," *Zeitschrift der Deutschen Morgenländischen Gesellschaft* 157:1 (2007): 105–7.

[18] *Smṛticandrikā*, pp. 38ff.

[19] *Vyavahāracintāmaṇi* 33 (Rocher's translation).

of empirical realities. At the same time, Dharmaśāstra provides us with only a jurisprudential account of that legal realm by establishing a viable technical argument for recognizing such conventional laws as part of the scholastic tradition of Dharmaśāstra.

The principal technique for achieving this recognition is to place such conventional rules (*samaya*) in the category of *paribhāṣā*, technical, supplementary, or meta-rules for determining the detailed interpretation of general rules of *śāstra*.[20] Under the technical rule categorization, conventions do not threaten the authority of the Dharmaśāstra itself, but rather operate where the *śāstra* is silent or ambiguous to supplement or clarify what the *dharma* is in any given situation. Here the limitations of the letter of the law in Dharmaśāstra are implicitly acknowledged, while the spirit of Hindu law is preserved by incorporating these rules as part of its jurisprudence. Understanding the Non-observance of Conventions in this way indicates that its practical import may be much greater than its middling consideration in Dharmaśāstra would suggest, for it presents an expansive realm of law beyond the texts.

As in all Dharmaśāstra discussions, the rules for Brahmins occupy a place of first importance in this title of law and act as an archetype for understanding other groups as ectypes.[21] In the end, however, Brahmins appear primarily as just another group that may make collective conventions for their communal governance. Indeed, the list of groups considered in the Dharmaśāstra includes "heretical" (e.g., Buddhist and Jain) monastic groups[22] and other groups beyond the pale of Ārya status. It is significant, therefore, that the conventions made by such groups are also called *dharma*s, since *dharma* normally connotes a deep exclusiveness and ethnocentrism.[23] The label *samayadharma* for the conventional laws of corporate groups does not call into question the supremacy of *varṇāśramadharma* as described in Dharmaśāstra because conventions are derivative and

[20] Donald R. Davis, Jr., "Intermediate Realms of Law: Corporate Groups and Rulers in Medieval India," *Journal of the Economic and Social History of the Orient* 48:1 (2005): 95–100.

[21] Patrick Olivelle (ed. and trans.), *Manu's Code of Law* (New York: Oxford University Press, 2005), p. 12.

[22] Olivelle, *Āśrama System*, p. 209 notes that it is likely that even the laws pertaining to Hindu *maṭha*s would have been included under this rubric. He generally discusses there the potentially powerful influence that such monastic institutions, whether Buddhist, Jain, or Hindu, may have had in the law of medieval India. The *Smṛticandrikā* excludes all Vedic groups from this category of "heretic" (*pāṣaṇḍa*), but does mention service in a *maṭha* as an example of a convention among such groups.

[23] Wilhelm Halbfass, *India and Europe: An Essay in Philosophical Understanding* (Albany: SUNY Press, 1988), pp. 172ff.

inferior *dharma*s that are never permitted to abrogate an explicit textual rule. However, the practical fact is, and this goes unstated but presumed in the texts, that the law of Dharmaśāstra and the law of corporate groups operated in largely independent realms. The question of conflict, though considered as we have seen, must have rarely had any practical import. The influence of Dharmaśāstra is rather at the level of ideas, approaches, and reasoning to be used in practical contexts.[24]

Perhaps unexpectedly, the figure of the ruler also appears prominently in discussions of the Non-observance of Conventions. Of course, the inculcation and maintenance of the system of castes and life-stages among his subjects is one of the ideal Hindu king's highest responsibilities. In this title of law, however, the king must also enforce and sanction the conventional rules established by the corporate groups in his realm. At the same time, the traditionally exclusive ascription of the right to punish that is given to kings in Hindu political theory is moderated to some extent in the texts. Under certain circumstances, it becomes not only necessary, but also desirable, for a corporate group itself to impose various punishments on members who transgress the group's laws. Provision is also made for the king to establish *dharma* by means of his decree, whether that means rectification or confirmation of established legal norms (common) or the legislation of new laws for a community (rare). As with the discussion of the conventions of corporate groups, the discussion of the king also points to certain legal realities and negotiations beyond the direct scope of the Dharmaśāstra. Again, this title of law does not undermine or challenge the standard presentations of the ruler's *dharma* in the texts. Rather, what we find is an attempt to jurisprudentially account for and authorize the practical legality of rulers' decrees and group conventions within the conceptual framework of Dharmaśāstra.

Turning to actual instances of Hindu law in practice, it would be impossible to give a comprehensive list.[25] Instead, I can only summarize the kind of evidence that is available in order to give readers at least some sense of the material for legal history in India in general, namely:

1 texts copied repeatedly over time;
2 inscriptions on stone and copper;

[24] Davis, "Recovering the Indigneous Legal Traditions," p. 199.
[25] The most recent survey can be found in Axel Michaels, "The Practice of Classical Hindu Law." In Timothy Lubin, Jayanth Krishnan, and Donald R. Davis, Jr. (eds.), *Hinduism and Law: An Introduction* (New York: Cambridge University Press, forthcoming).

3 documentary records from the archives of temple and royal courts; and
4 reports of foreign visitors and others.

The textual tradition in general must be used with caution for the reasons we have seen repeatedly in this study. As with so many aspects of India's history, the collection and cataloging of this evidence has barely begun.

The inscriptional corpus of India is truly huge.[26] Inscriptions are found carved into the stone walls of Hindu temples and other religious institutions, most often recording a donation to the temple for the maintenance of the deity and its priests. Larger temples existed at the center of economic redistribution networks that played a key role in many local economies. Both the donative information itself and the ancillary details given in inscriptions provide evidence for legal transactions. Similar details also occur on royal copper-plate inscriptions that might record donations of villages to Brahmins or gifts to temples. Again, other details of political, religious, and legal history are often incorporated into the panegyric to the donor, the description of the land's boundaries or the donees. Examples of legal details found in inscriptions include the caste dispute among Kammālas in AD 1118 and 1166 in which Brahmin councils were asked to determine the proper caste status of the so-called chariot-maker caste,[27] and the relatively old inscription of AD 592 which contains seventy-two *ācāra*s that were to be maintained in a community of merchants by order of the ruler Viṣṇuṣeṇa.[28] Such examples aside, few studies of inscriptions that focus on law have been undertaken, despite the great potential that epigraphy has to illuminate this and many other aspects of Indian history.

A second source of legal practice in history is found in repositories or archives of documents, usually on palm-leaf, from more recent periods. Temples, for example, often kept detailed accounting records of income and expense, including records of mortgage, lease, and sale of lands owned by the temple. Very often, the accompanying description of the temple's income and expenditure incidentally provides important information about the administration of law, jurisdiction, arrest, trial procedures, and

[26] Richard Salomon, *Indian Epigraphy* (New York: Oxford University Press, 1998) is the best survey of Indian inscriptions and their interpretation.

[27] J.D.M. Derrett, "Two Inscriptions Concerning the Status of Kammalas and the Application of Dharmasastra." In *Essays in Classical and Medieval Hindu Law*, Vol. 1 (Leiden: Brill, 1976), pp. 86–110.

[28] D.C. Sircar, "Glimpses of *Ācāra* and *Vyavahāra* in Early Indian Literary and Epigraphic Records." In Richard W. Lariviere (ed.), *Studies in Dharmaśāstra* (Calcutta: Firma KLM, 1984), pp. 3–14.

punishments. A good example of such description comes from AD 1607 in Kerala.[29] The record was made to account for the temple's receipt of the clothes and weapon of a man. The rest of the record, however, recounts that the man in question had murdered a Brahmin, that he was arrested and jailed in the temple, that superior political leaders were involved, and that the man was executed with their permission. In this way, a record made for one purpose can be the source of information about many other aspects of law in Kerala at the time. Repositories and archives containing such records have rarely been studied, much less edited and published.

Documents of a similar kind are also found in the form of formularies and other collections of exemplary legal documents. The most famous of these is known as the *Lekhapaddhati* and it contains a fascinating array of models for making legal documents, akin to modern forms, and other sample records of legal transaction designed to serve the scribes who wrote them out. There are, however, several such formularies and collections that have generally been noticed rather than studied. Again, the potential for legal history in such early archival material has yet to be developed.

One final source of information for legal history in practice has been fairly well studied, namely the reports of missionaries, travelers, officials, and others who visited or traveled through India. From Marco Polo onwards, we have a series of European visitors and travelers in India, many of whom recorded aspects of law that they witnessed or otherwise gleaned during their travels. Such observations and reports intensified in the run-up to colonialism during the eighteenth century and continued through the nineteenth century. That history is important but has too often substituted for a thorough history of law in classical and medieval India. Beside and before the Europeans, of course, came Buddhist travelers to India from China, some of whom described elements of legal practice, and Muslim travelers and officials, notably Alberuni, whose interest in legal matters became of increasing importance to Islamic rulers in India. Though this genre of travelers' reports has produced some insights into the practice of law in medieval India, the evidence is often eclectic or random in its focus and full of expected prejudices that together yield problematic and sometimes unreliable presentations of legal history.

In asking the question of Hindu law's practicability, therefore, we inevitably arrive at an intellectual impasse. Hindu law properly so called should refer to legal systems that are influenced by and have influence on the textual tradition of Hindu jurisprudence in Dharmaśāstra. Other criteria

[29] The full record is translated in Davis, *Boundaries of Hindu Law*, pp. 83–5.

for determining what is Hindu about a legal system – connection to a Hindu temple, to caste, or Hindu sects, for instance – all seem insufficient as descriptive bases for differentiating Hindu law from law generally. Rather these appear to be incidents only of a greater likelihood that a specifically Hindu law would operate in such contexts than in others. As we have seen from several perspectives, however, Dharmaśāstra was not written with the intention to produce a functional legal system. The practical implementation of law, as this chapter suggests, was left to communities of overlapping corporate groups and to political rulers. There is a gap then between what the texts imagine and present in terms of their own applicability or practicability and what may have actually happened in a given place and time. The practical influence of Dharmaśāstra and thereby the creation of a practical *Hindu* law occurred indirectly via the influence of the Brahmin caretakers of the *dharma* tradition, the rulers and others who may also have studied it. In many cases, it is quite possible to demonstrate such influence. Much more tangible and important, however, is the fact that Dharmaśāstra represents by far the most elaborate and systematic reflection upon law that we have from classical and medieval India, an unbroken tradition of more than 2,000 years. When it came to *thinking* about law, therefore, Dharmaśāstra was almost the only game in town. In terms of implementing law, by contrast, Dharmaśāstra was but one resource for substantive and procedural rules and ideas for the practical operation of law. The implications of this impasse for the study of law and practice still remain for consideration in the next section.

## AN APPROACH TO THE HISTORY OF LAW IN INDIA, AND OF HINDU LAW

It is a mistake to write a history of law in India on the basis of Dharmaśāstra. I mean this in two senses. First, Dharmaśāstra *by itself* cannot provide a direct witness to legal practices because it is composed within and for a scholastic tradition that privileges its own idioms and commentarial practices over a concern for relevance. It provides always a *mediated* witness to legal history, a "meta-discourse" in Olivelle's apt phrase.[30] Second, even if other historical sources are consulted, *starting with* Dharmaśāstra inevitably yields a view of law in which practice is seen as either congruent or divergent from the texts. This is the code-practice problem that has plagued Hindu law studies since their inception. Dharmaśāstra was not a

[30] Olivelle, *Manu's Code of Law*, p. 64.

code written to be consulted like a recipe-book for the proper ingredients and preparation of a legal system, or a religio-legal system. They are works of scholarship written by pandits not unlike contemporary professors, whose own work, including this one, tends to follow its own rules and veer away quite freely from real life, even if one of its purposes is to understand real life better.

The more appropriate focus for historical research on law in India is, therefore, what both the Dharmaśāstra and the epigraphical record call *ācāra* or some synonym. An approach to India's legal history that begins with *ācāra* has three distinct advantages:

1 it focuses first on the local, contextual, and particular histories of law that characterized different places and times; *ācāra* demands concreteness and specificity;
2 it appropriates the language of law found in dated historical evidence for legal institutions and practices; *ācāra* or its synonyms is almost always the word for "law" found in historical evidence from India; and
3 it maximizes our ability to use all available sources for legal history, including Dharmaśāstra, without privileging one kind of source unnecessarily.[31]

It should be emphasized here that beginning at the level of and with the language of *ācāra* takes us quickly outside the realm of "Hindu law," because it would again privilege a Dharmaśāstra-centered view of legal history to prejudge legal systems or practices as somehow Hindu prior to investigating them. Hindu law is not the default in the absence of other information. Rather, legal systems of classical and medieval India probably combined many influences, only one of which *may* have been the jurisprudence of Hindu law found in the texts studied here. The extent of overlap or influence between laws studied first at the historical level of *ācāra* and Hindu jurisprudence is a matter for empirical investigation and scholarly argument. To describe a legal system as a system of Hindu law, as I have done for medieval Kerala, demands justification and a clear demonstration of the influence of Dharmaśāstra on that system. Despite an academic turn away from such easy assumptions, collapsing the categories Hindu and Indian has become politically expedient in recent years. That tendency also manifests in some academic works, but I do not accept it in any form, because it not only misunderstands the realities of historical legal practice and institutions, but also makes diffuse and corrupt the coherent

[31] Summarized from Davis, *Boundaries of Hindu Law*, p. 150.

and beautiful vision of law contained within the Hindu tradition itself. The practical impact of Dharmaśāstra on law and religion can still be an interesting question, but not if approached by looking for Dharmaśāstra's traces in historical evidence. Rather, we must start with evidence for historically situated legal practice and from that begin to build up a picture of law in that place and time. Once a relatively clear picture of a historical legal system or of some small aspect of law becomes clearer, then one may profitably turn to texts like Dharmaśāstra to begin to ask whether Hindu jurisprudence, or any other textually represented legal thought, has influenced the law.

From these reflections emerges what the future of legal history of India might look like. What we need above all are many more micro-histories of law from different parts of India and in different periods. In some cases, such micro-histories can emerge only when scholars read existing evidence with a view toward developing a history of law. As a simple example, though it is widely recognized that the vast majority of India's gigantic epigraphical corpus consists of inscriptions that are also legal documents, especially records of legal donations, epigraphy has generally speaking not been read with legal history in mind. In other cases, micro-histories can emerge by examining as yet understudied or even unused historical materials. In my own case, a Kerala historian with whom I studied, M.G.S. Narayanan, introduced me to a genre of historical writing common in many parts of South India that contained a great deal of information pertaining to many aspects of law, even though the purpose of the records was financial record-keeping. I can only expect that records of a similar sort exist elsewhere in India and that other genres of historical evidence might also be used for legal history.[32]

As more micro-histories or regional histories of law are produced, we could begin to consider a scholarly consolidation and comparison of those for the purpose of discerning whether patterns emerge in the historical development of law in India generally or whether legal history follows more exclusively regional trends. The academic model in this instance is the revolution in Hindu studies created by the proliferation of ethnographic studies of Hinduism beginning in the 1950s. The many wonderful ethnographies that now exist on very local, regional, and transregional aspects of Hinduism can be used to produce nuanced formulations of both Hinduism's current structure and nature and as the basis for determining

[32] Axel Michaels, "The Practice of Classical Hindu Law," surveys the known possibilities.

its historical development. It is not that ethnographic work has neglected law in India. In fact, a few good ethnographic studies focused on law do exist.[33]

Rather, it is that the anthropological perspective on legal history has not found its way into studies of earlier developments in the Hindu tradition. As scholars of Hinduism, we have learned to read sectarian traditions, practices of renunciation, ritual, and devotion, and so forth from a perspective that always holds a very practical knowledge of these in mind.[34] We are thus open to a bottom-up view of these aspects of the Hindu tradition in a way that we have not opened ourselves to when it comes to law, in part because Hindu law was thoroughly dismantled and redesigned in very different form under colonialism. Stated in this way, my suggestion is simply that studies of legal history in India should mirror studies of history in India generally. The move to regional histories and to nuanced political histories has not yet produced thorough investigations of the place of law in the larger story.

Having a firm historical foundation grounded in regional and then transregional histories of law would finally allow us to re-read the normative texts such as Dharmaśāstra against a history that does not derive its trajectory from the texts themselves.[35] The textual trajectory has been the bane of both Hindu law studies and of Indian legal history for a long time. Our expectations change dramatically when the textual trajectory is demoted from a place of privilege. We should expect that texts did in fact influence both thought and practice, but also that they were influenced themselves by changes in society, religion, economics, politics, and so forth. It is almost commonplace now to invoke an expectation that social institutions be mutually constitutive. The level of detail in the texts and the fact that the authors of Dharmaśāstra wanted to be recognized as the final arbiters of *dharma* and law have encouraged hegemonic readings of the texts. Reversing the methodological approach, however, puts the texts in their proper place. In this view, texts still have power, power to create

[33] See recently, Robert M. Hayden, *Disputes and Arguments among Nomads: A Caste Council in India* (Delhi: Oxford University Press, 1999), and the extensive bibliography therein.

[34] Louis Dumont and David Pocock, "For a Sociology of India," *Contributions to Indian Sociology* 1:1 (1957): 7–22; J.A.B. van Buitenen, "On the Archaism of the *Bhāgavata-Purāṇa*." In Milton Singer (ed.), *Kṛṣṇa: Myths, Rites, and Attitudes* (Chicago: University of Chicago Press, 1966), pp. 23–40.

[35] For an experimental attempt to write a history of Hindu law without reference to Dharmaśāstra, see Donald R. Davis, Jr. "An Historical Overview of Hindu Law." In T. Lubin, J. Krishnan, and D.R. Davis (eds.), *Hinduism and Law: An Introduction* (New York: Cambridge University Press, forthcoming).

rhetorical worlds, to establish discourses, to educate thought, and even to provide substantive rules for practice. At the same time, texts never exist in a vacuum. The historical evolution of social institutions different from law most assuredly impacted the development of law, even if that development is muted and downplayed in texts like Dharmaśāstra.

In this connection, I must reiterate my view of the nature of Dharmaśāstra, because it comes from a particular lineage of academia and is somewhat at odds with some other prevailing views.[36] An established position in the study of Hindu law has been that the purpose of the later commentaries on Dharmaśāstra was to bring the older texts up to date and to add new material relevant to contemporary times.[37] In other words, according to this view commentators tried to adapt and revise the classic root-texts in accordance with changes in social, religious, and political circumstances. It is undeniable that historical change affected and must affect the contents of even the most closed-in scholastic traditions. It is another thing altogether to claim that scholiasts and later writers *intended* to introduce changes in order to update the tradition before them. In some cases, it is clear that they did – local laws were defended in Dharmaśāstra terms or new topics were introduced and elaborated in ever greater detail.[38] In most cases, it seems equally apparent that they did not intend to adapt texts to local situations or update them according to changed historical circumstances. More often the localization of textual norms or their contextual implementation happened outside the textual tradition itself. The commentators' primary interest must be understood to be the correct interpretation of the tradition that preceded them.

[36] Specifically, I have taken my basic understanding of the *dharma* textual tradition from the work of Ludo Rocher and his students Patrick Olivelle and Richard Lariviere. For further delineation of Rocher's views and their elaboration by his students, see my introduction to Ludo Rocher, *Studies in Hindu Law and Dharmaśāstra*, ed. Donald R. Davis, Jr. (Torino: CESMEO, forthcoming). A similar view of the history and development of Hindu law is expressed in U.C. Sarkar, *Epochs in Hindu Legal History* (Hoshiarpur: Vishveshvaranand Vedic Research Institute, 1958).

[37] A.S. Altekar, *Sources of Hindu Dharma in its Socio-religious Aspects* (Sholapur: Institute of Public Administration, 1952); and, more recently, Ashutosh Dayal Mathur, *Medieval Hindu Law: Historical Evolution and Enlightened Rebellion* (Delhi: Oxford University Press, 2007).

[38] The best example to my knowledge is the adaptive reformulation of Dharmaśāstra rules on adoption according to the practice of matriliny in Kerala. See Donald R. Davis, Jr. "Matrilineal Adoption, Inheritance Law, and Rites for the Dead among Hindus in Medieval Kerala." In Steven Lindquist (ed.), *Essays in Honor of Patrick Olivelle* (Firenze: Firenze University Press, forthcoming). New topics, including *satī*, *tīrtha*s, etc., were introduced and expanded in medieval Dharmaśāstra in ways that must correspond to some extent to the new prominence given to such issues in social practice.

If commentators in most cases did not intend to innovate on tradition, we might ask what it is they did intend in and by their work? A complete answer would have to examine the full gamut of scholastic academic traditions in India, traditions that addressed much more than law and religion. Nevertheless, we can say a few things about the models and metaphors that are most appropriate when considering these kinds of scholastic traditions. There are always different instruments or methods to use when trying to understand something. A microscope is objectively a more powerful tool for magnification, but it is much less useful for reading than eyeglasses or a magnifying glass. Similarly, the choice of theoretical and methodological perspective for viewing legal history in India, particularly Hindu law, greatly affects the resulting representation of that history.

What we are looking for is a theoretical framework that shares similar concerns with the Hindu law tradition. In the 1950s, a powerful and productive Marxist historiography developed in studies of India in the work of Kosambi and many others. In the 1980s, the Marxist approach in turn paved the way for the development of Subaltern studies in the work of Guha and others. Both of these, along with broader academic trends such as postcolonialism, have directed attention to the silent and silenced voices of history in an attempt to overcome both great-man and Orientalist histories of earlier generations. The important contributions of these "from below" historical approaches should not be neglected. Indeed, the general approach for the new history of law just described derives its primary inspiration from a similar desire to circumvent the restrictive lens of normative texts without discarding them altogether. At the same time, when one is interested as I am here in the nature and historical valence of those same normative texts, the suitability of a praxis- and subaltern-oriented method may be called into question because these do not share the values and social perspectives of the authors of the texts. As a result, we gain only transgressive readings that purposefully look behind and in between the contents of the text for clues about other matters of interest to the historian. Transgressive readings can yield exciting results, but they do not present us with the whole picture.

Sympathetic readings of the texts can also yield important insights and I want to suggest that an underutilized tradition of political, social, and cultural historiography exists that may be more appropriate to the study of Dharmaśāstra and Hindu law. There is no good label for this tradition,[39]

[39] This list of names will undoubtedly call to some readers' minds the unfortunate name "conservative sociology" for this line of thought, though the label refers more to current politics than to any inherent intellectual commitment.

but its modern intellectual history in Europe may be traced to Burke and, in India, the original Orientalists like Jones and Colebrooke through the work of Hegel, Tocqueville, and Durkheim to the more recent studies of Nisbet, Berger, and Luhmann. Perhaps the fundamental distinction of this line of thought is a commitment to a view that humans are innately and positively embedded in social institutions and traditions that existed before they did. Both society and tradition are reified or substantivized to a great extent in this view. Other features of this view stem from the tangible view of society and tradition.

Nisbet identified five characteristics that sufficiently summarize this view.[40] First, there is an emphasis on community and the positive valuation of belonging to communities as a part of both meaning and aspiration in human life. Family and the associations of civil society are prominent among the communities identified. Second, authority takes precedence over power and assertions of power are viewed with suspicion and severe restriction. Third, status is held to be the most powerful criterion for differentiating individuals within society. Rather than political, legal, religious, or economic distinctions, socially constructed recognitions of honor serve as the basis of status stratifications that determine the self-perception and self-presentation of both individuals and groups. Fourth, ideas of the sacred or the transcendent are held to be the ultimate source of wise tradition and positive prejudice that guide human action. Fifth and finally, alienation is the sense that holding fast to a once-perfect order and tradition inevitably involves loss and degeneration from the ideal. The vision of human progress is here inverted to emphasize rather an unavoidable diminution of humanity over time.

Though these five features are merely illustrative in terms of the detailed arguments of scholars in this tradition, they already suggest a correspondence with fundamental commitments of scholars in the Hindu law tradition. Both share a distrust of the state as an institution prone to corruption and abuses of power, preferring instead to emphasize the ordering capacity of communities and their traditional authority. Both view tradition and social status in substantial, even material, terms, considering other differences between people to be of less consequence. And, both imagine history in terms of a lamentable, but unstoppable, movement away from a primordial, transcendent ideal.

Hindu jurisprudence is fairly obsessed with the integrity and dharmic character of the ruler as the prime instigator of the state. Theologically, the

[40] Robert A. Nisbet, *The Sociological Tradition* (New York: Basic Books, 1966).

state is subordinate as we have seen within the system of castes and life-stages. At the same time, the good state is seen as the guarantor of *dharma* in the world and the only means by which any semblance of *dharma* can be maintained in the current age. Moreover, we have seen that the highest value is placed on tradition for the transmission and integrity of *dharma*, with the system of castes and life-stages being its ideal form. Placement of people within that system is a matter of personal substance, of a status-based and inherited set of traits within people. Finally, the familiar theme of time as loss recurs again and again in Dharmaśāstra and elsewhere in Brahminical traditions. The degenerate current age is precisely a progressive alienation of humanity away from the ideals set forth in the timeless Vedas.

As a whole, therefore, we might read the Hindu law tradition as a theological account of the ordinary life of a proper Hindu, especially a male Brahmin. As the culmination of a long scholarly tradition, that account intends to promote and justify the authority of tradition, to explain and reinforce traditional social status, and to situate human life in communities of livable scope and common interest. At no point in this view do the exigencies of contemporary life, the need to adapt tradition to changed circumstances, or even significant facts of history play an important part in Hindu jurisprudence. The texts recognize such realities, but, according to the principle of alienation, they desperately look more to the past for solutions than to the present or future.

With this very brief review in mind, I am simply arguing that a rich set of theoretical approaches to intellectual and social traditions such as Hindu jurisprudence should include approaches that treat the traditions sympathetically, using presuppositions that mirror or resemble those of the Hindu tradition itself. A largely untapped set of such resources is available, I suggest, in the lineage of thought called by most "conservatism."[41] Though I find the label confusing and prejudicial, I have no better alternative to offer and no expectation that it can be avoided in any case. Moreover, I do not think it will be surprising to any reader of this book that the tradition of Hindu jurisprudence is a "conservative" tradition. The approach to society and history in that tradition offers us a way to sympathetically understand the Hindu tradition in a way that makes its own self-presentation seem less remote or foreign.

In summary, the future of legal history on India should begin from dated historical evidence of legal practice, from the level conceptually identified

[41] I trust readers to kindly distinguish personal politics from intellectual inquiry.

in the Indian materials as *ācāra*. The collocation and the comparative interpretation of that evidence should be understood as the piecing together of different witnesses to the same history of law, each witness bringing its own biases, elisions, and agendas. Only after sorting out and adjudging the value of each witness with respect to a given historical context or issue, can the best possible description of law emerge. In some cases, Dharmaśāstra may be an excellent historical witness. In others, it may be terrible. The same goes for epigraphy, temple records, other textual genres, and foreign accounts. Together, however, the variegated sources have the potential to produce both a plausible account of legal history in India and the basis for even wider comparative legal history beyond the permeable cultural zone of India or South Asia. Furthermore, when the normative texts are re-read in the light of a history that does not tautologically depend upon them, that re-reading should be both transgressive and sympathetic, incorporating not only insights from subaltern views, but also views that link the hermeneutics of the Hindu legal texts with current intellectual horizons that similarly emphasize tradition, community, and authority.

# *Conclusion*

Comparison exposes us to the mistrust born of similarity without familiarity. The dangers and fears involved in discovering similarities that are not yet familiar lie at the root of tremendous human suffering. Similarity undermines hierarchy and discrimination; it thwarts power by exposing the weaknesses of power's ideological bases. Comparison by its nature should begin from a flash of similarity. Otherwise, there seems little point in selecting things to compare. Without a basis in similarity, the process of comparison becomes what it so often does in scholarship: a litany of differences accompanied by the relief of continued strangeness. The salves of relativism and pluralism have been applied to justify accommodation without comparison, but these have rarely been fully satisfying in the face of myriad points of sameness and connection. I do not insist that all is one, that everything is the same deep down, because looking for or presupposing similarity poses an equal risk of perennialism. Still, it is easier to see difference than commonality for the former is assumed while the latter must be shown when it comes to culture, religion, history, and language.

Comparative legal scholarship has moved from a phase in which categories of Common and Civil law dominated the descriptions of legal systems in Africa, Asia, and America[1] to a phase in which even basic categories such as law, trial, court, crime, verdict, etc., were held to be

[1] The benchmark for modern comparative legal history is Henry Sumner Maine, *Ancient Law: Its Connection with the Early History of Society and its Relation to Modern Ideas*, 10th edn (London: John Murray, 1906 [1861]). Maine's work exemplifies an evolutionary model of legal development in which characteristics of distinct phases in legal development are listed and compared along a scale from primitive to modern. Quite different in tone and approach is Montesquieu, *The Spirit of the Laws*, trans. and ed. Anne M. Cohler, Basia C. Miller, and Harold S. Stone (Cambridge: Cambridge University Press, 1989). Montesquieu's approach depends upon a deep connection between law and place and law and culture. Still, his descriptions of differences between Indian, Chinese, Egyptian, and Arab laws (insofar as he could know about them) are compared to equally wide differences between Gothic, German, Roman, Greek, and Common laws. Montesquieu thus appeals to descriptive terms of art (monarchy, contract, penal law, etc.) to enable a certain amount of mutual critique of the systems he examines.

inappropriate or unhelpful in understanding "non-centralized" or "non-state-based" legal systems.[2] The corrective provided by the latter approach coming out of legal anthropology – as important as it was in its time – has nevertheless not altered the continuing marginalization of non-Euro-American legal systems in discussions of law and legal theory. Basically, law school students, professors, and those interested in legal history have not been convinced that this stuff is relevant to them. The earlier phase attracted some interest from mainstream legal scholarship[3] but at the cost of severe distortions in the representation of comparative legal systems. The later phase corrected the distortions by attending to the linguistic, conceptual, historical, and political specificities of law in context, but, in so doing, argued implicitly or explicitly for the incompatibility and incommensurability of "law" and whatever it was that people in Africa, Asia, and America did.

The time has come for the pendulum to swing back. We should not be afraid to engage with the deep and rich legacy of legal language emanating from traditions of law found in Europe and America. At the same time, we must also not be afraid to insist that the formulations of even central legal concepts found in Euro-American scholarship are not hegemonic and irrefutable gospel. The model here is one of mutual modulation, the process of refining and rethinking categories that arises whenever different languages and semiotic systems are brought into comparative perspective.[4] Put simply, Hindu jurisprudence must be allowed to challenge current understandings of law, if a convincing case can be made that something important is revealed in the comparison. The same would go for any such comparison and for the understanding in turn of Hindu law itself. In comparison, nothing is immune from revision. The

[2] The classic rejection of law as an analytic category is Paul Bohannan, *Justice and Judgment among the Tiv* (Prospect Heights, IL: Waveland, 1989 [1957]). For Bohannan, law is "the 'folk system' of the English-speaking countries for dealing with their own institutions and ideas of social control" (p. 5). More nuanced is John L. Comaroff and Simon Roberts, *Rules and Processes: The Cultural Logic of Dispute in an African Context* (Chicago: University of Chicago Press, 1981). Comaroff and Roberts reaffirm "existing doubts about the value of distinguishing 'the legal' as a discrete field of inquiry" (p. 243) but also suggest "a variety of ways in which the analysis of the Tswana system can illuminate our understanding of arrangements in other societies" (p. 246).

[3] I think here of the Legal Realists interest in "primitive law." Llewellyn, for instance, set the kind of example for which I am advocating in his collaborative work with Hoebel. See Karl N. Llewellyn and E. Adamson Hoebel, *The Cheyenne Way: Conflict and Case Law in Primitive Jurisprudence* (Norman: University of Oklahoma, 1941).

[4] Jacob Neusner, "Judaism in the History of Religions." In James S. Helfer (ed.), *On Method in the History of Religions* (Middletown: Wesleyan University Press, 1968) discusses the issue in the context of religious studies.

problem has been, in fact, that immunity has been given to views of law that seem now so natural and obvious as to be indisputable, even though those views have a relatively recent historical origin and mixed pedigree theoretically.

The history of Hindu law studies has by and large been a history of listing differences and of providing justifications to show that Hindu law is just as sophisticated as any other legal system.[5] In large part, this tendency may be attributed to the real-world implications of the early studies of Hindu law. The fact that the early Orientalists' translations of Dharmaśāstra and their opinions about the applicability of Hindu law were paramount in actual legal cases made it essential to differentiate Hindu law from English law. The real-world consequences continued to the end of colonial rule in India and, to some extent, beyond as well. The misunderstandings, reductionism, and distortions introduced by the British administration of what they called "Hindu law" have been well documented.[6] For my argument here, however, the key point is that the political and practical interests and agendas at the origins of Hindu law studies outside of India have obscured and thwarted the humanistic engagement with the deeper ideas and history of the tradition.

In other words, the once pressing "need" to know the details of Hindu law for the sake of a "non-intrusive" colonial administration has put us in the habit of only learning *about* Hindu law, and not *from* it. The main purpose of this book has been to describe key conceptual ideas of Hindu jurisprudence in a way that allows us to begin to learn from the Hindu thinking about law. The resulting knowledge is not of the immediate, practical kind and will likely not enhance the efficacy of what is now administered and applied today as modern Hindu law in India and elsewhere. Rather, the descriptions of Hindu law in this book were meant to reveal understudied questions about legal systems everywhere and to provide an account of some Hindu answers to those questions.

[5] Many of the best studies by Indian scholars in the early twentieth century are motivated in part or in whole by the latter concern. For example, Priyanath Sen, *The General Principles of Hindu Jurispridence* (Calcutta: University of Calcutta, 1918), p. 38: "I do not, of course, mean to assert that Hindu Jurisprudence was in all respects as perfect as one could desire, but I hope to be able to show that, in the main, it will not compare unfavourably with even the most developed system of ancient Jurisprudence, the Roman."

[6] Bernard Cohn, "Law and the Colonial State in India." In J. Starr and J.F. Collier (eds.), *History and Power in the Study of Law* (Ithaca: Cornell University Press, 1989); Richard W. Lariviere, "Justices and Paṇḍitas: Some Ironies in Contemporary Readings of the Hindu Legal Past," *Journal of Asian Studies* 48:4 (1989): 757–69.

## THE SPIRIT OF HINDU LAW: A SUMMARY

In each chapter, I have tried to show how certain key theological conceptualizations and commitments of the authors of Dharmaśāstra have been worked out through a reflection on the implication of those commitments in ordinary life. The Hindu concept of law – and, I have argued, of law itself – emerges from this application of theology to ordinary life.

The expansive quality of *dharma* in Dharmaśāstra immediately challenged narrow conceptualizations of law as only connected to state institutions, courts, and legislatures. Furthermore, *dharma*'s connection to the household and family shifted the focus of law to perhaps the most ordinary of social locations. The Hindu tradition here reminds us that some conceptual and practical advantages emerge when law is not axiomatically sequestered from the business of ordinary life.

Within this far-reaching notion of *dharma*, we examined first the idea of *pramāṇa*, one of several terms for the sources of *dharma*, or how we may know it. The three main sources and their hierarchical relation to one another suggested collectively that law's authority depends upon the progressive elimination of choice in human action. It is a key task of law to eliminate choices that for reasons of history, culture, or politics are viewed as destabilizing, unnecessary, inappropriate, or even dangerous. Law presents rather a rhetorical ethos, the acceptance of which entails both the restrictions imposed by and the freedoms enabled by a reduction of the kinds of choices we can make in everyday life.

That reduction of choice does not eliminate the ongoing need for law to develop through time and to deal with ruptures in the order imagined by and established through law. Mīmāṃsā teaches us that law in its fullest sense emerges only after hermeneutical interpretation and the subordination of law to an ethical good. Hermeneutics, too, strives to eliminate the potentially endless choices presented in ordinary life about how to act by fixing both principles and details about the most important aspects of human action. The standard of judgment about these principles and details, whether explicit or not, is an ethical good in the mind of those faced with moments of decision and real choice. In the Hindu tradition, that ethical good is consistently identified with the system of castes and life-stages (*varṇāśramadharma*), the default notion of *dharma* underlying all of Dharmaśāstra.

Substantively, Hindu law focuses first on the idea of *ṛṇa*, both the specific and general debts that human beings owe congenitally and contractually to one another. The pervasive and paradigmatic role of debt in Hindu jurisprudence makes a claim that law defines and recognizes certain roles of law as being just as important as the rules of law. People find recognition and protection in the law through their assumption of legally recognized roles. Those roles in turn enable a host of otherwise chaotic human endeavors to have structure and purpose.

These various roles of indebtedness are complemented in Hindu jurisprudence by a notion that the material objects that humans use, create, and possess embody and concretize legally idealized human relationships through the recognition of *svatva*, property and ownership. *Svatva* confirms for us, on the one hand, the uncomfortable truth that property tends to reinforce intransigent inequities and perpetuate exploitative social relations encoded into the rules and roles of law. At the same time, property in the Hindu view insists, on the other hand, that all people have an inalienable ownership stake in the material world of which they can never be fully dispossessed. The ethical claim of the latter view provides at least some check on the unbridled continuation of the former.

In every sphere of substantive engagement with the law, conflicts, disagreements, and uncertainties regularly appear. The idea of *vyavahāra* is the Hindu solution to such problems in the domain of *dharma*. As the province of the ruler, *vyavahāra* offers a set of real world procedures for managing a system premised on underlying theological and transcendental connections. In the end, legal procedure in Hindu jurisprudence teaches us that real justice is to be found only through the conflictual, but necessary liminality between tradition and reason. In this liminal social position, *vyavahāra* holds fast to both a deontological idea of justice as fairness and a contextually constructed idea of justice as an ethical virtue.

The result of a legal procedure is almost always *daṇḍa*, punishment in one of several forms. Apart from its deterrent and sometimes retributive effects, punishment also permits *dharma* to exist in the world at all in two distinct ways. First, *daṇḍa*, as another of the ruler's *dharma*s, acts as the worldly means for *dharma* to enter the mundane world. It is the essence of the ruler's idealized realm (*rājya*) and the practical guarantor of *dharma*'s observance and preservation. Second, *daṇḍa* permits mistakes in the worldly zone of *dharma* it has made possible. Every legal and religious system needs a mechanism for expiation, for repairing tears in the fabric of legal order. *Daṇḍa* is that mechanism in Hindu law. Punishment is very often viewed in terms of its capacity to thwart threats to the state's dominion and to inflict pain on transgressors of the legally imagined social order. Without denying the value of this view, we should also remind ourselves of the positive effects of punishment to permit and define the existence of the state in the first place and to allow failures of many kinds within the legal order to be repaired at the levels of the individual, community, and society at large.

Finally, the picture of Hindu law presented by these seven concepts derives from the realm of legal imagination or legal cosmology as given in the Dharmaśāstra texts. The important question of legal practice is somewhat remote, though not entirely separate, from this textual realm. The texts themselves do provide their own take on legal practice by recognizing *ācāra*, customary law or community standards, as integral to the ongoing life of the law on the ground. Here, the texts point to a world of lawmaking and legal institutions that goes well beyond what they describe. The texts recognize and validate *ācāra* as a legitimate source of *dharma*, but stop short of entering into the details of practical historical legal systems. As a result, if we are concerned with the *history* of Hindu law in practice, then we cannot begin from a study of Dharmaśāstra, but rather from whatever historical evidence we may be able to find of *ācāra*.

Other concepts might have been chosen, but I believe the eight selected give the proper emphasis to the various actors, processes, and ideas of Hindu law given in the texts. Among the concepts that could have been addressed, the first is the idea of *varṇāśramadharma*, the system of castes and life-stages. There is more to be said about the integrity of this specific notion, but its fundamental premises are encoded in the idea of *dharma* itself as described in Dharmaśāstra. In this way, the idea appears throughout this work as the main underlying notion to be understood whenever *dharma* is invoked in Hindu law. Another important idea that might have merited a chapter of its own is that of *prāyaścitta*, or penance, that I addressed in some detail in Chapter 6. Penance formed an early pillar of the full explication of *dharma* and, therefore, could be viewed as essential to the spirit of the tradition. Huge sections of Dharmaśāstra are devoted to the topic and intimate its importance. Still, its role seems related to and often subordinated to *daṇḍa* in my view, hence its description in that chapter.

Finally, some might question my somewhat oblique treatment of the figure of the ruler or king within Dharmaśāstra. My primary reason for not giving *rājadharma*, the duties of a ruler, separate consideration is my conviction that previous studies of Hindu law, particularly those of Lingat and Derrett, have placed too much focus on the ruler and his role in the Hindu legal imagination and in the practice of Hindu law for which we have evidence. The ruler appears regularly here under the heading of other concepts and is indeed, along with the Brahmin, a centrally identified actor in the spirit of Hindu law. At the same time, both of these figures seem to me structural parts of the system of castes and life-stages, the explanation of which in Chapter 1 sufficiently shows the prominent positions of these two ideal figures. Within that structure, of course, the historical agency of Brahmins and rulers both constituted and deviated from the norms expressed in Dharmaśāstra. To think of Dharmaśāstra in terms that make it into a code, however, risks serious misunderstanding of the issue of text and practice Hindu law as described in Chapter 3.

Together, the eight concepts give us a solid framework through which to understand the spirit of Hindu law and to make a case for law as the theology of ordinary life. However, as we saw in the previous chapter on *ācāra*, it is quite possible, perhaps even necessary, that we also consider the opposite formulation of this thesis, namely that religion is the legalization of extraordinary life or the transcendent. The expression is admittedly awkward but reveals an important process at the heart of religious institution-building. The institutions of religion attempt to capture and to translate the transcendent, out-of-the-ordinary experiences of religious life into repeatable rituals, ethical and moral rules, and processes for atonement or rectification – all characteristics of legalization. There is a chicken-and-egg problem here, but we might obviate a search for origins by simply acknowledging that both processes must have been at work at the same time and both demonstrate the inextricable connection of religion and law in India, and perhaps elsewhere. If we imagine religion to be the product of placing rule-based limits on extraordinary experience, worship, belief, persons, objects, and events, then we must acknowledge that in some cases acts of legalization preceded and formed the basis for religious ideas and institutions. Conversely, viewed from the angle of law, the theological placing of ordinary actions in a framework of transcendent religious significance occurs through the specification of the how, when, why, and what in the form of legal rules. Stated simply, law makes the extraordinary humanly manageable; religion makes the ordinary humanly purposeful.[7]

## CRITICISMS OF CLASSICAL HINDU LAW

Having presented a summary of the spirit of Hindu law, it seems worthwhile to reflect for a moment on weaknesses of its jurisprudence and criticisms that might be made of its legal imaginings. There are many criticisms

[7] Compare John Witte, Jr., "Introduction." In J. Witte, Jr. and F.S. Alexander (eds.), *Christianity and Law: An Introduction* (Cambridge: Cambridge University Press, 2008), p. 1: "[R]eligion

that might be made, but I want to focus on only one significant weakness. In this connection, I have found the work of Hannah Arendt helpful in identifying certain blindspots in the Hindu view of law in relation to larger questions of humanity, justice, and equality. Consider first the following quotations:

> One of the surprising aspects of our experience with stateless people who benefit legally from committing a crime has been the fact that it seems easier to deprive a completely innocent person legality than someone who has committed an offense ... the deprivation of legality, i.e. of *all* rights, no longer has a connection with specific crimes ... The calamity of the rightless is ... that they no longer belong to any community whatsoever. Their plight is not that they are not equal before the law, but that no law exists for them.
>
> The crimes against human rights ... can always be justified by the pretext that right is equivalent to being good or useful for the whole in distinction to its parts ... A conception of law which identifies what is right with the notion of what is good – for the individual, or the family, or the people, or the largest number – becomes inevitable once the absolute and transcendent measurements of religion or the law of nature have lost their authority.[8]

Arendt's studies of the plight of stateless persons in relation to the law points to the most significant shortcoming of classical Hindu law. By emphasizing the ethical goods of the Veda and of *varṇāśramadharma*, classical Hindu jurisprudence measures the worth of individuals against those standards, in the hierarchical manner so familiarly associated with India.[9] In so doing, what we today consider to be fundamental rights of human existence could be, as in totalitarian regimes, suppressed with little ideological dissonance. More specifically, lower castes were denied status within the scheme either of the Vedic world or of the *dharma*s of caste and life-stage. Lower castes had no rights (*adhikāra*) in those domains. Without legal status, these groups could have no voice and no standing from which to effect changes and improvements to their condition, at least within the system.

It is telling that within Hindu jurisprudence, little or no law is described for lower castes. From the perspective of Dharmaśāstra, these lower castes approximate the status of Arendt's "stateless persons." According to this system (not the only one to be sure), they belong to no clear community and, therefore, have little or no law or legal protection.

gives law its spirit and inspires adherence to ritual and justice. Law give religion its structure and encourages its devotion to order and organization."

[8] Hannah Arendt, *The Portable Hannah Arendt*, ed. Peter Baehr (New York: Penguin, 2000), pp. 36, 40.

[9] The classic work on hierarchy in India is Louis Dumont, *Homo Hierarchicus: The Caste System and Its Implications*, trans. Mark Sainsbury, Louis Dumont, and Basia Gulati (Chicago: University of Chicago Press, 1980).

Thus, the main criticism to be leveled against traditional Hindu law is its failure to incorporate a balancing sense of right, to counter its emphasis on a narrowly defined sense of what is good. Intimations of this balance are found in the notion of "common *dharmas*" (*sādhāraṇadharma*) and the fundamental moral values they portray. But, Dharmaśāstra provides few, if any, means of bringing such values into judicial contexts. As such, the system is basically rigged to relegate certain groups of people to a non-legal, anomic, and community-less existence.

The retort to this criticism would certainly begin by invoking the flip-side of Arendt's point, namely that human rights cannot be delivered or guaranteed outside the context of a living human community of practicable scale and with real institutions. Dharmaśāstra provides or at least recognizes this context, even if it merely reflects its historical age in denying to lower classes the same rights and privileges of upper classes. What jurisprudence of its antiquity did not do the same?

The description of classical Hindu law as lacking a concept of legality analyzed in Chapter 5 makes an implicit, though perhaps unintended, claim that no one had legal rights because no centralized political state existed. Similarly, Arendt argues that claims of human rights outside the context of national states are doomed to failure and actually produce worse consequences for stateless persons. Limited to the modern world, the argument appears sound, but the argument for classical India pertains to a political situation that is notably distinct. Legality was for the most part defined by and enforced by intermediate communities in medieval India. As such, legal protections were provided by those communities, and only rarely by the militarily superior state in a region.

Nevertheless, the systematic presentation of the spirit of Hindu law found in Dharmaśāstra is hardly concerned to ensure that all people find legal protection and political security. In fact, the opposite seems true. People of lower castes, non-Hindu communities, and foreigners are more or less relegated to a position of legal agnosticism, a kind of we-don't-care-what-*you*-people-do attitude. Halbfass has written incisively on the fundamental ethnocentrism and exclusivism encoded in the orthodox discussions of *dharma*.[10] To deny these aspects of *dharma*'s formulation in Hindu legal texts would remove a central feature of what its authors seem to intend by writing them, namely a cogent presentation of what may be properly called orthodox Hinduism. Dharmaśāstra provides a theology

[10] Wilhelm Halbfass, *India and Europe: An Essay in Philosophical Understanding* (Albany: SUNY Press, 1988), pp. 172ff.

of householder Hinduism that defines clear boundaries of what a good Hindu life should look like, and law plays a prominent role in that theology. Moreover, that life is concerned with both status and substance in such a way that many people in the world are effectively not even eligible to participate in the fullness of the Hindu life that unfolds in the *dharma* tradition.

In this exclusiveness, I find nothing outrageous or unexpected given the time period in and during which the tradition began and developed. Every religious tradition of the ancient world had similar theologies. Moreover, in the recent history of Hinduism, Hindu theologians of various persuasions have increasingly emphasized precisely that balancing sense of right that early Hindu traditions played down. In other words, Hindu theology has developed an even more subtle notion of *dharma* that incorporates an explicit and strong appeal to fixity, naturalness, and foundational moral truth.[11]

Other criticisms of Hindu law may surely be found and argued. The scholastic nature of the Hindu legal texts, for example, highlights the lack of systematic practical legal rules and promulgation that can often afford greater protection of individual rights and consistency in legal processes over a certain area. I have generally avoided the question of practice in this work, primarily because complex arguments for the relationship of Dharmaśāstra and legal practice have been made elsewhere and referred to in the previous chapter.

When we ask instead about the spirit of Hindu law, however, it seems incumbent upon us to start with ideas that are compelling and attractive to a modern reader interested in law and religion. This perspective and attitude motivated both the structure and the content of this work. Rather than end on criticism, therefore, I will conclude with a few observations about the beauty of Hindu law.

## ON THE BEAUTY OF HINDU LAW

In order to both describe and justify the search for beauty in the Hindu law tradition, we might begin with Gadamer's suggestion that "legal hermeneutics serves to remind us what the real procedure of the human sciences is."[12] The manner in which a judge or lawyer must be both legal historian

[11] For example, see the expansive and universalized notion of *dharma* in Sarvepalli Radhakrishnan, *The Hindu View of Life* (London: George Allen & Unwin, 1927).

[12] Hans-Georg Gadamer, *Truth and Method*, 2nd rev. edn, trans. Joel Weinsheimer (New York: Continuum, 1989), p. 327.

and logical jurist in order to find solutions to legal problems in the present strikes Gadamer as the most tangible model for humanistic engagement with texts and ideas of the past. Gadamer is concerned to demonstrate the manifold ways in which our reading of texts from the past in conjunction with our prejudices and "foreunderstanding" of ideas serves to give us a consciousness of the present that is forged both by and through history. He wants to universalize the act of hermeneutics as the unavoidable and essential activity of a knowing humanity.

The texts of Hindu law, the Dharmaśāstra, doubly fulfill and exemplify Gadamer's thesis. First, at a direct level, the Hindu law tradition appropriated and developed its own hermeneutical system to accomplish that very same task of making tradition alive in the present. At this level, Hindu legal hermeneutics, like legal interpretation generally, helps us "distinguish what is truly common to all forms of hermeneutics: the meaning to be understood is concretized and fully realized only in interpretation, but the interpretive activity considers itself wholly bound by the meaning of the text."[13] The activities and texts produced by scholars and commentators in the Hindu tradition grapple exactly with this dilemma of stating the meaning of earlier texts under circumstances and with prejudices that may have greatly affected the application of ideas and rules. Readers of Dharmaśāstra must attend to the intricacies of its hermeneutical principles and presuppositions in order to understand and describe the Hindu legal imagination at work.

But, second, what the modern *mere* historian of Hindu law has perpetuated is the idea that "it is fundamentally impossible for him to regard himself as the addressee of the text and accept its claim on him."[14] Modern historians have instead distanced themselves from the ideas of the Hindu texts: both *that's what* THEY *used to do* and *that's what they* USED *to do*. Gadamer shows us a way forward from or out of this position and its often distorting entailments.[15] Within Dharmaśāstra, we can find legal hermeneutics at work, but outside of it, we are forced to ask whether the texts can and should have any meaning or relevance for us today. Following this line of thought, therefore, I have made a case for certain lessons of the old Hindu law texts that can impact our present ways of thinking – and should. I have tried to accept the Dharmaśāstra's claim to address

[13] *Ibid.*, p. 332. [14] *Ibid.*, p. 335.

[15] Compare Edward Said, *Humanism and Democratic Criticism* (New York: Columbia University Press, 2004).

even me and us and to explore what that acceptance might mean for an understanding of law and religion.

The most important and most beautiful thing I have learned from the Hindu tradition is the value of thinking about law in close connection to both religion and ordinary life. So many studies of law presume a strong measure of state control, a separation of legal and religious life, and a yawning chasm between court and home. It has become natural to associate and limit law to the activities of courts and legislatures. Even otherwise fascinating studies fall victim to the pitfalls of these presuppositions.[16]

It was, for instance, this kind of mistaken restriction that led Huizinga to connect law and play in his classic *Homo Ludens*. For Huizinga, all play is "a stepping out of 'real' life into a temporary sphere of activity with a disposition all of its own."[17] In this view, law resembles play because it is a contest in which the outcome is either winning or losing.[18] Abstract notions of justice and of right and wrong are all later cultural accretions. It is no accident that Huizinga focuses on litigation, ordeals, and judicial wagers to illustrate the law's resemblance to play. I have no quarrel with the comparison in these areas, but rather with the artificial line drawn around those domains as somehow the full extent of law's role in human life. As we have seen, extracting law conceptually from ordinary life leads to a crass instrumentalism in which law becomes a mere tool for the real work of culture. Huizinga's restriction of law, however, actually reveals how deeply embedded law is in everyday life, because law's play-like elements are exposed as such a small piece of its larger presence in society. Moreover, the agonistic, rule-based play of litigation, ordeals, and wagers is itself a distillation and recreation of the play of life itself, in which the rules become more technical, intense, and conscious. Therefore, to argue that law, like play, necessitates placing oneself outside "real life" involves the concomitant claim that law is defined solely by litigation and other judicial activities. This view impoverishes our understanding of law

[16] For instance, Marci Hamilton, *God vs. the Gavel: Religion and the Rule of Law* (New York: Cambridge University Press, 2005) is a trenchant and provocative critique of the evil and criminal actions undertaken in the name of religion in contemporary America. Presumed throughout, however, is a distinction between religion and law and between law and ordinary life that Hamilton takes to be the natural state of things, an unquestionable, or at least unquestioned, truth. The view presented here does not undermine Hamilton's argument, least of all by suggesting that religion is good by default. Instead, what most legal studies of religion need is a more nuanced understanding of religion and greater openness to the workings of law in ordinary life.

[17] Johan Huizinga, *Homo Ludens: A Study of the Play-Element in Culture*, trans. R.F.C. Hull (London: Routledge, 1949), p. 8.

[18] *Ibid.*, p. 78.

in general, even as it provides insight into certain aspects of law's place in formal litigation.

The point of this digression on Huizinga's connection of law and play is to lay bare the pervasiveness of limiting law to the work of courts and legislatures. In one way, the post-French Revolution period of Euro-American legal history is the story of progressively restricting law to precisely the court and the legislature, two domains controlled by the state. What so many scholars who study legal pluralism, religious law, or legal anthropology have shown, however, is that while this narrative has worked effectively in terms of how many people understand law conceptually, it has also hidden the reality of plural legal orders, alternative normative regimes, and religious or traditional self-appropriations of law's creative, coordinating, good-producing potential. Hindu law, by contrast, calls all of this *dharma* and we would be well served to ask what might be gained by calling it all law as well.

Hindu law, moreover, demands an engagement with "real life," an acceptance of the very ordinariness of life that Huizinga wants to sequester away from legal contexts. Law is more than the breakdown of normativity or the restoration of a legal equilibrium through punishment, the situations imagined by the Hindu legal terms *vyavahāra* and *prāyaścitta*, respectively. Law is also, and more often, the routine performance of normativity – people obeying the law – signaled in Hindu jurisprudence by the term *ācāra*.

In the context of modern secular legal systems, the idea that law pervades human life sounds intrusive, even dangerous. And, in this era of rights-talk, democracy, and appropriate limitations on governmental power, there are good reasons to maintain also a view of law that has boundaries, because of the close and potentially exploitative connection of law and the state. The need for limitations on the law relates also to the professionalization of law in recent centuries, a shift that also requires that the law has manageable practical boundaries. Nevertheless, even if good reasons exist for a more narrow view of law, equally good reasons also exist for maintaining a contrary view of law that is pervasive, in which normative regimes of many varieties are accommodated and juxtaposed under the heading of law. Religious legal systems such as Hindu law remind us that legal, or at least law-like, processes and institutions function in even the most ordinary of human contexts, that law is not necessarily the sole province of the state, and that law enables human flourishing as much as it constrains human vice.

The beauty of Hindu law lies in the reorientation to law that the tradition's emphases put into play. First, the tradition insists that law knows no bounds, that everything in human life is part of law's scope. Law's domain is coextensive with life itself. *Dharma* is a collection of duties and rules that affect and are expected of everyone and, in some views, of everything as well. From this emphasis in Hindu law, we glean the intimate connection of law and ordinary life. But, the tradition, secondly, reverses the usual description of law as an institution that merely controls human behavior by describing law rather as primarily an institution that makes human flourishing possible. That notion of flourishing entails the teleology described throughout this book, a promulgation of the system of castes and life-stages as the ideal framework for the full realization of human potential. The systemic goal toward which Hindu law works in turn theologically privileges the household and the family as the central social locations of law's religious effects.

In the end, what we learn comparatively from the lessons of Hindu law is that, whatever else law may be in part, it is also the theology of ordinary life. In addition to the reorientations toward law just described, this formulation challenges any conception of religion as being demarcated solely by what is otherworldly and ultimate, because such views give little room for the application of religious ideas to ordinary life. The final conclusion of this study, therefore, can be stated as follows: whenever and wherever a set of religious or theological questions (and I mean the big ones like: what does it mean to be fully human? What is the place of humanity in the world? What is the meaning of life?) are asked in relation to the actions of daily life, the response and the result is invariably that special configuration of norms, institutions, rhetoric, and ritual that we call law.

# *Bibliography*

PRIMARY WORKS IN SANSKRIT, BY TITLE


*Baudhāyanadharmasūtra*. In Olivelle, *Dharmasūtras*.

*Bṛhadāraṇyaka Upaniṣad*. In *The Early Upaniṣads*. Ed. and trans. Patrick Olivelle. New York: Oxford University Press, 1998.

*Daṇḍaviveka of Vardhamāna Upadhyāya*. Trans. Bhabhatosh Bhattacharya. Calcutta: The Asiatic Society, 1973.

*Dharmakośa. Vyavahārakāṇḍa*. Ed. Laxman Shastri Joshi. Wai: Prājña Pāṭhaśaḷā Maṇḍala, 1937–41.

*Gautamadharmasūtra*. In Olivelle, *Dharmasūtras*.

*Mānavadharmaśāstra*. Ed. and trans. Patrick Olivelle, *Manu's Code of Law*.

*Manusmṛti with the Manubhāṣya of Medhātithi*. Ed. and trans. Ganganatha Jha. 10 Vols. Delhi: Motilal Banarsidass, 1999 [1920–39].

*Mīmāṃsānyāyaprakāśa of Apadeva*. Ed. and trans. Franklin Edgerton. New Haven: Yale University Press, 1929.

*Mīmāṃsānyāyasaṃgraha (A Compendium of the Principles of Mīmāṃsā) by Mahādeva Vedāntin*. Ed. and trans. James Benson. Wiesbaden: Harrassowitz, forthcoming.

*Nāradasmṛti*. Ed. and trans. Richard W. Lariviere. 2nd edn. Delhi: Motilal Banarsidass.

*Sarasvatīvilāsa: Vyavahārakāṇḍaḥ*. Ed. R. Shama Shastry. Univ. of Mysore Oriental Library Pubs. Sanskrit Series No. 71. Mysore: Gov't Branch Press, 1927.

*Smṛticandrikā of Devaṇabhaṭṭa*. Ed. L. Srinivasacharya, Vyavahārakāṇḍa. Vol. 3. Part 2. Gov't Oriental Library Series. Bibliotheca Sanskrita No. 44. Mysore: Gov't Branch Press, 1914.

*Tantravārttika of Kumārila*. Trans. Ganganatha Jha. Delhi: Sri Satguru, 1983 [1903–24].

*Vasiṣṭha-Dharmasūtra*. In Olivelle, *Dharmasūtras*.

*Vyavahāracintāmaṇi of Vācaspati Miśra. A Digest on Hindu Legal Procedure*. Ed. and trans. Ludo Rocher. Gent: University of Gent, 1956.

*Yājñavalkyasmṛti with the Mitākṣarā of Vijñāneśvara*. Ed. Narayan Ram Acharya. Delhi: Nag, 1985.

SECONDARY WORKS

Abel Richard L. (ed.) *The Law & Society Reader*. New York: New York University Press, 1995.

Alexander, Frank S. "Property and Christian Theology." In *Christianity and Law: an Introduction*, eds. J. Witte, Jr. and F. S. Alexander. Cambridge: Cambridge University Press, 2008.

Altekar, A. S. *Sources of Hindu Dharma in its Socio-religious Aspects*. Sholapur: Institute of Public Administration, 1952.

Arendt, Hannah. *The Portable Hannah Arendt*, ed. Peter Baehr. New York: Penguin, 2000.

Aristotle. *Nicomachean Ethics*. 2nd edn. Trans. Terence Irwin. Indianapolis: Hackett, 1999.

Ball, Milner S. *The Word and the Law*. Chicago: University of Chicago Press, 1995.

Beccaria. *On Crimes and Punishments and Other Writings*, trans. Richard Davies, ed. Richard Bellamy. New York: Cambridge University Press, 1995.

Benjamin, Walter. "Critique of Violence." In *Reflections: Essays, Aphorism, Autobiographical Writings*, trans. Edmund Jephcott, ed. with an intro. Peter Demetz. New York: Harcourt, Brace, and Jovanovich, 1978 [1921], pp. 277–300.

Berger, Peter. "Sociology and Freedom," *The American Sociologist* **6** (1971): 1–5.

Berman, Harold J. *Law and Revolution: The Formation of the Western Legal Tradition*. Cambridge: Harvard University Press, 1983.

"Toward an Integrative Jurisprudence: Politics, Morality, and History," *California Law Review* **76** (1988): 779–801.

Bohannan, Paul. *Justice and Judgment among the Tiv*. Prospect Heights, IL: Waveland Press, 1989 [1957].

Bourdieu, Pierre. "The Force of Law: Toward a Sociology of the Juridical Field," *Hastings Law Journal* **38** (1986–7): 814–53.

Bowles, Adam. *Dharma, Disorder, and the Political in Ancient India: The Āpaddharmaparvan of the Mahābhārata*. Leiden: Brill, 2007.

Brick, David. "Transforming Tradition into Texts: The Early Development of Smṛti," *Journal of Indian Philosophy* **34** (2006): 287–302.

Buitenen, J. A. B. van. "On the Archaism of the *Bhāgavata-Purāṇa*." In *Kṛṣṇa: Myths, Rites, and Attitudes*, ed. Milton Singer. Chicago: University of Chicago Press, 1966.

Carmichael, Calum. *The Spirit of Biblical Law*. Athens: University of Georgia Press, 1996.

Certeau, Michel de. *The Practice of Everyday Life*, trans. S. Rendall. Berkeley: University of California Press, 1984.

Chatterjee Śāstri, Heramba. *The Law of Debt in Ancient India*. Calcutta: Sanskrit College, 1971.

Clooney, Francis X. "Jaimini's Contribution to the Theory of Sacrifice as the Experience of Transcendence," *History of Religions* **25**(3) (1986): 199–212.

"Why the Veda Has No Author: Language as Ritual in Early Mimamsa and Post-Modern Theology," *Journal of the American Academy of Religion* **55**(4) (1987): 659–84.

*Thinking Ritually: Rediscovering the Pūrva Mīmāṃsā of Jaimini*. Vienna: De Nobili, 1990.

Cohen, Abraham. *Everyman's Talmud: The Major Teachings of the Rabbinic Sages*. New York: Schocken, 1995 [1949].

Cohen, David. *Law, Violence and Community in Classical Athens*. New York: Cambridge University Press, 1995.

Cohn, Bernard. "Law and the Colonial State in India." In *History and Power in the Study of Law*, eds. J. Starr and J. F. Collier. Ithaca: Cornell University Press, 1989.

Comaroff, John L. and Simon Roberts. *Rules and Processes: the Cultural Logic of Dispute in an African Context*. Chicago: University of Chicago Press, 1981.

Cover, Robert M. "Foreword: *Nomos* and Narrative," *Harvard Law Review* **97** (1983–4): 4–68.

"Violence and the Word," *Yale Law Journal* **95** (1985–6): 1601–29.

Das, Veena. *Life and Words: Violence and the Descent into the Ordinary*. Berkeley: University of California Press, 2006.

Davis, Jr., Donald R. "Recovering the Indigenous Legal Traditions of India: Classical Hindu Law in Practice in Late Medieval Kerala," *Journal of Indian Philosophy* **27**(3) (1999): 159–213.

"Being Hindu or Being Human: a Reappraisal of the puruṣārthas," *International Journal of Hindu Studies* **8**(1–3) (2004): 1–27.

*The Boundaries of Hindu Law: Tradition, Custom, and Politics in Medieval Kerala*. Corpus Iuris Sanscriticum et Fontes Iuris Asiae Meridianae et Centralis. Vol. 5. Ed. Oscar Botto. Torino (Italy): CESMEO, 2004.

"*Dharma* in Practice: *Ācāra* and Authority in Medieval Dharmaśāstra," *Journal of Indian Philosophy* **32**(5) (2004): 813–830.

"Intermediate Realms of Law: Corporate Groups and Rulers in Medieval India," *Journal of the Economic and Social History of the Orient* **48**(1) (2005): 92–117.

"A Realist View of Hindu Law," *Ratio Juris* **19**(3) (2006): 287–313.

"Hinduism as a Legal Tradition," *Journal of the American Academy of Religion* **75**(2) (2007): 241–67.

"Maxims & Precedent in Classical Hindu Law," *Indologica Taurinensia* **33** (2007): 33–55.

"The Non-Observance of Conventions: A Title of Hindu Law in the Smṛticandrikā," *Zeitschrift der Deutschen Morgenländischen Gesellschaft* **157**(1) (2007): 103–24.

"On Ātmatuṣṭi as a Source of Dharma," *Journal of the American Oriental Society* **127**(3) (2007): 279–96.

"Before Virtue: Halakhah, Dharmaśāstra, and What Law Can Create," *Law & Contemporary Problems* **71**(2) (2008): 99–108.

"Law." In *Studying Hinduism: Key Concepts and Methods*, eds. Sushil Mittal and Gene Thursby. New York: Routledge, 2008.

"An Historical Overview of Hindu Law." In *Hinduism and Law: an Introduction*, eds. T. Lubin, D.R. Davis and J. Krishnan. Cambridge: Cambridge University Press, forthcoming.

"Matrilineal Adoption, Inheritance Law, and Rites for the Dead among Hindus in Medieval Kerala." In *Essays in Honor of Patrick Olivelle*, ed. Steven Lindquist. Firenze: Firenze University Press, forthcoming.

Day, Terence P. *The Conception of Punishment in Early Indian Literature*. Waterloo: Wilfred Laurier University Press, 1982.

Derrett, J. Duncan M. (ed.), *An Introduction to Legal Systems*. New York: Praeger, 1968.

Derrett, J. Duncan M. *Religion, Law, and the State in India*. London: Faber, 1968.

*History of Indian Law (Dharmaśāstra)*, Handbuch der Orientalistik Vol. 2. Part 1. ed. J. Gonda. Leiden/Köln: Brill, 1973.

"Two Inscriptions Concerning the Status of Kammalas and the Application of Dharmasastra." In *Essays in Classical and Medieval Hindu Law*, Vol. 1. Leiden: Brill, 1976, pp. 86–110.

*Essays in Classical and Modern Hindu Law*. 4 Vols. Leiden: Brill, 1976–8.

Douglas, Mary. *Purity and Danger: an Analysis of Concepts of Pollution and Taboo*. London: Routledge, 1966.

Dumont, Louis. *Homo Hierarchicus: the Caste System and its Implications*, trans. Mark Sainsbury, Louis Dumont, and Basia Gulati. Chicago: University of Chicago Press, 1980.

Dumont, Louis and David Pocock. "For a Sociology of India," *Contributions to Indian Sociology* **1**(1) (1957): 7–22.

Engel, David. "Law in the Domains of Everyday Life: the Construction of Community and Difference." In *Law in Everyday Life*, eds. A. Sarat and T. Kearns. Ann Arbor: University of Michigan Press, 1993.

Fuller, C.J. *The Camphor Flame: Popular Hinduism and Society in India*. Rev edn. Princeton: Princeton University Press, 2004.

Gadamer, Hans-Georg. *Truth and Method*. 2nd rev. edn. Trans. J. Weinsheimer and D.G. Marshall. New York: Continuum, 1989.

Ganguly, J.N.C. "Hindu Theory of Property," *Indian Historical Quarterly* **1** (1925): 265–79.

Geertz, Clifford. "Local Knowledge: Fact and Law in Comparative Perspective." In *Local Knowledge: Further Essays in Interpretive Anthropology*. New York: Basic Books, 1983.

Ghoshal, U.N. *A History of Indian Political Ideas*. Bombay: Oxford University Press, 1959.

Gladstone, W.E. "Proem to Genesis," *The Nineteenth Century* **19** (1886): 1–21.

Goffman, Erving. *The Presentation of Self in Everyday Life*. New York: Anchor, 1959.

Gordon, Robert. "Critical Legal Histories," *Stanford Law Review* **36** (1984): 57–125.

Hacker, Paul. "Dharma in Hinduism," *Journal of Indian Philosophy* **34** (2006): 479–96.

Halbfass, Wilhelm. *India and Europe: An Essay in Philosophical Understanding.* Albany: SUNY Press, 1988.

*Tradition and Reflection: Explorations in Indian Thought.* Albany: SUNY Press, 1991.

Hallisey, Charles. "The Surprise of Scripture's Advice." In *Religious Identity and the Problem of Historical Foundation*, eds. Judith Frishman, Willemien Otten, and Gerard Rouwhorst. Leiden: E.J. Brill, 2004.

Hamilton, Marci. *God vs. the Gavel: Religion and the Rule of Law.* New York: Cambridge University Press, 2005.

Hart, H. L. A. *Essays on Bentham.* Oxford: Clarendon, 1982.

Hayden, Robert M. *Disputes and Arguments among Nomads: a Caste Council in India.* Delhi: Oxford University Press, 1999.

Hegel, G. W. F. *Elements of the Philosophy of Right*, trans. H. B. Nisbet, ed. A. W. Wood. New York: Cambridge University Press, 1991.

Heim, Maria. *Theories of the Gift in South Asia: Hindu, Buddhist, and Jain Reflections on Dāna.* New York: Routledge, 2004.

Helmholz, R. H. *The Spirit of Classical Canon Law.* Athens: University of Georgia Press, 1996.

Hopkins, Thomas J. *The Hindu Religious Tradition.* Belmont: Wadsworth, 1971.

Huizinga, Johan. *Homo Ludens: A Study of the Play-Element in Culture*, trans. R. F. C. Hull. London: Routledge, 1949.

Huxley, Andrew (ed.), *Religion, Law and Tradition: Comparative Studies in Religious Law.* London: Routledge, 2002.

Jameson, Frederic. *The Political Unconscious: Narrative as a Socially Symbolic Act.* Ithaca: Cornell University Press, 1981.

Jha, Ganganath. *Manusmṛti: with 'Manubhāṣya' of Medhātithi*, 10 Vols., 2nd edn. Delhi: Motilal Banarsidass, 1999 [1920–39].

Johansen, Baber. "Secular and Religious Elements in Hanafite Law: Function and Limits of the Absolute Character of Government Authoity." In *Islam et Politique au Maghreb*, eds. E. Gellner and J. Vatin. Paris: Centre National de la Recherche Scientifique, 1981.

Jolly, Julius. *Hindu Law and Custom*, trans. Batakrishna Ghosh. Calcutta: Greater India Society, 1928.

Kamali, Mohammad Hashim. *Principles of Islamic Jurisprudence.* 3rd edn. Cambridge: Islamic Texts Society, 2003.

Kane, P. V. *History of Dharmaśāstra.* 5 Vols. Poona: BORI, 1962–75.

Keller, Nu Ha Mim (trans.),. *Al-Maqasid: Nawawi's Manual of Islam.* Rev. edn. Beltsville, MD: Amana, 2002.

Kirfel, Willibald. "Frühgeschichte des Eigentums in Altindien," *Anthropos* **60** (1965): 113–63.

Klostermeier, Klaus K. *Survey of Hinduism.* 2nd edn. Albany: SUNY Press, 1994.

Kumar, Dharma. "Private Property in South Asia? The Case of Medieval South India," *Comparative Studies in Society and History* **27**(2) (1985): 340–66.

Kuttner, Stephan. "Harmony from Dissonance: An Interpretation of Medieval Canon Law." In *The History of Ideas and Doctrines of Canon Law in the Middle Ages*. London: Variorum Reprints, 1980.

Lariviere, Richard W. "Witness as the Basis for all Other Modes of Proof in Hindu Law," *Adyar Library Bulletin* **51** (1987): 60–70.

"Justices and Paṇḍitas: Some Ironies in Contemporary Readings of the Hindu Legal Past," *Journal of Asian Studies* **48**(4) (1989): 757–69.

"Law and Religion in India." In *Law, Morality, and Religion: Global Perspectives*, ed. Alan Watson. Berkeley: University of California Press, 1996.

"Dharmaśāstra, Custom, 'Real Law,' and 'Apocryphal' Smṛtis," *Journal of Indian Philosophy* **32** (2004): 611–27.

Lingat, Robert. "Les Quatre Pieds du Procés," *Journal Asiatique* **250** (1962): 489–503.

*The Classical Law of India*, trans. J. D. M. Derrett. Berkeley: University of California Press, 1973.

Litowitz, Douglas. "Gramsci, Hegemony, and the Law," *Brigham Young University Law Review* **2000**(2) (2000): 515–52.

Llewellyn, Karl N. and E. Adamson Hoebel. *The Cheyenne Way: Conflict and Case Law in Primitive Jurisprudence*. Norman: University of Oklahoma, 1941.

Logan, William. *Malabar*. 2 Vols. New Delhi: Asian Educational Service, 1995 [1887].

Lubin, Timothy. "Authority." In *Hinduism and Law: an Introduction*, eds. Timothy Lubin, Jayanth Krishnan, and Donald R. Davis, Jr. Cambridge: Cambridge University Press, forthcoming.

MacCormack, Geoffrey. *The Spirit of Traditional Chinese Law*. Athens: University of Georgia Press, 1996.

MacIntyre, Alasdair. *After Virtue: A Study in Moral Theory*. 2nd edn. Notre Dame: University of Notre Dame Press, 1984.

Mahmood, Saba. "Ethical Formation and Politics of Individual Autonomy in Contemporary Egypt," *Social Research* **70**(3) (2003): 1501–30.

Maine, Henry Sumner. *Ancient Law: its Connection with the Early History of Society and its Relations to Modern Ideas*. London: John Murray, 1861.

Malamoud, Charles. "The Theology of Debt in Brahmanism." In *Cooking the World: Ritual and Thought in Ancient India*, trans. David White. Delhi: Oxford University Press, 1996.

Mantena, Karuna. *Alibis of Empire: Social Theory and the Ideologies of Late Imperialism*. Princeton, Princeton University Press, forthcoming.

Marriott, McKim (ed.), *India through Hindu Categories*. New Delhi: Sage, 1990.

Mathur, Ashutosh Dayal. *Medieval Hindu Law: Historical Evolution and Enlightened Rebellion*. Delhi: Oxford University Press, 2007.

Mayne, John D. *A Treatise on Hindu Law & Usage*. 1st edn. Madras: Higginbotham, 1878.

McCrea, Lawrence. "Hindu Law and Scriptural Hermeneutics." In *Hinduism and Law: an Introduction*, eds. Timothy Lubin, Jayanth Krishnan, and Donald R. Davis, Jr. Cambridge: Cambridge University Press, forthcoming.

Mendelsohn, Oliver. "How Indian is Indian Law?" In *Enculturing Law: New Agendas for Legal Pedagogy*, eds. M. John and S. Kakarala. New Delhi: Tullika, 2007, pp. 132–57.

Menski, Werner. *Hindu Law: Beyond Tradition and Modernity*. Delhi: Oxford University Press, 2003.

Michaels, Axel. *Hinduism: Past and Present*. Princeton: Princeton University Press, 2004.

"The Practice of Classical Hindu Law." In *Hinduism and Law: An Introduction*, eds. T. Lubin, D. R. Davis, and J. Krishnan. Cambridge: Cambridge University Press, forthcoming.

Montesquieu. *The Spirit of the Laws*, trans. and ed. Anne M. Cohler, Basia C. Miller, and Harold S. Stone. Cambridge: Cambridge University Press, 1989.

Moosa, Ebrahim. "Allegory of the Rule (*Ḥukm*): Law as Simulacrum in Islam?" *History of Religions* **38**(1) (1998): 1–24.

*Ghazālī and the Poetics of Imagination*. Chapel Hill: University of North Carolina Press, 2005.

Narayana Rao, Velcheru, David Shulman, and Sanjay Subrahmanyam. *Textures of Time: Writing History in South India 1600–1800*. New York: Other Press, 2003.

Nelson, J. H. *A View of the Hindu Law as Administered by the High Court of Judicature at Madras*. Madras: Higginbotham, 1877.

Neusner, Jacob. "Judaism in the History of Religions." In *On Method in the History of Religions*, ed. James S. Helfer. Middletown: Wesleyan University Press, 1968.

Nimmer, David. "'Fairest of them All' and Other Fairy Tales of Fair Use," *Law & Contemporary Problems* **66**(1–2) (2003): 263–88.

Nisbet, Robert A. *The Sociological Tradition*. New York: Basic Books, 1966.

Ocko, Jonathan K. and David Gilmartin. "State, Sovereignty, and the People: A Comparison of the 'Rule of Law' in China and India," *Journal of Asian Studies* **68**(1) (2009): 55–100.

Olivelle, Patrick. "Renouncer and Renunciation in the Dharmaśāstras." In *Studies in Dharmaśāstra*, ed. Richard Lariviere. Calcutta: Firma KLM, 1984, pp. 81–152.

*The Āśrama System: the History and Hermeneutics of a Religious Institution*. New York: Oxford University Press, 1993.

(ed. and trans.), *Dharmasūtras: The Law Codes of Āpastamba, Gautama, Baudhāyana, and Vasiṣṭha*. Delhi: Motilal Banarsidass, 2000.

"Manu and the *Arthaśāstra*: A Study in Śāstric Intertextuality," *Journal of Indian Philosophy* **32**(2–3) (2004): 281–91.

"The Semantic History of Dharma: The Middle and Late Vedic Periods," *Journal of Indian Philosophy* **32** (2004): 491–511.

(ed. and trans.), *Manu's Code of Law: a Critical Edition and Translation of the Mānava-Dharmaśāstra*. South Asia Research Series. New York: Oxford University Press, 2005.

"The Power of Words: The Ascetic Appropriation and Semantic Evolution of *Dharma*." In *Language, Texts, and Society: Explorations in Ancient Indian Culture and Religion*. Firenze: Firenze University Press, 2005.

"Explorations in the Early History of Dharmaśāstra." In *Between the Empires: Society in India 300 BCE to 400 CE*, ed. Patrick Olivelle. New York: Oxford University Press, 2006.

(ed.), *Dharma: Studies in Its Semantic, Cultural, and Religious History*. Delhi: Motilal Banarsidass, 2009.

"Dharmaśāstra: A Textual History." In *Hinduism and Law: an Introduction*, eds. Timothy Lubin, Jayanth Krishnan, and Donald R. Davis, Jr. Cambridge: Cambridge University Press, forthcoming.

Penner, J. E. *The Idea of Property in Law*. Oxford: Clarendon, 1997.

Pollock, Sheldon. "The Idea of Śāstra in Traditional India." In *Shastric Traditions in Indian Arts*, ed. A. L. Dallapiccola. Wiesbaden: Steiner, 1989.

"Playing by the Rules: Śāstra and Śāstric Literature." In *Shastric Traditions in Indian Arts*, ed. A. L. Dallapiccola. Wiesbaden: Steiner, 1989.

Postema, Gerald. *Bentham and the Common Law Tradition*. Oxford: Clarendon Press, 1986.

Prasad, Leela. *Poetics of Conduct: Oral Narrative and Moral Being in a South Indian Town*. New York: Columbia University Press, 2007.

Radhakrishnan, Sarvepalli. *The Hindu View of Life*. London: George Allen & Unwin, 1927.

Radin, M. *Reinterpreting Property*. Chicago: University of Chicago Press, 1993.

Rawls, John. *A Theory of Justice*. Cambridge: Belknap/Harvard University Press, 1971.

Reinhart, A. Kevin. "Islamic Law as Islamic Ethics," *Journal of Religious Ethics* **11**(2) (1983): 186–203.

"Transcendence and Social Practice: *Muftīs* and *Qāḍīs* as Religious Interpreters," *Annales Islamologiques* **27** (1993): 5–28.

Ricoeur, Paul. *Interpretation Theory: Discourse and the Surplus of Meaning*. Fort Worth: TCU Press, 1976.

*The Just*, trans. David Pellauer. Chicago: University of Chicago Press, 2003.

Rocher, Ludo. "Ancient Hindu Criminal Law," *Journal of Oriental Research Madras* **24** (1954–5): 15–34.

(ed. and trans.), *Vyavahāracintāmaṇi by Vācaspati Miśra: A Digest of Hindu Legal Procedure*. Gent: Vanmelle, 1956.

"'Lawyers' in Classical Hindu Law," *Law and Society Review* **3** (1969): 383–402.

"Hindu Law and Religion: Where to Draw the Line?" In *Malik Ram Felicitation Volume*, ed. S. A. J. Zaidi. New Delhi: Malik Ram Felicitation Committee, 1972.

"Schools of Hindu Law." In *India Maior: Congratulatory Volume Presented to J. Gonda*, eds. J. Ensink and Peter Gaeffke. Leiden: Brill, 1972.

"Karma and Rebirth in the Dharmaśāstras." In *Karma and Rebirth in Classical Indian Traditions*, ed. Wendy Doniger O'Flaherty. Berkeley: University of California Press, 1980.

"Inheritance and *Śrāddha*: The Principle of 'Spiritual Benefit.'" In *Ritual, State and History in South Asia. Essays in Honour of J.C. Heesterman*, eds. A.W. Van den Hoek, D.A. Kolff, and M.S. Oort. Leiden: Brill, 1992, pp. 637–49.

*Jīmūtavāhana's Dāyabhāga: The Hindu Law of Inheritance in Bengal.* New York: Oxford University Press, 2002.

*Studies in Hindu Law and Dharmaśāstra*, ed. Donald R. Davis, Jr. Torino: CESMEO, forthcoming.

Rocher, Ludo and Rosane Rocher. "Ownership by Birth: the *Mitākṣarā* Stand," *Journal of Indian Philosophy* **29** (2001): 241–55.

Roy, Kumkum. "Defining the Household: Some Aspects of Prescription and Practice in Early India," *Social Scientist* **22**(1–2) (1994): 3–18.

Said, Edward. *Humanism and Democratic Criticism.* New York: Columbia University Press, 2004.

Salomon, Richard. *Indian Epigraphy: A Guide to the Study of Inscriptions in Sanskrit, Prakrit, and the Other Indo-Aryan Languages.* New York: Oxford University Press, 1998.

Sarat, Austin and Thomas Kearns. "Beyond the Great Divide: Forms of Legal Scholarship and Everyday Life." In *Law in Everyday Life*, eds. A. Sarat and T. Kearns. Ann Arbor: University of Michigan Press, 1993.

Sarkar, Benoy Kumar. "The Theory of Property, Law, and Social Order in Hindu Political Philosophy," *International Journal of Ethics* **30**(3) (1920): 311–25.

"The Hindu Theory of the State," *Political Science Quarterly* **36**(1) (1921): 79–90.

Sarkar, U.C. *Epochs in Hindu Legal History.* Hoshiarpur: Vishveshvaranand Vedic Research Institute, 1958.

Scharfe, Hartmut. *The State in Indian Tradition.* Handbuch der Orientalistik 3:2. Leiden: Brill, 1989.

Schofer, Jonathan W. *The Making of a Sage: a Study in Rabbinic Ethics.* Madison: University of Wisconsin Press, 2005.

Sen, Priyanath. *The General Principles of Hindu Jurisprudence.* Calcutta: University of Calcutta, 1918.

Shapiro, Scott J. "Authority." In *The Oxford Handbook of Jurisprudence and Philosophy of Law*, eds. Jules Coleman and Scott Shapiro. New York: Oxford University Press, 2002.

Sircar, D.C. "Glimpses of *Ācāra* and *Vyavahāra* in Early Indian Literary and Epigraphic Records." In *Studies in Dharmaśāstra*, ed. Richard W. Lariviere. Calcutta: Firma KLM, 1984, pp. 3–14.

Sontheimer, Günther-Dietz. *The Joint Hindu Family: its Evolution as a Legal Institution.* New Delhi: Munshiram Manoharlal, 1977.

"Religious Endowments in India: the Juristic Personality of Hindu Deities." In *Essays on Religion, Literature and Law*, eds. H. Brückner, A. Feldhaus, and A. Malik. New Delhi: Manohar, 2004.

Spellman, J. W. *Political Theory of Ancient India*. Oxford: Clarendon Press, 1964.

Tamanaha, Brian Z. *On the Rule of Law: History, Politics, and Theory.* Cambridge: Cambridge University Press, 2004.

*Law as a Means to an End: Threat to the Rule of Law*. New York: Cambridge University Press, 2006.

Umphrey, Martha Merrill, Austin Sarat, and Lawrence Douglas. "The Sacred in Law: an Introduction." In *Law and the Sacred*, eds. A. Sarat, L. Douglas, and M. M. Umphrey. Stanford: Stanford University Press, 2006.

Vikør, Knut. *Between God and the Sultan: a History of Islamic Law*. New York: Oxford University Press, 2005.

Waldron, Jeremy. "Property Law." In *A Companion to Philosophy of Law and Legal Theory*, ed. Dennis Patterson. Malden, MA: Blackwell, 1996.

Weiss, Bernard G. "Interpretation in Islamic Law: the Theory of *Ijtihād*," *American Journal of Comparative Law* **26** (1977–1978): 199–212.

*The Spirit of Islamic Law*. Athens: University of Georgia Press, 1998.

Wezler, Albrecht. "Dharma in the Vedas and the Dharmaśāstras," *Journal of Indian Philosophy* **32** (2004): 629–54.

White, James Boyd. "Rhetoric and Law: the Arts of Cultural and Communal Life." In *Heracles' Bow: Essays on the Rhetoric and Poetics of the Law*. Madison: University of Wisconsin Press, 1985, pp. 28–48.

Whitman, Walt. "Song of Myself." In *Leaves of Grass*, ed. Jerome Loving. New York: Oxford University Press, 1998 [1855].

Wilson, Stephen. *Feuding, Conflict, and Banditry in Nineteenth-century Corsica*. New York: Cambridge University Press, 1988.

Witte, Jr. John and Frank S. Alexander (eds.), *Christianity and Law: an Introduction*. Cambridge: Cambridge University Press, 2008.

# *Index*